Every Town
Needs A Castle

Every Town Needs A Castle

Dwayne Hunn

To order additional copies of this book, contact:
Xlibris Corporation
1-888-795-4274
www.Xlibris.com
Orders@Xlibris.com
87527

Contents

Dedication

"Michael, do you believe in an after life?"

"Oh, I dunno . . ." he kept repeating, as I pestered him with different versions of the same question.

Finally, on this occasion he offered, "When you die, I think maybe your energy goes up there somewhere and flies around with a bunch of other energies, kind of like electricity. Then, maybe, someone or something sends it back down to zap," and he made a little zap movement with his hand, "someone down here with that energy . . . But who knows." he said, as he then folded his hands over his stomach and closed his eyes that had been looking out on California's largest tool shed floating in the peaceful Castle reservoir.

This book is dedicated to . . .

Those dreamers
who work hard
and like doing so . . .

Who during their workdays
wonder if they should, could, or
would live their dreams . . .

Who might have been
considered strange
by the suburban surrounders and surroundings . . .

deemed unfit to fit
inside the walled and gated communities . . .

heckled, booed, or ignored for
holding too old or too new or too uncharted views and
rules to live by . . .

Whose built dreams
would harm no one,
enlighten wonder,
and expand chuckles in time, space and even your
neighborhood . . .

Who wonder what are the life living skills
that every household
every community
needs more of . . .

This book's dedicated to you.

And to those who think they might like to be like you.
And to the leadership qualities you'll need.

And to Michael Clarke Rubel
And to the many who cherished him.

And to those who recycle, build, and make things
        that one can see, feel, touch, and wonder about
And is not dedicated to those
who shuffle and trade paper with pompous airs,
        who supposedly create money and prestige yet default
during the best of times under the test of time.

For MCR personified and brought to life
        the character, humor,
Love of life, and hard work . . .
        leadership skills, business ethics, and love of kids
        that we, our communities, and the world
        needs much more of . . .

And to wizened old timers like Grandfather, Stanley, and Odo
        who like all treasured guides
Turned the obstacles
        scattered along life's roads and gullies
        into signposts to keep the young
        from constantly miring in ditches or falling into abysses.

Teachers they were
        interesting, challenging, and different in the best sense of
        each of those words.

So, this is particularly dedicated to:

Grandfather Harry Austin Deuel, III, 1872-1967
Stanley Baird, Died 1972
Odo Stade, July 2, 1892-March 5, 1976
Michael Rubel, April 16, 1940-October 15, 2007
Kaia Rubel, August 13, 1942-June 22, 2009
And those like them, or growing to be like them.

So, it was said

Stored in Granddad's Pueblo, Colorado garage was his fine, black 1937 Buick four door sedan. As one who loved driving fine cars and 16 wheelers, grandson Christopher Rubel asked Granddad how much he'd take for it. Granddad said:

> **"You're in the Air Force, going**
> **overseas, and too poor."**

Besides, he added,

> **"There's a rich kid down the street who wants it. He**
> **doesn't know anything about cars, and his father will**
> **pay a good price for the Buick. It needs a ring job,**
> **and he'll have to overhaul it, which will teach him**
> **something. You already know how to do all that stuff,**
> **and I don't want to sell you a car that needs work."**

I suggested that it was kind of mean to sell the car knowing it needed work.

He said,

> **"It would be mean if I sold it to you. Selling it to that**
> **kid will give him an education just getting it to run**
> **and having to overhaul it."**
> *Chris Rubel, Michael's brother and Grandfather Deuel*

> **"Mike's sole purpose in life seems to be to keep**
> **anything from going to the dump."**
> *Dorchen Rubel Foreman, Michael's sister*

Acknowledgments

Thanks to Michael and Kia Rubel for sharing so many words, pictures, experiences, meals, and smiles, some of which I hope were captured in this book.

Thanks to Suzie (Kia's daughter), her husband Darren, and their son, rookie All Star Christopher Armstrong, for sharing their hospitality during Kia and Michael's later years.

Thanks to Scottford Rubel and his father Christopher for helping me track down stuff, remember names, dig up a picture here and there, and gently nudge this book along.

Thanks to Dr. Tom King for his non-pharmers' literate literature eyes in doing more than fixing quotes, attaching apostrophes, capturing outrageously poor syntax, and making lies lay properly.

Thanks to the visionary and exquisite artists who made the spirit of Rubelia come alive with their pen and ink drawings that fill the book and adorn its covers. Thank you Sally McHann, Criswell Guldberg, Scott Rubel, whose artwork, I reckon, kept him from drilling my wall, and maybe a couple other artists whose inkwells we've lost.

Introduction

"I never watched a man work more on a
place to make it totally worthless,"
said Grandfather Deuel to Mayor Finkbinder . . .

Initially, this book was titled *Grandfather Used to Say*. Chapter 2 tells why. It is filled with Grandfather's sayings, and much of the book hinges around that chapter and what other wise elders used to say.

Embedded within Chapter 2's adages lies the wisdom and understanding supporting why *Every Town Needs a Castle*.

Final work on this book is taking place in 2010, as the world peers at bushwhacked economies that has billions peering into a looming cyclone of recessions or depressions. People are cost consciously seeking to build and care for their homes and communities, get along with others, have old-fashioned fun, and even recycle. All old stuff to Rubelian Pharmers.

Consequently, methinks that for those who read between the lines herein, this is a timely book, for:

Michael's grandfatherly upbringing would often lead him to say,

"This is how people live when everything goes wrong."

And sur'nuff, lots seems to have gone wrong out in the real world that surrounds the gated, well-fortified, and moated Castle of Rubelia. Yet, inside that Rubelian gated citadel an exemplary community developed that got along with everyone, lots of old fashioned phun was had, and our recycling rate was like 98.28%.

Michael would also often say,

"Of course, there's something wrong with me."

But fer'certin it wasn't Michael's lifestyle, spending habits, or philosophy that today has so many outside the Rubelian Pharmland planting gardens of carrots, for fear they may soon be picking grapes of wrath.

For those who:

- Fiddled at the Pharm a lot,
- Enjoyed working on the Castle a bit, or
- Undertook Quixotic Rubelian ventures sometimes,
- MCR would, with a smile and puff of his pipe, echo Grandfather with,

"There must be something wrong with him."

Michael's memories were filled with deeds by old timers and characters who:

- Worked hard,
- Fixed mechanical, electrical, physical, and radio things,
- Recycled by nature,

- Relied on inventiveness to "Make do" through a depression and wars, amidst an abundant, and once resource rich America and California—where yanks made things that worked simply, long, and well for themselves and others.
- Found time for friends, and
- Had little time for twits or twittering through or about the nonessentials in life.

These points might be reasons enough to give this book to someone you'd prefer not twitter through life. On the other hand, you might not want to read this book for it may tilt you, or those you give it to, toward "different." And if you become "too different," people will say, "Something's surely wrong with . . ." and then, *where oh' where will you fit in?*

Yes, Michael's upbringing made him different. It attracted people to him. Perhaps, by extension, those who hung with Michael were strange, too engaged, or became estranged. Nonetheless, led by a different man, the strange, engaged, and estranged stone-buggied hundreds of tons of rocks, cement, and junk into a Castle far from Europe's 16th century Renaissance.

Michael gave many of us pharmers, and may give you, a glimpse of how the experiences, wit, and sayings of the old and wizened are not always wasted on the young.

For some of us lucky ones, many Pharm mornings started with *Breakfast with Michael.* Gargantuan portions of oatmeal and brown sugar or honey, with side slices of Pharm oranges and avocadoes would be followed by eggs, potatoes, meat, whatever vegetable was left over from previous meals, and toast (usually with way too much butter). In the winter months, the stuff was boiled and fried on one of the many cast iron skillets over the wood burning stove by the big guy in flannel shirt and blue denim overalls.

When heaping portions were distributed to all in attendance, Michael would then sit to eat—and finish before the rest of us. Before, after, and during his cooking sojourns, we all loved eating up Michael's stories and food.

Then, long before Mortensen, Michael would push more than three gargantuan cups of kettled tea to all. Filled with loose tealeaves, honey, and milk—*Chai*, in the sweetest sense, was pushed on all of us. Chatting would ensue, punctuated with good humor and its guffaws, laughter, smiles, and talk of pursued projects or the pursued, undertaken on Pharm land and/or in the world outside. It's the kind of tea drinking that Mortensen learned long after MCR that builds peace and understanding everywhere.

During one of these now much-missed breakfasts, I first discovered the black notebook filled with Michael's recollected scribbled sayings. During the tea drinking portions of breakfast, often when Michael was trying to stoke up his pipe during a conversational interchange, Michael would remember something that *"Grandfather used to say" (GUTS).*

Michael would often add the GUTS of his grandfather's life to the conversation, and then ask one of us to pass him that black notebook, into which he'd bend his left arm and record grandfather's words for posterity, his own memory, and to build that little book, *Grandfather Used to Say.*

This is not a traditional book. Hopefully, you will figure out how to read and visualize it. Hopefully, some of you will capture the spirit of a nontraditional man and the unorthodox projects that gravitated from and revolved around him.

The world needs more straightforward, sensible, revolutionary Michaels. It needs more people to live and spin the stories he spun.

After *the glendoran* magazine ran one of my Pharm stories, Michael summed up why there are a number of pictures scattered throughout this book.

September 15, 1992

Dear Dwayne,

We really like your story . . . With pictures to help the reader comprehend these things is essential, we think. It is totally incomprehensible to the reader without some graphics, and even then?

. . . Keep up the wonderful work—you may prove certifiable soon with these tales from our past.

MYK

As a pictorial starting point you, a reader, might want to keep this picture in mind. From somewhere around this recycled Bottle House point, a kid named Michael, a Castle of Junk, and many phunny buildings and people magically grew up.

"It is a perfect project. It has everything against it."

While growing up differently, Michael and some of the Pharmers moved around quite a bit. Several of the Pharmers, and particularly Michael, also didn't seem to consume the right books that would properly inculcate them into *America's Consumer Society.* While moving around in the world, Michael lived in many different environments. Even in his 2.5-acre domain, he lived in many different environs.

In the 1960's, Michael lived in one of the refrigerators in the Tim Palace, a.k.a. Packing House. The wooden refrigerators had been used by Singer Sewing Machine and farm owner, Al Bourne, to cool his citrus. By the

"Yes, (I) lived in one of Mr. Bourne's refrigerators. If we latched the doors, we'd suffocate." MCR to a reporter

1970's, as the Castle started rising from the one-time irrigation reservoir, one-time frog farm, one-time emptied but silt-bottomed reservoir turned plastic-sheeted cucumber garden, Michael moved into less comfortable quarters in the under construction, messy castle building area. His new residence became known as the Troll's House.

The Troll's House had a single bed, a 1930's vintage gas range that always needed the kiss of a match to go into heat; an aged, chipped, beat-up sink; a 1940's finicky-handled refrigerator; another of the Pharm's typically wonderful four legged porcelain tubs; and a single guest chair. Upon visiting, Michael used to refer to Thoreau, repeating something from Walden's Pond about one chair being all a man needed to entertain true friends.

Oh, yes, next to the chair and bed was the warmth source, a wood-burning stove.

Why Michael choose to live in the Troll's House probably had something to do with *whatever it was he learned* by living in the Bottle House during his early building-the-Pharm and escaping Mother Dorothy's party phase.

Whatever it was Michael learned made him make . . .

- Me live in the Bottle House (BH) while building my rail road-tied house . . .
- Some woefully selected others rough it in the 6'x8' Bottle House with only one chair . . .
- All of us BH residents stuff the tiny pot bellied stove to gain no more than a few hours of warmth . . .
- All of us sleep on a lumped-beyond-comfort loft mattress squeezed under an intimately touching and sometimes heat crackling tin roof . . .

"Living there will inspire you to get your house built quicker," opined the King of Cemented Rocks, Creosoted Beams, Grandfatherisms, and Tortuous Logic.

Therein must have been a twisted mix of what Michael Clarke Rubel learned from his travels amidst Emerson, Thoreau, American Consumerism, and the world.

As Michael built the Castle higher and higher, he elevated himself to the second and third floors, and many more rooms, recycled chairs, and used furniture. His kitchen got bigger and better, even adding a hand pumped source of sink water. The stove got bigger and older. It was, however, still flamed by the smack of a match, but it could also cook, both food and the room, by filling its ironed caverns with lots of wood.

Michael's travels and grandfather had taught

Michael how to keep the wood cooking portion of that old stove fueled, while recycling old world fuel. At the foot of the staircase leading to his more upscale and upstairs Castle accommodations, Michael always had a huge stack of wood. Metal buckets hung around the stack, awaiting ascension from a human's touch. And humans wanting to rise to the occasion were in abundance.

So, Michael altered Thoreau's rule and added four or five old chairs along with several crate stools to his back deck view.

The result? It seemed that lots of Rubelia knowing American consumers wanted to climb the stairs to ruminate and cast their eyes upon the expanded Walden Pondish Castle of Salvaged Junk.

In climbing those stairs, they would often hear the MCR Thoreau imposter saying,

"Would you bring up a bucket of wood with you?"

Sounded a lot like Grandfather saying,

"Put wood by the outhouse and carry a stick in."

didn't it?

First, a little about Grandfather . . .

When Grandfather's Colorado mining work hit a shaft of bad luck, he, instead of going west, went east. He piled his family into the back of a friend's new 1914 truck, paid his friend 2/3rds of what it cost to buy a gallon of gas today ($2.00), and got out near the Lamola River. Friendly Vermonters helped keep inflation in check by offering his family an abandoned trailer, collecting and storing fire woods for the looming winter, and giving them some sickly pigs.

Grandfather's Colorado's mine-shafted luck was followed by Vermont's flooded-out luck in 1915. From page 842 of RDI (Rubel's Diary, I believe), the results were described this way:

> "The Lamola River would rise with warm weather and then freeze again—then flood and freeze with the ice backing onto itself in great layers tipped this way and that making the river appear like some small mountain range. Hardwick's townspeople were resolved, however, when an

unusual warm spell created a flood making this river of mountainous ice rush down stream. In its path, it carried away Hardwick's pride. Three bridges, numerous houses, a new gas station, and the one and only Cafe.

"Grandfather's family survived to the spring with their little gypsy trailer, firewood, and a stout 300-pound pig, named Hungry Pig in good spirits.

"Grandfather said that living in that tiny trailer with no wheels was one of the happiest periods in his life. The family pulled together in those cramped quarters and his wife kept them neat and spotless with a cheer that warmed his heart."

That tranquility was bumped on a particularly cold Spring day when grandmother was in the woods collecting fire wood with a push cart, the kids were in school, and grandfather's pride, Hungry Pig, became ill. Before searching for a neighbor who might know what to do for Hungry Pig, grandfather used boards to push the pig into the warmer trailer and then corralled the pig with some chairs.

Upon returning from his search for the neighbor, grandfather joined a sobbing grandmother's sitting in front of the trailer. While he was away searching for pig health care, the sick pig revived and, "tore the whole place apart—shitting and pissing on everything and then up and died in the middle of the floor."

Like so many hard working Americans of the early 20th century, the Deuels took the setback as a dueling opportunity. After some discussion with his helpful neighbor, grandfather's pork laden tragedy became a pork feeding opportunity.

Grandfather, his helpful neighbor, and family quickly issued tight-lipped invitations to "friendly" neighbors. In a nearby field, a slowly turned and well-hung, spitted Hungry Pig was eaten all day by a gathering of friends. Much like, I reckon, our Rubelia's pig-roastings were eaten around Glen Spear's built railroad-tied circular pig pit (now torn down) near the gas pumps. The Hungry Pig trailer disaster and ensuing celebratory feed led grandfather's family:

"Down the road to an old house that was available for $1.00 per month. The roof needed work as well as everything else, however, with a lot of work it could be made livable. Grandfather moved in with the promise that the dollar would he forthcoming when he got one.

And so those who had been at the feed and other family and neighbors chipped in to . . .

"Put the place in order. The firewood that *was* up the road by the trailer was hauled with the pushcart down to the new place and the cardboard was layed thick to be placed in the window-holes. The prize in this old place was the large kitchen stove, which Grandmother made shine and which brought the whole house alive.

And grandmother's "prize," the large wood burning stove, probably looked a lot like the wood burners Michael had on the Pharm and in the Castle for the flavor, memories, and toastiness they added to all eating or sitting near.

Not too many of us Pharmers probably knew or thought much about the genesis of the *slow eating, slow cooking, gummy building, and good talking* that was so much a part of Rubelia. Methinks, however, that the genesis of all this healthy phunny community building sprouted from grandmother's warm genes that worked around the "prize."

Michael probably used some of his pipe puffing time to remember the "prize" his grandmother made shine. Michael probably often imagined the warmth that came with friends and neighbors gathering for coffee, pig, and food amidst the warmth of a wood fired stove and pig pit, because he replicated such warmth in his Pharmer's Castle.

"Neighbors began to stop by for coffee around the old stove and drop a penny in a can near the door as they left to help compensate. Then Grandmother would sometimes serve something with the coffee and to the family's delight at the end of the day find nickels and an occasional dime. Gradually and imperceptibly, the old house became a social center with dinners and luncheons being served with the can near the door, where louder and louder noises would be heard as the coins got bigger and bigger, Grandfather explained that that old can became the conscience of the area for everyone knew what you had for lunch or dinner and what the sound in the can should be to be right. There was never a mention of how much should be charged per plate—simply a sense among the patrons that kept things in line."

As noted elsewhere in this book, Michael had an aversion for inspectors and for garnering too much public attention. The aversion seemingly ran in the family tree.

"Problems were to follow, however, with the ever increasing popularity of the place. Grandfather said it all started when they painted a big cardboard sign and hung it under the porch to keep it dry. The sign read in big white letters, "THE HUNGRY PIG."

"Even in these early days of American History there were health inspectors. Some like in Hardwick, Vermont, self-appointed and with no salary to speak of. Their general compensation being free meals at any Cafe in their territory—being that Cafe owners were not really sure as to what these inspectors really could do or not do.

"The first order to be given with great solemnity and authority was that the back door had to be fixed to keep the baby pigs out of the house. My Grandfather was amazed at how badly his wife took this. She waited calmly until the inspector left and then flew into a rage. She claimed that people were paying for their meals and giving the leftovers to the piglets on the floor with great joy and this in turn increased their profits. How many times, she raged, have you seen a man holding a piece of meat to his mouth, looks into those begging eyes of the piglets and decided to lower his fork to the floor. Food (would be) lost with the pigs left outside. No one is going to go outback and share their paid for dinner. An outrage that someone can walk into their house and tell them what to do. She would quit cooking before she would put those beautiful little pigs out back during lunch and dinner."

Aha, said I after reading this. Here, I figured, was where MCR got his idea to train all Pharmers and guests to put their plates of food on the floor for the bevy of politely waiting Pharm dogs, Yes, the Pharm dogs got the last lick at all lunches, dinners, parties, and even breakfasts, which sits perfectly with his contently smiling and crocheting grandmother sitting on some heavenly cloud above.

"Breakfast was out. Pigs in the house early in the morning offended Grandmother.

"Grandfather was perplexed and confused. They had such a good thing developing and now it may all end. The things Grandmother said were serious and when she said she would not cook without pigs in the house, that was exactly what would happen. She was mule headed and nothing would change her mind, no matter how *wrong* she was."

As this book hints, Michael was often "perplexed and confused." He believed his Castle was a "good thing developing" but always worried, "it may all end." He knew he needed an early warning system that went beyond radar, trip alarms, motion detectors, concertina wires, etc., which lined the Castle's walls. Michael built his early warning system with his network of people, who liked visiting and hanging around Michael's "prize" and would warn him of attacks by the likes of inspectors. A large part of Michael's realization that he needed such a good alarm network came from grandfather's stories that often ended up in his RDI (Rubelian Diary).

"Talking the problem over with the patrons, who feared the closing of the best place in the region, they set up a system whereby everyone in the township would help notify Grandfather as a pre-warning system to the arrival of the health inspector. People took this task with a seriousness that startled Grandfather and his wife.

"Even the policeman would help out. A code system was developed with car horns from neighbor to neighbor with periodic breaks of shotgun blasts or bells. People were so excited over this new form of communication that there were town *meetings* over the possibility of adapting this system for the county volunteer fire department. Grandfather stated that there was absolutely no way the inspector could get within two miles of his Cafe without him knowing. That even with the one attempt by the inspector to hide in the trunk of a car to get to the Hungry Pig without detection, the warning sounded more vigorous than ever. The inspector was furious and stamped in one day to announce that no Cafe in his territory would be allowed to operate with holes in the floor.

"A new floor was out of the question. The Cafe was doing well, but not that well, and all their earning had been plowed back into dishes and sinks and a big hot water system and glass for the windows and countless other things necessary for a Cafe.

"My Mother came home from school and filled up one tiny hole with some chewing gum she was chewing. Grandfather's eyes lit up and exclaimed that he would simply put free chewing gum by the door and ask everyone to stick it in a hole when they left. A little sign read, *"Free Gum Chum. Leave Gum When Done."* The projects of the various groups amounted to great engineering feats. The larger holes took the co-operation of many people to chew and pool their resources and slowly, over a period of weeks, fill in a hole. Then those who had managed a particular fill would forever take credit for their hole. Children began to come by leading the way to selling candy and pop from a table. The house had to have a room added for dining. And when the winters came and the gum got cold—dropping out of their holes, Grandfather was able to put in a new floor and add a room out back for the two dishwashers who once worked out of tin tubs amongst the trees.

"And our family became prosperous because Hungry Pig died in our trailer in 1916 or thereabouts."

First Memories
By
Michael C. Rubel

One of my first memories was when I was five or six years old sitting in the principal's office on a hot afternoon listening to my mother explain to my teacher and principal that I was really all right. My mother told them that the reason I talked funny was that the milkman was Italian; Her late husband spoke German in the house and the cleaning lady spoke French. Mother's best friend was from Hungary and all day long the boy (me) spent his time running about in the orchards where only Spanish was spoken. The mailman stuttered badly and my best friend, Klaus, had not learned English yet since arriving from Germany. The radio was always on some shortwave band with code beeping since my father was an avid "HAM" Radio operator.

My mother went on to explain that it was only after my father died that the boy (me) stopped going around beeping in Morse code. I remember how they looked at me. My mother began to talk in French with my teacher who had been to Paris and the principal yelled out the window to the grounds man with instructions in Spanish.

Mother forgot to mention that the trash men only spoke Armenian.

And they wondered why I played with ants all the time.

Golden Pecks
"When I was about ten years old, I used to go up to the Pecks to work for Papa Peck hauling rocks, for he was building his house. In his kitchen, which was finished, he had, I think it was two quart jars of gold nuggets. Filled to the top with gold nuggets. And men would stop by once in awhile and ask him where would be the best place to pan for gold, or which canyon would be the most promising, and some of

those kept staring at those bottles (Laughs). And they'd say, 'Where did you find those?'

"And he said, 'Well, I found them in Heaton Canyon near such and such a place.'

"Well, they'd be off like a shot.

"Well, one morning I got there and he sez, "Someone came last night and stole all our gold nuggets."

"I said, 'Oh my goodness . . .' because there was no theft in those days and I was just, you know, devastated because I thought that was their life savings, you know.

"And he sez, 'Would you come help me, we need to make more.' (Laughs).

"And I said, 'How do you make gold?'

"He said, 'I'll show ya.'

"I said, 'Does anybody else know? Because it's so valuable.'" (Laughs)

"'Well, let me show ya.'"

"So we got the big Bunsen burner, which I now have in the big machine shop. And we heated up this big cast iron bowl and put this plumber's lead in it. You know, they used to use lead in drain systems. Anyway, he put a bunch of this lead in there, and we melted it, and put a bucket of water next to it, and I took a big spoon and spooned the molten lead into the water, and it would explode almost, scattering. And after we'd made a whole bunch of nuggets with the lead, he threw them out on a towel, dried 'em, and then we put some gold paint, and spread 'em around on it. Let 'em dry and then put them in the quart jars, filled the quart jars full of water, put the caps on, and put 'em back on the shelves."

Michael saves the day

Michael started kindergarten and elementary school somewhere in the mid-40s. Along about the time he was in the third or fourth grade, Michael was sent to Harding Military Academy. With the postwar political climate and the Korean conflict on horizon, the cadets were receiving a lot of indoctrination as part of their education.

The lessons that most impressed Michael were the films about fighting off attacking invaders . . .

As a boyhood activity, Michael used to go off camping in the hills above Azusa Canyon. He would take a shotgun, pistol, and fishing pole with him and stay up there for days and even weeks at a time, hunting for his food. He ate a lot of squirrel and fish.

When he was about 12, Michael was on one of his camp outs. He had been out for the better part of a week when one day while he was out looking for food, he looked up and saw parachutes coming out of the sky.

He knew that he was, in fact, witnessing an invasion. With his "training and expertise" in antiwar intruder tactics he took it upon himself to go thwart these scoundrels. With his shotgun and pistol locked and loaded, he went to the clearing where he saw the paratroopers landing.

As he came upon the soldiers, who by then were getting out of their harnesses, he loudly yelled with the best authority he could muster, "Stay right where you are!"

Imagine the surprise of these professional military men at the sight of this young lad, shot gun and pistol at the ready, demanding their surrender. The truth was that they were American paratroopers on a survival training mission and they were unarmed . . .

"It's okay, kid . . . We're American."

"I don't believe you."

"No, really we're on a training mission. Just take your finger off the trigger of that shotgun and unlock the pistol."

"No! It's not a double action pistol . . . Put your hands up!!!"

"Kid, look at our uniforms . . . They're American."

"You could've stolen 'em."

"Believe me . . . We're just out here on a survival training mission and we're all pretty hungry. How 'bout you?"

About this time, young Michael caught sight of the sea rations and their equipment . . . "Are those the kind with the noodles in them?"

"They sure are."

"I'd really like to have some noodles. Want to trade for some squirrel meat or fish?"

"C'mon kid, let's just sit down and eat, huh?"

"Why do you guys have to do all this survival stuff, anyway? Follows Camp is just over the ridge. Flo Flo is the cook over there . . . she used to cook for Eisenhower . . ."

And so goes the story of how Michael became a hero that day, single-handedly warding off the great Azusa Canyon invasion of 1951 (... Or was it 1950? ... Whatever ...)

4-29-04 (Michael's notation)

Recently Bill (a.k.a. Blanchard) Crawford visited Kia and myself. He is 92 years old and lived at Williams Camp in the 1950s. He told of his memories of this event with the Air Force, and I asked him to write it down for us.

Some who visited

Rubelia as it morphed from Phunny Pharm to Castle included:

Dwight and Mamie Eisenhower in 1962 after MCR's friends Papa and Flo-Flo Peck took them to a Church of Open Door reception.

Bob Hope had a blast as Dorothy Rubel's guest at the 1964 Party for the Birdbath, powered by the 7-ton steam engine hooked up to squirt 8 inches of water, while flushing the neighbors toilets . . .

Sally Rand, the original Fan Dancer, was best of friends with Mother Dorothy and greatly amused Grandfather with all the strip poker games she would lose to him. One of her dances ushered in an awakening for some at Scott Rubel's 10th birthday party, and headaches for MCR.

Frequent '60's visitors included that "Dirty Rat" Edward G. Robinson, Comedian Jack Benny, Producer Alfred Hitchcock, and Keystone Cop Frankie Walrus.

In between wedding scenes filmed at the Lavern Presbyterian Church in 1966, an old dusty red car plated as "Dusty" led the "Graduate" to visit. That's Dustin Hoffman, for those who don't know where "plastics" came from. He came bearing no crosses . . .

Newsman Harry Reasoner snuck through a closing gate in pursuit or Michael's ancient and bouncing Volkswagen. In time, "George, the Janitor" quit dodging his filming requests until, over tea, Reasoner's personality won Michael over. Not so lucky was Barbara . . .

Barbara Walters, and her bodyguard, followed up after Reasoner's Castles in the World show with a visit. Her hopes to do another Rubelian show for her network were waylaid by Michael feigning his easily assumed idiot routine, which he performed so capably when he wanted to camouflage Rubelia from the outside world.

Two who rode up in anything but a dusty old red car were Prince Philip and the Archbishop of Canterbury. In the Prince's 1983 "Secret State Visit," more than a few neighbors noticed more than the Pharm's peacocks strolling through their neighboring yards and roadways. The Queens's hubby and friends brought M16, who backed off when confronted with the RTTF, Rubelian Tunneling Security Forces.

Another revolutionary State Visit came when a helicopter landed in 22 acres of weeds near Palm Drive. There, Henry Kissinger stepped out of the whirly bird and downed three cups of tea with Flo-Flo in the Pharm's Big Kitchen. It noticeably sweetened his heavy accent, which many believed moved the Vietnam Peace Talks forward and ended the Falling Red Dominoes War.

So, it was said

"But Dorothy, he's the most interesting kid on
the block . . .

"You've raised two very successful children.
Let's have fun with this one."
Grandfather Deuel

I've learned . . .
That the best classroom in the world is
at the feet
of an elderly person.

I've learned . . .
That just one person saying to me,
"You've made my day!"

Makes my day.
Andy Rooney's Thoughts on Life
From one of MCR's 2001 large envelop mailers

Chapter 1

Grandfather on enterprise and reservoirs

Grandfather Deuel
<u>Rubel Farms</u>

Grandfather and the reservoir
By M.C. Rubel, written around 1969

Oh, I suppose it isn't worth mentioning. By and by, though, everyone finds it out . . . about the reservoir and my Grandfather, I mean.

He is a friend, my Grandfather. We like one another a lot. He likes to talk. He has a whole lot to talk about, being ninety-six and all. We would all have a lot to say at ninety-six. Anyway, he is my friend.

In 1963, he *was* ninety-four, and we're sitting by the kitchen window. He drinks wine there. He wanted to know what I wanted to do. I'm his grandson, so he banks on me a bit to amount to something. I like it, being it isn't difficult to amount to something in Grandfather's eyes. He thinks everyone is just one hundred per cent. Almost everyone.

To understand his suggestion you have to know that on my place there is a big reservoir. It holds 3 ½ million gallons of water if you fill it UP, but it had so many fish in it that it began to smell bad, and the City inspector said I'd have to empty the water out because it was a public nuisance. The reservoir covers a half-acre in square feet if you could square it off, but it was a seventeen-foot circular wall around the edge and a drain in the bottom, which goes out into the streets of the subdivision down below. We found this out when we unplugged the drain and when the neighbors went out to get their Sunday papers the streets were flooded with smelly water and small fish batting their tails frantically trying to get back: into deep *water*. I joined them in consternation and wondered with them where the water was coming from. I offered to go up the canyon back of the place to see where the water was coming from, in-fact, and they appreciated my help. The City had to send a crew out to clean up the dead fish that Sunday afternoon.

Now that there wasn't any water in the reservoir, everyone we know thought something ought to be done with it, and Grandfather decided I should be a farmer. He admitted land was expensive, but be insisted that here we had a place made to order . . . the bottom of the reservoir. Grandfather was taken back by the profit you could make in strawberry growing. But with land so expensive, and strawberries taking some land to grow in, Grandfather decided we should grow strawberries in coffee cans hung on wires, row above row, as high as the eye could see. For every row of hanging coffee cans, the land use doubled. Who could beat that? It was *a* hundred per cent. Never a better idea.

The Agricultural people from the United States Government all drove out to talk with my Grandfather. They explained that the top two rows would be just top grade. No problem as far as they could see. The under one may not turn red, they surmised, but would be just as sweet probably.

Grandfather decided advertising was too expensive. Trying to change the nation into buying yellow strawberries was a big job for a little beginning farmer. Rubel Farms had not yet gotten off the ground, let alone change the taste of a nation.

Mushrooms came next. Grandfather likes to ride around in my 1932 Ford. We drove a long ways off to see a Mushroom Farm. They had a bulldozer pushing their compost piles about. Grandfather did not *like* the smell. We walked into cavernous dark buildings made out of old Army barracks and it *was dank* and dismal. Grandfather claimed it was a dirty kind of building . . . no sunlight and all that. We drove home in silence. Grandfather was thinking. Orchids came next. So we went downtown to meet Mr. Sherman, the Orchid man. He was sure friendly. Grandfather did not like him. I guess because we listened to him talk for such a long time . . . about how many years it took before a flower would develop into a plant; the temperature which had to be kept just so; the watering which bad to be on schedule. Grandfather decided orchids would take too long, and since I had never grown anything yet, perhaps a little touchy. They needed care. No question about that.

Grandfather decided we could grow frogs in the big half-acre reservoir. Just put a tab of water and dump in some frogs. They'll sell like hot-cakes, Grandfather decided. It was settled. We drove up into the Canyon to talk to Papa Peck. He always claimed frogs grew their leg back if cut off right. Grandfather said Peck was the man to talk to, since he knew something about the business. We got some real fine frogs at a dollar apiece. Grandfather chuckled all the way home. Why, we would have a million frogs in no time and every restaurant in the country would come buying.

It was a happy day. My future was settled. Rubel Frog Farms—in Lights and all—like downtown. It did not take too long for the area around the reservoir, nestled at the foot of the hills just north of the swank subdivision, to echo the sound of frog barking. It was inspiring. The noise sort of grew out of the reservoir and mega-phoned all over the neighborhood. Grandfather said it would remind all the people in their freshly built homes of the country. Grandfather said people wanted to be reminded of the country and they proved it by planting lawns around their homes.

Grandfather was mad when the City inspector came and said to kill all the frogs.

Grandfather seemed upset for weeks after the City Council said we were disturbing the peace, but good old Grandfather was never put down for long. He said we could grow cucumbers in the reservoir and make them climb up strings and put a plastic root over the reservoir to make a hot house. Cucumbers bring twenty-five cents per each one when winter hits field crops and kills lots of them . . .

We could get seven dozen on each climbing plant, claimed the United States Government Official who came out from Los Angeles to talk with

Grandfather. The grower got 12 cents apiece and Grandfather decided we could get 3300 plants in the reservoir if we planted right. Well, after a lot of pencil work in the dirt on the driveway, Grandfather blessed the damned neighbors. Grandfather said that if I stuck to it we could buy up the neighborhood and do any damned thing we liked before long.

I *asked* Grandfather how one could grow cucumbers on cement in a reservoir. Grandfather just stated that with 3300 plants and seven dozen cucumbers on each plant, we would have $33,264 per year and we would do it, and do it fast. People like Grandfather just put this whole country right where it is today. No wonder the politicians have such a hard time destroying it. That's what Grandfather thinks, anyway.

We got a truck from a friend and dumped thirty truckloads of dirt into the reservoir. My cousin wanted to help, but I would not let him. I wanted all the money. I'm not dumb. Grandfather agreed with that.

Taking the dirt in a wheelbarrow and dumping it into the tin troughs, which I made to hold it was three months of hard work. There was no money for the roof, so I planted anyway. I got the seeds wholesale, and hundreds of seeds for cucumbers would go in my wallet. Enough to plant the whole reservoir didn't weigh a half a pound.

On cold nights, I lit the smudge pots to keep the reservoir warm. I slept one cold might and everything died.

Grandfather told me something about Mr. Edison.

So I decided to try again, but thought that maybe my cousin would be help after all. He always did things after thinking about them. He told me that the troughs did not have enough dirt in them to support a cucumber. He was probably right. We rented a big dump truck and dumped twenty loads of dirt and five loads of sand and four loads of redwood sawdust from a redwood mill out by San Bernardino. I was glad Austin helped haul the dirt and sand.

We worked almost all night every night. Grandfather slept during the night. Austin and I had big lights that lighted up the reservoir. We worked hard. Hour

Reservoired cucumbers, not pickleable.

after hour of hauling. We had to work at night because my cousin worked during the day where they paid money for his time. He was a bill collector. I wanted to be one too. No one would hire me, excepting the old paper mill in San Dimas. I began to work there for a dollar-fifty per hour from 3 PM to 11 PM. I pushed cardboard into a big crunching machine. It then was made into pulp for the big machines in the other rooms.

Covered cucumbers—almost

I was tired, but Austin and I worked from mid-night to four AM every night.

We were happy in our project. We had big ideas. Grandfather smiled all the time. He kept telling the new neighbors that they had had made our fortunes with their damned criticism and complaints. If it hadn't been for them we might still be wasting our time on frogs. The neighbors always listened to my Grandfather.

When our plastic arrived, we draped it over the wires that had strung across the top of the reservoir to hold it. The plastic came in wide sheets. The plastic made it so big and warm looking inside. We were proud . . . almost cried with that rare sense of accomplishment . . . accomplishing on our very own. Our plants were three inches high. Thirty three hundred and six plants growing . . . making our fortunes. Austin and I went to bed, leaving the big gas *heater* running to keep the farm warm.

Austin thought there *had* been a terrible explosion, but Grandfather said the Santa Ana winds from the desert had come up with hurricane force and ripped off the plastic. It was banging hit and amiss on a lot of the new neighbor's homes. It was all over their trees and gardens too. It was a sad Sunday morning. Austin and I were feeling rather low. Grandfather tried to cheer us up but we could see the tears in his eyes. That did not help. We loved the old man and we hated to see him disappointed.

Austin and I gathered up some of the re-usable plastic and went to the town Banker, Mr. Hodges. He said we could have five hundred dollars to buy new plastic. He said he had driven up to see our project several times and was impressed with the way we worked. We thanked Mr. Hodges and bought new plastic. Our second roof was really better than the first. We still had our plants alive too. Austin made sure they were irrigated correctly. They were six inches high and we were starting to guide them onto strings. Most everyone thinks that cucumbers can only lie on the ground, but we did a lot of research, and know better.

Our second roof rippled in the breeze. All our friends said we were crazy, but Grandfather said for us not to pay any attention to them. Nothing ventured, nothing gained. They did not have a brain in their head is what Grandfather believed.

When our first heating bill came, Austin and I were somewhat impressed. It was an expense we had not counted on. Grandfather paid it. He said it was the least he could do. He walked, around among the plants a lot. He was never in the way. The gas heater burned his coat once, but he got it out in time.

The whole project went very well. We were planning on buying trucks and more land and building other doomed greenhouses.

When the roof blew again, and it rained and froze the following night, we had no energy to begin again. Our crop would have come after the field crops were marketable anyway.

Blown cucumbers make tired farmers.

So Grandfather convinced us to plant eggplants to recover some of our lost investment. They could stand more cold than cucumbers. He meant well and it was worth a try. We planted eggplants and they grew.

But the excess nitrogen from the decaying redwood sawdust, which we had mixed into the earth in the troughs, made the eggplants look beautiful but remain hollow and tasteless. At least that was what the men from the United States Agricultural Division said.

Grandfather told us something about Edison.

"What about those Rubelian bullfrogs?"

Michael was asked, "What about those Rubelian bullfrogs?"

"Well, I tried raising strawberries in an old reservoir which is now in the center of where I'm building the castle. But the darn things wouldn't turn red. They just ripened to a dull yellow and my grandfather figured I couldn't change the nation's taste in color, so he suggested I try raising bullfrogs and sell them to high-class restaurants.

"It was a great idea (to 21 year old Michael in 1961), so I got a bucket of (bullfrog) larva from a friend.

"I didn't figure there was enough in that bucket to make me a millionaire, but the first thing I knew I was dumping shovels of liver and sacks of dog food into the pond were more than 1 million frogs were croaking away.

"The reservoir served as huge bullhorn for the bullfrogs' croaking and the noise became so unbearable that the neighbors started to complain.

"My grandfather, who was 91 at the time had prepared the frogs haven and the pond and let the water drain out through an old abandoned sewage line. Trouble was, however, a new housing development down the hill had closed it off and the water ripped up the street and sidewalks and all the frogs went everywhere—hell, you can still find frogs all through the town and that's been nearly 20 years ago."

Said Michael Rubel to a reporter

So, it was said . . .

"Granddad, where's your hearing aide?" asked Chris Rubel, Michael's older brother.

Waving the question off, Granddad retorted, "I don't need it . . . There's nothing being said worth hearing. Besides, if I'm wearing the hearing aide, I have to wait for others to quit talking before I talk.

Without that thing, I can talk any goddamn time I want."
To Christopher Rubel

Some people were walking through the packinghouse and they asked Grandfather, "How did all this stuff happen?"

Grandpa replied, "We just forget to take things to the dump.

Chapter 2

Grandfather's tunneling codes

What follows are Grandfather's sayings culled from Michael's wrong-handed penmanship, remembered sometimes in the midst of talking over tea, or telling a story and then scribbled into the diary.

For today's budding Ben Franklin or today's wise and penurious, Grandfather's sayings will be used in lieu of expensive visits to psychiatrists, psychologists, yoga studios, ashrams, fitness centers, bars, walks along the beach, or inhalants. Of course, if you could just stick to building for decades your own Castle of Junk, you may not need Grandfather's wise words, since you would have worked out your own set of wisdoms . . . while pilling rocks, junk, and wine bottles with friends.

Interspersed with Grandfather's sayings are some Pharm pics and stories.

Rubelian Tunnel Blasting

Tunnel Area

Ask an original Pharmhand to explain them, and you'll likely get a wise, or preposterous, story.

Then, it is your decision whether to undertake the disappearing art of investigative journalism that ferrets out the conclusive truth of Pharmhand lore. This journey of truth may bring wisdom to your life, rollicking smiles to your jowls, or a lot more of both to everyone's rocking chair.

Your assignment, should you choose to accept, involves reading the sayings, and then the stories, and determining which saying most closely caused or resulted from which of Grandfather's coded guides to life. After honing your penetrating reasoning, inform Rubelia's Head Janitor of your conclusions, or check with one of its tunnel workers first. Either is likely to have the gritty details beneath his dirty fingernails.

Checking Rubelia's tunnel pumps

The Head Janitor then may forward your insights to the Rubelian Tunnel Crew Supervisors, who know better than any the meager impact of words on moving dirt, clearing heads, and protecting same with hard hats and facts.

Grandfather Used to Say . . .

Sin? The greatest sin is to hurt someone.

Beware of a man with too many friends.

To love is to die a little. There is no greater joy.
(See Curt's story later in this book.)

There is someone wrong with everyone.

The greatest war is the war that rages within me.

The greatest joy is the joy that I have given.

The greatest pain is the pain that I have caused.

It is rich to live like a poor man.

If we had a fire here, it would help make the place worth something.

Thinking stops many good things from happening—just shut up and dig.

Don't worry about it until you can do something about it.

Offending others is stupid—don't bother people with the.

Don't bore people with the truth—laughter is the song of men.

"Now, Michael, I want you to learn something. Just be quiet."

Enthusiasm is a gift from the Gods.

Cry alone—laugh with others.

Don't talk too wise. People love others to be a little foolish—we all want to be loved.

Caption: Carol Dunstan drives MCR's imagination into overdrive

How do we prove we are not crazy?

Blessed be our imagination—it makes life a joy.

You can do anything sitting in a chair.

But, Michael, with my Porsche girl?

Experience all the emotions so you can sympathize with others.

Laugh at yourself—Taking yourself seriously means you have not looked at the heavens.

Men are fragile—be gentle.

Everyone must benefit from a relationship—or the ship will sail away.

Pregnancy is the consequence of a man poking fun and a girl taking him seriously.

If you let a girl have what she wants—then she will want something else.

"This would often lead
to Michael telling a story about a pretty
woman pursuing him with matrimony in mind . . .
Once this led him to respond by walking his pharm
burros back to Mexico, giving them to Mexican farmers, and
then heading to New York to work a seagoing freighter . . .
Even with all that she proposed the day before her
wedding to cancel the marriage, if he would just say
her wish could happen . . ."
[See Ted's story later in this book]

The face you have is the one you deserve.

An unhappy six-year-old Michael at Halloween

Kid MCR's Model X Castle

Children are fragile flowers—don't step on them.

Michael don't you realize by now that you're a very special person?

Change is one guarantee we have through life.

The word "No" never built anything. It is simply the easiest answer.

Ewoks did something phunny to Rubelia

The final journey is death—a great adventure.

Don't tie anyone down in rough times or the rope will break.

Keep your own corner swept—examples are your strongest gifts to others.

A clean bird is a happy bird.

This was Mrs. Frlezner's abiding rule. As the Castle-keeper, she kept the rest of us Pharmhands shoeless and in line—with her own magic witch-crafting. See her story later in the book.

You get what you deserve and deserve what you get.

Getting rich quickly has to be hurting someone. It's wrong.

Health is wealth.

Your best friend can be your worst enemy.

Business must be based on reputation—not trust.

Lead the herd if you want to get stepped on.

You can buy all the trouble you want.

Money does buy happiness.

Beware of those who talk of the "theys" and "thems" of the world.

Eliminate the "I" from your thoughts. We and you are of interest to the other person.

Live to work—it's fun.

MCR & Lambert lying while Pharmhanders sweat

If you think about yourself—you are not working hard enough.

Plow deeper.

Man is the only animal who loves; hates; helps; kills; who has all the facets of a diamond and all the imperfections. Isn't it wonderful?

Man is only as big as the things that bother him . . .

Constructing Rubelia's Apollo Launch Pad

Getting to the moon first bothered us Pharmers too. So we built to go there too.

Advice? Memorize Kipling's poem: "If . . ."

If you can keep your head when all about you
Are losing theirs and blaming it on you,
If you can trust yourself when all men doubt you,
But make allowance for their doubting too;
If you can wait and not be tired by waiting,
Or being lied about don't deal in lies
Or being hated, don't deal in hating,
And yet don't look too good or talk too wise:

If you can dream—and not make dreams your master
If you can think—and not make thoughts your aim,
If you can meet with triumph and disaster
And treat those two impostors just the same;
If you can bear to hear the truth you've spoken

Twisted by knaves to make a trap for fools,
Or watch the things you gave your life to, broken,
And stoop and build 'em up with worn-out tools;

If you can make one heap of all your winnings
And risk it all on one turn of pitch and toss,
And lose and start at your beginnings
And never breathe a word about your loss;
If you can force your heart and nerve and sinew
To serve you long after they are gone,
And so hold on when there is nothing in you
Except the Will which says to them: "Hold on!"

If you can talk with crowds and keep your virtue,
Or walk with Kings—nor lose the common touch,
If neither foes nor loving friends can hurt you,
If you can fill the unforgiving minute
With sixty seconds worth of distance run,
Yours is the earth and everything that's in it,
And—which is more—you'll be a man my son!

I knew my grandfather and he knew George Washington. Our country is very young.

Think abut it like sex, if you want to concentrate. Wears you out.

Las Vegas? Wasn't built out there from winners.

Notice how the Willow tree survives? It bends.

Nothing is worth anything until it is being used.

"This morphed into MCR's Pharm rule that the first to use the 15' high piles of stacked railroad ties, rows of company discarded telephone poles, piles of recycled wood, bricks, electrical stuff, river bed rocks, cement, etc. deserved to have the stuff for his Pharm project."

Grandfather on his mom . . .

My mother was the wisest person.

If she said it once, she must have said it a thousand times—

'Harry! Go out and play.'

To make others happy, you have to make yourself happy first.

It is a great luxury not to like something.

Grandfather's Mom

Good news can wait. Bad news will hunt you down.

*Every man is worth $2 from the neck
down—unlimited from the neck up.*

*If Hitler would have been drinking, there would not
have been a war.*

The truth surfaces every 20 years.

*If you are happy with where you come from, you'll
be happy where you are going.*

*Behind every great disaster goes a lot of work . . .
Grandfather used to add,*

*"If they would have lived in a tent, they would not
have had all those problems."*

All Mud did NOT turn left . . .

> *Michael Rubel sitting on bag, Walt Wiley working, Glen Speer in clear coat, and Dwayne Hunn in yellow coat.*
>
> *National Geographic, October 1969.*
>
> *Workers, including high school cutting volunteers, are ten foot above the street on their third hand built, sand bagged wall, trying to stop the mud flooding down from San Gabriel Mountains after Noah's LA deluge.*

Mayor Finkbinder was expressing concern about the castle (proposed and visualized in drawings only) collapsing in an earthquake and Grandfather responded:

"Why look at all the money it'll save us. Rather than go to Europe to see ruins, people can just come here."

We would not have all these problems if we lived in a tent.

> *While Michael was trying to fix the leaky Tim Palace roof, Grandfather made the above remark to Michael.*

"Grandfather, do you ever pray?"

"Of course I do. I pray all the time. Won't do any harm if there is not a God. Could do a lot of good if there is a God.

There wouldn't be any upholstery in cars if it wasn't for women.

> *Michael elaborated on Grandfather's upholstering rule by commenting on drive-ins and the fairer sex . . . "Everyone was going to drive-ins," socially observant Michael explained. "No one knew what the movie was at drive-ins when they went with a girl. Everyone was making out in cars at the drive-ins . . . And that forced luxury into all the cars . . ."*

If you think you are beaten—you are.

If you want your dog run over, keep him pinned up. *

Grandfather *was always*
saying give *animals*
and *children*
freedom or *they'll get*
run over.

Long live the boyish spirit

To Dorothy Rubel, *Michael's mother,*
he'd often say:

"You've raised two *very successful*
children. Let's have *fun with this one."*

It wouldn't *be worth*
nothing, *if it*
weren't for *people . . . .*

I wish *everyone*
could be *happy . . .*

of Mykee Rubel

When you cry, I cry. When you laugh, I laugh.

Everybody can't ride in the wagon.
Someone has to push.

Women have clean minds. They are always
changing them.

Marry a girl that has more to lose than you do.

Give a man a good wife and he becomes happy. Give
a man a bad wife and he becomes a philosopher.

Kaia and Mykee were happy Pharmers.

Pain is the human condition.

If we were any smarter, we would probably worry more.

If you want to enjoy sausage or respect law—don't watch either being made.

When you're out of money start laughing.*
(Look for Golden Peck story.)

How do we prove we are not crazy?

Free advice? It is sometimes worth its price.

If you cannot smile—don't open shop.

If you smile a lot, then your wrinkles will develop in the right places.

The brighter the bulb—the shorter it burns.

The older the tree—the rougher the bark, the more gorgeous it is.

Michael, I want you to be a romantic. Romantics are always disappointed. But cynics always expect the worst.

More and more I want less and less.
("Comes with age," Michael said his grandfather would say.)

Privacy is a rare and precious thing.

Bethlehem is the same latitude as Tombstone, Arizona.

We cannot conceal what we are.

The best work is done for love's sake.
(Which must account for so many helping Mykee turn all this junk into a castle?)

Warren Asa's Blacksmithing Area.

Delete your need to understand. Things are as they are.

I don't live here in peace and harmony by being pleasant to everybody. Be selective.
(Harry Reasoner, Barbara Walters, tours, the later years recharged grandfather's words.)

It is a compliment to be hated by some people.

Aristocrats' ancestors stole sheep . . .

Reminiscing on Grandfather's words, Michael puffing from his pipe in his chair, said:
"Quayle's (Dan Quayle, Vice President to George H. Bush) grandfather was a smuggler. Also, the Kennedys got rich on prohibition."

Keep your own corner swept. Examples are contagious.

Lose your dream—you die.

Things do not matter. People do.

Life must be gotten through with as little self-contempt as possible.
Michael added:
"Grandfather said self-contempt leads to suicide."

Self-contempt and suicide run parallel.

People are like fruit trees—near their last crop they go berserk . . .
(Michael added that it reminded him of a friend who had just jumped into his third marriage to a very young lady.)

"Guess it is better to bank with a young teller, your account may last longer."

Too much wisdom is obnoxious.

Life is difficult. If it were easy—everyone would still be alive.

Put wood by the outhouse and carry a stick in.*

"Would you put some sticks in one of those buckets and bring it up with you for the fire."
(Grandfather said it when Michael was a kid . . . MCR would repeat it to visitors decades later. Sitting in his chair outside his office on the second floor, visitors would ask if they could come up to visit with him, and he say . . . "When you come up, could you bring up a bucket of wood with you? Sitting there by the staircase . . .)

California is the only place where you eat outside and pee in the house.

If you feel too happy—borrow money.

Men prefer broken horses and married women.

It is a free country—unless someone does not like what you are doing.

If you smile when everything goes wrong, you are either a nitwit or a repairman.

If you don't want your roof to leak—don't build one.

When I forget something—what is lacking in the head is made up for in the legs.

Rubelia's Carpeted Ladies Room

(Curt's story, later in this book, would give Michael a different take on the above.)

When accused of being a womanizer, he replied, "I don't waste my time chasing boys."

When you always expect the worst, you can't be disappointed.

Good taste is the enemy of creativity.

It is not wise to leap over a chasm in two hops.

Yes, I had a dream come true once and it turned my life into a nightmare.

As the years piled on, Michael would often say:

"The castle is a young man's dream and an old man's nightmare."

Regarding people that don't have something wrong with them:

"If you want to live a long time, get something wrong with you and take care of it."

My wife ran off with my best friend. I sure miss him.

Old sins cast long shadows.

Happiness must be earned.

I just want to live long enough to see what happens next.

I'm too old to die young.

Death is nature's way of saying hello.

He is a sinking ship. His life pump is not working.

Success has many fathers. Failure is an orphan.

Truth is a very special thing. I only use it on special occasions.

Perception is frequently more important than the truth.

It is none of your business what other people think of you.

I quit school. I was losing all my dumb friends.

I knew I was different as a little boy. Other boys wanted to be fireman and policemen while I wanted to be a bachelor when I grew up.

It is a perfect project. It has everything against it.

If the good lord wanted me to be rich, he would have tended to it a long time ago.

Wisdom is depressing. It alters happy perceptions.

Lord—why me!

No lie is more corroborated than the lie that causes a person pain.

Keep a cat or feed the mice.

Feminism is always an indicator of eminent collapse.

Do not say anything you do not want to be heard.

I never met a girl who didn't teach me something.

What is wrong with him? He set his hair on fire and put it out with a hammer.

If you want to have problems, contact an attorney.

If you want to worry, buy something shiny.

Man is incomplete until he is married. Then he is finished.

With a little more wine, she would have had fewer tears.

If you want a house—build one.

If you are contemplating suicide, don't put it off.

It is a very cold day when people run out of excuses.

I look funny when the sun is out.

Don't defend yourself. History will.

We are all so fortunate to have something to complain about.

I rise early but take a long time to wake up.

I am not illiterate. I know who my mother is.

I am blessed with selective amnesia.

You can lead a man to Congress, but you can't make him think.

What is it about the word 'No' that you don't understand.

Marriage is a triumph of hope over experience.

Praise the man who plows and remember the horses who do the work.

My lack of knowledge is terrifying.

On July 27th 2003, I criticized Michael, who all of us Pharmhands know is the world's foremost termite expert and Creosote sprayer, for not knowing if termites communicate to their brethren to stay away from a termite trail site touched by humans.

I also asked him another world shaking policy question, which revolves around one of the issues we had been studying for hours, when I asked him why Rubelian humming birds empty their watering bottles in random fashion. You can see from my questioning why MCR so often wondered how I was able to know or do anything.

MCR responds, while rocking in his chair and then punctuating his answer with his trademarked opening and closing of his mouth at the end of his statement, by saying, "I am so tired of having my opinions be proved wrong that I have given up thinking about things . . ."

The Pharm, with dunderheaded-like questioning, was always the place to raise and find the yawning answers to life's persistent questions for which even Guy Noir yearned . . .

Things are as they are and will end as they must.

Michael's perception of reality is not quite adequate.

The devil lives in the fine print.

If you do not care where you are, you can't get lost.

Good people get to die first.

The universe is not run by the merit system.

In every paradise there lives a serpent.

A clean shop means nothing is being done.

From a sheet in MCR's diary book, where he jotted down Grandfather's sayings when they came to him, came the following.

Grandfather was possessed with an uncanny memory for numbers. He could remember a number, no matter how insignificant, for the remainder of his life. It used to worry my mother.

One of my earliest recollections was Grandfather being pulled home in a shiny car by a team of horses. It stuck in my mind, I think, because the horses signified milk to me, since they came daily with a milk wagon driven by Mr. McCream, as we called him.

Years later, I asked Grandfather about this event and he said that was lesson number 4,783.

He and a friend were on a remote road on the way to hunt up a week's meat. A jackass was walking in the middle of the road and no amount of hollering and stone throwing by his companion could persuade the donkey to pull over to the side.

With confidence, Grandfather told his friend to watch this. He pulled right up behind the donkey and blew the horn. With one flick of the donkey's heel, he put his hooves right through the grill and radiator, ruining the rest of their trip.

The lesson in Grandfather's mind was that when dealing with mule-heads stay clear and be patient.

When you keep looking back on your memories, you quit getting things done. Nostalgia is fun, but if you want to accomplish something look to the future.

☺ ☺

Don't trust people that don't die, they have something wrong with them.

Remember to fulfill your anxiety.

What the hell, I'm a Rubel.

If it does not work, don't fix it.

One man can't fix everything.

On July 26, 2003, Michael added this to his black notebook of Grandfatherisms:

Some people were walking through the packinghouse and they asked, "How did all this stuff happen?"

Grandpa replied, "We just forget to take things to the dump."

Packing House, aka The Tin Palace

One day when Michael complained about how much work it was mixing the cement for one of the endless Pharm projects, Grandfather replied,

"Don't tell people about the labor pains. Show them the baby."

People really don't care about your problems . . .

*"I hit my finger with a hammer and cried out saying how it hurt."
Grandpa said,
"I don't feel anything."*

MCR called him "Grandfather." Mrs. Rubel, Michael's Mom, called him Harry. Everyone else called him Mr. Rubel.

*Walking through the packinghouse with some people, they asked him,
"Are you worried about a fire?"
"Gad, if this placed burned down it might be worth something,"
Grandfather replied.*

If you loan out your tools, they come back BROKEN. If you loan out your wife, she comes back happy.

Every time you predict the future, the future changes.

It takes a thousand people to build a bridge and only one to destroy it.

Michael Clarke Rubel used to say . . . .

To love is to die a little. There is no greater joy.

Your *life* is in my hands. Do you understand that . . .?"

Cliff Notes on Kid Michael

Michael Rubel's father died when he was six.

Michael, through a variety of luck, unplanned connections, and genetically sparked wonderful humor, purchased in the 1960's the Pharm from Al Bourne, the then owner of Singer Sewing Machine. Soon his mother, and then his grandfather, came to live at the Pharm, to help Kid Michael figure out how to make the Pharm work, earn a living, and build a life.

Kid Michael probably got confused with the saying that goes . . .

> *"One makes a living by what one gets, one makes a life by what one gives."*

For in chasing his dream of fort and castle building, he didn't seem to make much of a living but made a very expansive life for himself and the hundreds of others whom he allowed to enter his quixotic castle-chasing dream of life.

Kid Michael probably also got confused about what the meaning of a house was, after having lived in too many childhood observatories, forts, and open roads circumnavigating the world via mules, ships, Harleys, trains, flat bed trucks, and thumbs. Fortunately, for thousands of commoners who have come to visit and work, as well as the likes of Prince Philip, Michael continued confusing suburban home dwellers with his Romantic Era Castle of Junk.

(Yes, the Prince married to Queen Elizabeth—and a repeat visitor to Rubelia—since he claims, "It is the only American castle I care to visit.")

Grandfather's words and attitudes had a huge impact on Michael's approach to life. Even the book, <u>Castles by Mike</u>, inspired by Grandfather back in 1967 glimpses the playful approach to life that sunk so deeply into Michael's head. Castles by Mike opens with a picture of an experienced fortress and castle builder, Michael, smiling and saying:

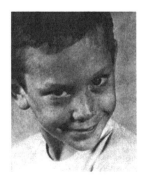

**General Contractor
Mike**

I'm Mike. I build castles.

Everybody dreams of castles now and then, but I build 'em.' I'd like the chance to be your General Contractor when you decide you really want to build one.

Let me show you some pictures I took of my work. I think you'll agree I have to be the most experienced castle builder anywhere around, these days. Experience is important in a project of this nature.

In closing, the <u>Castles by Mike</u> book shows Michael's latest work at that time. Kid Mike adds:

Yes sirree! This is it. My masterpiece.

And ecologically pristine—never cut down a single tree.

You know that if you are going to stay in style today, you gotta build highrise. That top deck is 65 feet above the ground.

MCR's 14 story fort

I can build you a bomb shelter and a penthouse and put as many floors and rooms in between as you want.

What do you think? I doubt that you can find a more experienced castle builder anywhere. After all—I went into this business when I was 7. I'm 9 now.

Let me hear from you when you're ready to build. I'll take all of the details off your hands. I'll see that the job is done right and you get exactly what you want.

It's been nice talking to you. Don't forget to give me a call. I'll see you again soon—I hope.

It's amazing what a little kid can accomplish who listened to things he had heard all his life from wise elders who cared . . . and who thought Kid Michael was special. And who valued kidhood.

> For those who like to see the result of an upbringing that pivoted around hard word, some sweat, phun talk, good thought, and community . . .
> "This is how the Castle was shaping up as Michael went through what he called the Golden Years."

Official 1970's U-2 photo of Rubelia

This official 1970's U-2 photo of Rubelia was supplied by the guy who'd do whatever the Prez asked him to, G. Gordon Liddy, a secret phone tap visitor to the Pharm and friend to our Crazy Bill. Well, we guessed G. Gordon signed the Rubelian Guest Book as "Friend," but his penmanship was so bad it could have been "Fiend." Oh, well, Grandfather sometimes said to look for the best in all kinds of people.

National security concerns required these stealth security photos and others to be done to satisfy national security concerns regarding Pharmhands and their nefarious, troubling, and hidden activities so that their danger assessment can be properly calibrated. Under the FOIA (Freedom of Information Act), these pictures were obtained prior to the Bush II Administration. Since the Bush II administration, all Rubelian related information, even that shared with the FBI during MCR's earlier compliance with the Commie scare days, has been reclassified.

Pharmhands presently have no access to even their Nixonian tapped phone conversations, even though the splitters and taps may still be there in the old phone box behind the parking shed.

Even under today's early 21st century conditions trying the souls of True Patriots, however, one of Rubelia's Security Team Tunnel mottos, adapted from Grandfather's approach to life, still applies;

"They can spy, but we can still hide."

What you see in the U-2 photo would not exist today were it not for the seasoned and smile-evoking wisdoms of the old timers who raised Michael Clarke Rubel. Even in today's political world, the roles Grandfather played in front of Michael came back to be replayed in Michael's life.

Here's one of those molding roles Grandfather played that allowed many Pharmers to ramble down Rubelia's old bricked driveway—which over decades turned into railroad-tied, then marbled-stone, then packed dirt, which were always artfully portrayed with domesticated animal droppings.

> The Glendora City Council was always trying to do things to me and the Pharm. One day they tried to pass an ordinance saying people couldn't live in tin packinghouses. Grandfather was there and stood up and said to Mayor Finkbinder,
>
> "Joe, it seems to me that you forgot how a lot of people got to this town. Why don't you recall how your family came to town and moved into the pump house on Leadora (Avenue), because they couldn't afford anything else?"
>
> After Grandfather rambled through his unique historical perspective, the Glendora City Council DID NOT pass an ordinance to keep Pharmers from living in the Packing House's refrigerators, and the other tinny sheds that circled the reservoir from which the Castle would rise.

So, it was said

Grandpa looked in on MCR when Michael was living in the bottle house.

He came with a bottle of wine, sat down in the one mangy blue chair, and said,

"Michael you've taught me something . . .
There's more than one way to stay single."

House available for Paris Hilton . . .

For those interested in and keeping track of
how "perfect projects" and people grow . . .
"The Bottle House is the castle in embryo."
And where several of us lived for some spells.

Chapter 3

Quiet giants who formed Michael

Odo Stade and Stanley Baird

Head Janitor Michael talks about the people who taught him how to use a broom and dust pan.

"The Biggest influences on my life were probably Odo Stade #1, Stanley #2, and Grandpa #3. Stanley and Grandpa used to always stick up for me and answer Mother with one-liners . . ."

"Your grandfather loved you, Michael," I interjected, as Michael paused looking into space.

"Well, I don't remember him saying that. But he did say I 'was fun to watch.'"

This reminiscence starts with Michael adorned in his stained, greasy overalls, bottomed off with another pair of unmatched loafers. He was in the reservoir working on something—pushing bottles in squiggly cement, tying mattress springs to some rebar for the next day's cementing, or tugging on some rusted lug nut on one of the aged vehicles. I can't remember exactly which of those important business ventures he was doing, with his floppy, creosoted hat topping his giddy smile.

Glen and I entered the reservoir and started talking with him, expecting a couple whimsical stories to tumble from his mouth while he tool-puttered. After continued putterings, some stories, and several chuckles, the time of day was mentioned.

With important rulers who become absorbed in establishing their empires, the track of time is often ignored. So it was so often with the Castle's benevolent dictator.

Michael's ignoring of time during the pursuit of his loves—hard work, funky building, and castle raising—accounted for many broken dates and stunted romances.

Several times, Michael's ignorance as to how to conduct (according to inhabitants of Venus) the pretty woman chase left broken hearts in the wake of his persistent trips to the tool shed. Ah, but consider, had there been fewer broken hearts there probably would have been fewer Pharm antiques laid in the concrete of broken dates. The old gas tank, for one, obvious on driving down the driveway of the big gate, was cemented around one of those many crushed dates.

On that Pharm replica, Michael remembered a date—the day after spending 15 hours laying and connecting the donated 42 year old bubble head gas tank from some old service station claimed from an era preceding the high finned, V-8 times. Such *forgettenences* by Men from Mars done unto Women from Venus don't bond the heart as well as arriving with a flower on time. But . . . such *forgettenences* sure do plough a phunny Pharm and build a goofy Castle.

Michael's hands were fiddling with some contraption while his mouth was playfully fibbing us with some escapade of life when the hour of day came up. Michael's smiling head slowly rose up from his chore.

"Is today Wednesday?" he asked.

"Yeah," we answered.

"You said it's 5:55?" Michael asked.

"Right."

"Oh, my . . . Stanley will be here! Will you put these tools away? And when Stanley comes, will you send him up. I've got to clean up."

Stanley's day

With that Michael rushed off, acting as though the place was on fire, or he was about to grievously offend his mother. Glen knew Michael and Stanley much better than newcomer I. But even Glen had forgotten the weekly day of gratification etched in Michael's very being.

Wednesday was Stanley's Day.

Every Wednesday at 6:00 p.m., Stanley would come by. Often Michael and Stanley would go out to dinner. Sometimes Michael would cook for him in the big kitchen. If friends had invited Michael over for dinner or a party on Stanley's day, Michael politely refused, or asked if Stanley was also invited. Then he'd check with Stanley. If Stanley didn't feel like doing it, they did whatever else Stanley preferred.

Stanley was one of Michael's loved ones. Stanley was one of those who raised Michael to be the character and man so many of us love.

So, who was Stanley?

Stanley Baird

I long wanted to tell the Stanley story that Michael told to me. Michael had said I couldn't until Stanley and a pair of brothers had passed away.

Now if you knew or read about Michael you will know he learned from the old timers he loved to live by several phunny rules. One was that the straight truth and nothing but the truth (not to be confused with the recently maligned straight talk bantered about in political campaigns) wasn't as important as making people happy. So, you can judge your belief in this story . . . Or go to NPR, find the Prairie Home Companion, and hire Investigator Guy Noir who is also searching for answers to life's persistent mysteries. Me, I always loved being a believer in MCR, with or without NPR and Guy Noir. (NPR = National Public Radio for those who only get their purported news from FOX Views) You can also research what's here and find that the story stands on its own without a chalk board and prop man.

As a young man, Stanley worked at a variety of manual and menial jobs. He worked hard and quietly and saved pennies when pennies were worth more than its copper.

One day two of Stanley's more "A Personality" friends, who hadn't saved nearly as many pennies, came to Stanley with a business proposition. Stanley, in his gentle way, was not willing to part with so many of his hard-earned pennies to these brothers.

But his persistent friends did not quit.

Sometime later Dorothy Rubel, Michael's always statuesque mother with the flamboyant style gleaned from her Gibson Girls and singing Duell Sister days, where she hobnobbed with Bing Crosby, Bob Hope and others, was having a party at her home for Glendora's notables; many of whom were her real estate clients. Stanley's investment-searching friends offered to provide food for the party.

As Stanley was enjoying the party, his brothers asked him more than once how he was enjoying the food. "Wonderful . . ." was Stanley's reply, which matched the response of many others at the party.

"This, Stanley! This food is what we want you to invest in . . . This is what we need your money for to launch our business . . ."

Well, Stanley was a hard worker. A quiet, gentle man. And a soft touch.

Dishwashing investor

Stanley lent them the money. His driven friends did the business. In return, Stanley had a job in one of the food stores washing dishes, serving out food, and working the cash register.

Stanley continued renting a room from a lady friend in Pasadena and being one of Michael's quiet mentors, along with Odo Stade and Grandfather.

One day his friends excitedly came to Stanley to discuss their business deal. Politely, Stanley listened.

"Well, why are you telling me this?" Stanley asked.

"Stanley, you are a partner. Someone has offered to buy our 14 (or some such number) stores."

"But I have always left the business decisions up to you. Do what you want."

"Stanley, this is different. You are a partner. Without your investment, this offer would not be there."

So gentle Stanley, the dishwasher, began thinking a little like a partner. He came up with one requirement that must be met before he would sell. He took his requirement with his partners to meet the entrepreneurial buyer.

Stanley's requirement had little to do with business. It had a lot to do with friendship.

In their first San Bernardino store, Stanley and his black friend shared the stocking, sandwich creating, milkshake-making, dishwashing, cash registering chores, which in their systemized eating place was just about all you had to do. Stanley's requirement? One local store in their chain, where he and his black friend worked, had to be kept. "Sell all the stores for whatever you feel is fair but keep this one so Eddie (may not be correct name) and I will always have a job."

The potential buyer had nice offices. His revenue was made selling milk shake machines. This man, however, was not smooth and easy going, as milk shakes were meant to be. During their meeting, he was the un-tastefully lumpy, pugnacious, pushy, hardnosed businessman.

The pushy businessman made a take-it-or-leave-it offer to buy every one of their feeding stores.

Stanley, in his easygoing manner, tried more than once to explain how they needed to withhold one store. Harshly, and maybe with expletives, the buyer repeated his all or nothing offer.

To these beratings, mild mannered Stanley merely got up and quietly walked out of the room.

The pushy buyer ranted, raved, and roared.

In the end, the well-heeled buyer caved to the dishwasher's demands.

Stanley and Eddy kept working at the orphaned store, but the irked businessman did not forget, forgive, or turn the other cheek.

Upset at being bested by a towel man and floor sweeper, the well-heeled new chain owner opened a new store of his recently acquired chain across the street from the store Stanley retained. The angry owner was ready to do whatever was needed to monopolize the block. He slashed the price of his food and drinks by several pennies, when pennies bought a lot of milk shake. Brilliant, strategic, and cut-throat entrepreneur that he was, he knew he would soon drive Stanley and Eddy out of business.

But a funny thing happened on the way to the bank, back in those days when friendships stood taller than checkbook deposits.

During those lean and good times, Stanley's food had been there for his patrons. When lean times hit in the late 30's and 40's, patrons often did not have money to cover all they and their families may have wanted or needed. Even his brotherly business partners criticized Stanley's response to the needs of his patrons, but it was Stanley's way.

"Well, you come back and pay us when you can," Stanley would say to young and struggling patrons and families.

"Come back and pay us when you can . . ."

That strange approach to business came back to haunt the big businessman's monopoly plans for Park Place.

The new owner with big business plans kept lowering his price well below that of Stanley's, yet instead of drawing crowds through his doors he garnered picketers with signs saying, "Don't eat here! Eat at Stanley's!"

And eat at Stanley's the people did. Stanley's shop survived. The big owner counted the dollars he was losing and left that losing store to open others elsewhere.

What to do with all this money?

The brothers and Stanley suddenly had a lot of money. The brothers bought mansions in Palm Springs and enticed Stanley to do likewise. With so much money, yet with great reticence, Stanley did as they suggested. Yet, according to Michael, Stanley visited his gated Palm Springs Estate only once. Stanley continued renting his one room in Pasadena and visiting his protégé Michael every week.

In the early 70's, Michael was living in one of the wood paneled, character rich refrigerators in the Packing House. After darkness had set and the whimsical daylight power that Michael somehow cast over us to keep working had waned, that refrigerator often served as a gathering place for wine drinking, out of shrimp cocktail or canning canisters, and talk. Sometimes it would be just Glen, Michael, and a couple others. Other times there would be twenty or thirty sitting on the floor and outside of the 6" thick, steel handled door.

Sometimes the room would fill with raucous stories about the Pharm or other adventures. Mostly we'd want to hear Michael tell stories about the Pharm or his dozens of worldwide hijinks. Sometimes there would be political debates with Michael and Skipper telling us how wonderful and needed it would be to have America swing to the right. Glen and I would counter with how unhealthy that would be. Most of the room had to grapple with choosing on which branch of the Pharm's citrus or avocado trees they would choose to stand. On those nights a jovial crowd could argue, laugh, and roar while gallons of Gallo jug wine were sipped through shrimp cocktail glasses and jars, which only added to the raucous cheers from jarheads to pencil heads' worldviews.

As the decades piled up, however, Michael moved his quiet muscle toward the side Glen and I envisioned in the world. In recent years he would often say, "What a wonderful President Bill Clinton was compared to that dumb Bush."

They were wonderful gatherings, unmarred by television, cell phones, or fanciness. They were filled with straight talk from the Pharm land, mirth, and fanciful playfulness, always lightly fueled by gallon Gallo jugs of wine.

To provide such sustenance, every month or so jarhead Michael rolled out his mechanized division to add just enough sweetness to all such gatherings. By stuffing his ancient Beatle Bug Volkswagen, with the wooden arm signals, full of 30 four-pack boxes of Gallo jug wine purchased from a San Bernardino winery, MCR always had enough wet stuff for his debating teams to cheer or cry into.

One night I went to the Tin Palace, aka Packing House, removed my shoes per Mrs. Friezner's commandment, and walked hopefully through the Tin Palace's open door to MCR's refrigerator to partake in another round of Pharmers' repercussive discussions.

The freezer door was open, the lights were on, soft music was eking out of the wood framed radio from the early 1900's, and I stood there looking at the room's only two chairs. Two hundred + pounds of Michael, in a clean flannel shirt, with his arms on the arm cushions, his head straight, and his mouth only slightly open, was asleep.

In the other leather chair, Stanley slept.

My stockings and I quietly left the Packing House. It was a quiet Wednesday.

A few days later, I asked, "Michael, do you and Stanley ever run out of things to talk about?"

"Oh, sure," he responded.

"What do you do?"

"Oh, sometimes nothing. Sometimes we just sit there."

"Don't you get bored?" I asked.

"No. Not me . . . Whatever Stanley wants to do, I'll do . . . I just love that man . . ."

"Do you guys sometimes just fall asleep?

"Sure. Sometimes we say nothing all night long. When he falls asleep, I'll just carry him into a bedroom where he can sleep . . . I owe him so much . . . I love that man."

Not any of us Pharmhands could carry the man Michael was. But many of us could repeat those last two sentences in reference to Michael.

"I owe him so much . . . I love that man."

Birthing the Golden Arched Big Mac

Stanley Baird died in 1972. His partners Mac and Dick McDonald died in 1971 and 1998, with 99 billion burgers sold under their names. Ray Kroc died in 1984. Michael Clark Ruble died October 15, 2007.

Odo Stade

Michael, while recovering from a medical setback in 2005, talking about three of the men he admired and loved . . .

"Odo (Stade) was more intellectual than my grandfather and Stanley. He knew the biography of Brahms and Beethoven. All this stuff my grandfather and Stanley weren't interested in. So there wasn't too much in common to talk about, but they all got along fine. It's just they weren't close friends. They didn't sit around together and . . . (CHEW the fat, I interject) . . . Yes, chew the fat."

"When you said he was very formal . . . Would Grandfather cuss and swear sometimes and Odo wouldn't?" I asked.

"Well, grandfather ran a big crew in Denver, Colorado in a steel mill, and they were primarily Swedes, and his language was very coarse. But when Grandfather was around anyone other than that, he never used bad language. And one time my mother and the Lawtons, Landons, and my grandfather were down at the big auditorium at Citrus (Citrus College) and they had what they call the San Gabriel Valley Symphony organization . . .

Well, we're all sitting there . . . listening to the music and you know how sometimes the music stops and you don't know if it's over or not?

"Well, my grandfather looks around when the music stopped and no one was applauding and he says, "Boy . . ." and it's heard all over, ". . . What the fu _ _, I thought it was pretty good."

"And my Mother was mortified, absolutely mortified. And he looks around and they start playing again and Grandfather says, "Wha . . . what happened there?"

My mother says, "Grandfather, I'll explain it later."

Odo and Pancho

Odo Stade standing to Pancho Villa's right.

"Odo Stade rode with Pancho Villa. He was there when Villa was assassinated in 1923. And Odo got wounded also. When I saw the wounds on Odo's chest . . . I just cannot believe that he could have lived through that because they were huge bullet holes. And I just cannot understand how he could have survived it.

"How many?"

"I think there were like three . . . But maybe they were just ricochets or something."

"But a big black car pulled up at the hacienda and when Villa went out with about five friends to greet them, they opened up with a machine gun. Killed everybody but Odo and one other man.

"And Odo changed his boots with Pancho Villa because his boots were better and he put his boots on Villa and took his boots. Villa's girlfriend had his 45 and it was a much better 45 than his so for about $4-5 dollars or something, he traded the guns. And then Villa's scabbard for holding his rifle, his boots, and his pistol were given to me when I was about 15 years old . . . ."

Odo came to Hollywood. He got a job doing stunt piloting. They called it barn storming, where he'd crash into a barn for Buster Keaton. I think he broke a leg the first time, broke an arm the next time, decided there was no future. So, he got a job at a Hollywood bookstore because he could speak six languages and that's how he met his wife, Maria, because she could only speak German and she would come in for German books. So anyway, the owner of the bookstore, when it crashed in 1929, gave the whole thing to Odo.

And then Odo went broke, because no one was buying books.

"And he was diagnosed with tuberculosis and the doctor said he had about six months to live. (In 1929) So he went up to the High Sierras and camped and fished and whatever and then got better. And he met a man named Sahib. Sahib was a multi-millionaire, I guess. He had about 20 mules and pack animals and tents and men working for him and he offered Odo a job helping with the mules, called a muleskinner. And so Odo got this job and a more luxurious way of life.

"And then Odo asked him if he could go to Hollywood and propose to a lady that he knew and bring her back. Sahib and Odo got along really well. In fact, I met Sahib because he used to come and visit the Stades. They called him Sahib, I don't know why.

"Maria accepted, understanding she'd be living out in the mountains in tents and stuff. But Maria said it was so luxurious because they had canvas bathtubs and they'd heat water up with fire. And she could take a bath, and she said that was just unheard of in the High Sierras. And the food was good, and everyone was very nice. So, they did that for about four years and then Odo came down and worked for the US Forest Service. He was the only patrolman on the north side of the Angels National Forest. He worked for the Valleyermo National Forest, on the desert side. He had to patrol on a horse between Apple Blossom and Big Pine, back and forth. He had a house at Valleyermo with Maria. But he'd be gone like for a week at a time. He said there was nothing to do, but he just rode back and forth. Then when they needed a dispatcher, in about 1940, when everyone was going to war, they needed a dispatcher down in Glendora, at the forest service building, to run the radio. They asked him to come do that and he did. That's when they moved to Glendora. They lived in a Forest Service house on Lorraine Avenue, right on the southeast corner of Bennett and Lorraine . . .

"That was just a block away from where we lived . . . I'd go there to get candy from Maria. I didn't know Odo at that time.

"But then my mother gave Odo and Maria a half acre north of our house, where the Scotty house is now. And she gave that with the hope that they'd build a house there and help raise me, since she was always off at work. And they agreed to that. That was about 1952, I think. They built their house there.

Odo Stade at Colby Ranch, August 1917
Photo by Harold Miles
Wandalee Thompson Collection
Sierra Madre Historical Archives
(2002.1.33)

"And then I lived in the observatory, which was a little block house building that my father had built for a telescope. We used to call it the observatory. And that's still there actually. So, I lived there and that was about 20 feet away from Odo and Maria. So, I would go over there and read and listen to music and listen to Odo's stories. That's why Odo became so important in my life. He was a very proper and honest, ethical . . . just a perfect person . . .

He told stories about Villa, Loomis Ranch, about Buster Keaton, who he said was as funny off stage as he was on stage. He liked Keaton. He said Keaton would have a script for each of his films and they were supposed to follow the script. And there would always be somebody who would think up something funnier and then someone else would respond with something funnier . . . And then Buster Keaton would say, 'Throw all those damn scripts away and just do what you want. It's better than the stuff I wrote for you.' And everyone would laugh and carry on and then he'd cut out stuff he couldn't use and use what he could and everyone liked him.

"Odo had a very interesting life."

Buster Keaton and Michael's scripts

Michael was the phunny Head Janitor of the Pharm, and King of the Castle who would often let us play in his childish game of life by letting us,

> *"Throw all those damn scripts away*
> *and just do what you want . . ."*

And Michael would often say,

> *"It's better than the stuff I wrote for you."*

Then we Pharmers would tally-ho,

> *"And everyone would laugh and carry on and then he'd*
> *cut out stuff he couldn't use and use what he could and*
> *everyone liked him."*

And sometimes, we'd get Michael to sing "The Fox" . . . and we'd laugh even more. And no one would try to match The Fox script because no one could sing it better than the Phunny Head Janitor.

Michael built a lovely, phunny Pharm, a wondrous Castle, and an army of admirers following the wisdoms of his elders. And we all had fun, phun, and puns hanging around Michael and the stunts he would run.

May Michael, orbiting above with all his electrifying energy, send down his wonderful spark to all those who knew and loved him, especially when we earth-bounders need his energy and moxie. And may he also help those trying to understand this book.

And in order to understand, may all those reading remember the mottos that filled Rubelian air:

"Hard work is fun."
"A clean bird is a happy bird."
"Safety Third."

And happily consider grandfather's phun puns that filled the cavities of Michael's head and the tunnels of his Rubelian Castle,

"I never watched a man work
more on a place
to make it totally worthless."

For Grandfather Deuel knew, and taught Michael who taught most of his tunneling crews, that digging life in overalls was a helluva lot more interesting than Gucci shopping.

Passing it on

Like families so often do, grandfather passed lessons, thoughts, and dreams onto his grandson. Since Michael lost his father at an early age, many younger-than-grandfather old timers joined the game of passing on more of the same to MCR.

Michael, to some of us, was a big guy wizened well beyond his years living his life like a kid just a few yards outside the sandbox. Being so tied to playing in the sandbox, or sand/cement box, Michael relied on wisdoms passed down from grandfather and the old timers. Those wisdoms mixed well with the rules learned playing in kindergarten sandboxes.

Michael lived the wisdoms of old timers in building a castle of boys' dreams. Many were blessed to share in the building and soaking in of some of those wisdoms.

What follows are some stories of a few of the many Pharmers who learned what

"Grandfather used to say . . ."
by hanging around the sand/cement box with the Head Janitor, who turned grandfathers' words, and the cement mixer, into Castle play.

Chapter 4

Other best friends

"My fate was ever safest in your hands."

If you read the previous story about Stanley Baird, it started as a story about Michael's friend, whose name was changed in my first draft from Stanley to Bradley. After doing 752 words of that "Bradley" story, the King of Rubelia read the draft and wagged his finger at me. I obediently wagged my tail, took my bony fingers to the keyboard, and hid the Stanley story in a folder until restarting it in this 2009 day. In the meantime, I punched out this "Other best friends" story.

In the end, the heart and soul of both stories is the same.

They are stories about a friend and his friend.

So, after Michael's bark, I temporarily buried the story of one of Michael's humble and dearest friends, for whom MCR would have fetched anything. Well buried was the Stanley story, if you believe Pharm stories, about a man who may have helped launch an American business venture that arches above almost any other. Instead, a little bark from Michael back then drove me to write about one of his humble and dearest friends, who seldom barked or uttered a harsh word.

Maybe dogs are man's best friends. Maybe they are . . . the only things on earth that love you more than they love themselves . . . smarter than some people, because they wag their tails and not their tongues . . . best friends, because they are not always calling for explanations.

Maybe those doggone truths are why, back in its frontiering and castle building days, when the Pharm was an all-male bastion; there were so many dogs around. Pharm guys needed that doggie camaraderie and moral support that Pharm fireplaces, big beams, and tool sheds didn't supply enough of to us of the weaker gender.

When this stumbling alphabet picker took up residence at the Pharm, Nadia (in adjoining picture) was ruler of the Pharm's Dog Pack. On any outing, she expected the respect afforded any top-notch Master Sergeant. If Michael's 28-year-old Willys jeep (still parked between cactus and garage) was to lead the patrol, Nadia would point the way as she tried to balance herself as the hood ornament behind the wench and over the rusted tan engine cover. If she wasn't hood pointing, while trying to dig her sliding paws into the metal of the jeep, she barked orders from her shotgun seat with its worn to the foam and busted through front springs, as us mere boys and other dogs piled into the back's metallic rumple seat.

Then Nadia was still an imposing 80+ pound black and white mostly German Shepherd. She seemed fearless and didn't hesitate to remind other dogs who was Ruler of the Pharm Pack.

Of course, even dogs get old and their rules wind down. In winding down, however, unlike some packs of jungle animals, the Pharm's dog pack lived by a more civilized rule. Since Nadia had always ruled with a fair paw, the other dogs still followed and gave her the comforts she was due. Pharmhands as well as the errant Knights of the Pharm Round Table even more respectably followed their point dog's lead into any quixotic escapade.

That is not to stay Nadia totally had her way. Even a ruler is burdened with a headache or two.

After a year or two at the Pharm, the Pharm hands recognized that I was in need of a companion who, without ever reading the book, could help me "Win Friends and Influence People." One Saturday, they forced such a gorgeous companion on me.

I was up early that day pounding nails into 2x4s, hoping this puzzle of wood would soon stand and turn into a home. Nail pounding may not have been my preferred early Saturday morning activity, but Michael had deviously imprisoned and shackled me—by cuffing and limiting my sleeping hours with an alarm clock made of corrugated tin switched on by the early morning sun.

Gift of tin roofed alarm clock

How is one fettered by a tin-made alarm? You receive such a Rubelian Tin Man made gift by spending months in the Virgin Islands trying ineptly to help Pharm architect Glen Speer build a St. John business, only to return to the Pham to find someone else residing in what was once your tree house. As you sit in the big kitchen with Michael, asking if there might be another place on the Pham for you to be, he pours you the customary Pharm chai and gives you an uncustomary fortune cookie that says something like: "You can build your house on the Northeast corner of the Pharm . . . Maybe . . ."

After diligently studying the crumpled words, I queried, "What's the 'maybe,' Michael?"

"Well, you can try to build the place, but I won't buy anything for it. You either build it with what's around here or you buy what you need," said the dumb Head Janitor, and cunningly keen landlord.

"Okay," said I, understanding the Pharm rule that he who nails the piled-around-the-Pharm junk first—homesteads it. I figured I'd road runner those piles of Feather River project rail road ties, junk wood, beams, 2x4's and other stuff lying around into the walls of my house. For the rest, I'd rely on that special Pharm genie who always seems to come by and fill the need. (As usual, she did.) The genie just required that I supply the labor in recycling old barns and wineries into the wood that would eventually surrounded bed, fireplace, windows, glass, kitchen, bathtub, etc.)

"Oh, and one other thing . . ." said the Tin Man.

"What's that?" said innocent I.

"Until you finish. You have to live in the bottle house," continued the keen, yodaish one.

"The bottle house?" swallowed I.

"Yeph. The bottle house. It'll inspire you to work hard and fast," smiled the cunning one, as the big guy encased in his levied apron marched away with a R2DT waddle, "Gotcha" smile, and Yoda twinkle in his eye.

Bottle House living

For those of you who haven't "lived" in the bottle house, which includes most everyone in the western hemisphere, except for Michael and some of Michael's cousins, and maybe for a night or two the Moffets, Jim Lambert, Dan Sugden, Scott Rubel, Bruce Burr, and myself—allow me to describe.

Michael built the bottle house around his eighteenth year, while parts of his brain still functioned at warp maturity speed 12. It was made of neighborhood donations—bags full of emptied colored wine, ketchup, and soda bottles, which appeared on the driveway most every morning. Neighbors left MANY MORE than enough bags of bottles, as the Castle's walls attest, so building a cemented 6'x8' bottle house was "nada problemo."

Sitting smack dab in the middle of the reservoir (now ensconced by the Castle), the bottle house's interior was designed by some degenerated decorator from centuries back. It held a chair that Salvation Army threw away long before Michael was busy being 12. Its heating system was a Civil War state-of-the-art pot bellied stove. Chuck-full of wood, this high-techie burned for an hour or two to stem the chill of the night before reverting to its refrigeration mode—by sucking in the night's cold through the eaves' gaps between tin and the last row of cemented bottles and gaps in the hand made, lumbering door.

Visitors to this lavish retreat reached the second floor via a ladder that bumped one's head into the corrugate tin ceiling. Nestled on the unevenly beamed floor of the loft was something reminiscent of an old mattress, covered by a wounded World War I sleeping bag. Both these garments of nighttime repose fleas refused to share, even with as tasty a red-blooded body as mine and whoever else might dare. That, except for a couple bottlenecks that stuck out enough to function as a hook, on which one could hang one's trouser and shirt, was each and every one of the bottle house's lavish amenities.

Escaping Sally Rand, Bing Crosby, Bob Hope, Joe Penner . . .

Michael built the bottle house as his and his dogs' hideout from Mrs. Rubel's (Mother's) Tin Place orchestrated theatrical productions, which included her friends: Fan dancer Sally Rand, Bing Crosby, Bob Hope, Joe Penner . . . . In addition to being an escape during those dramatic times, Michael used the bottle house, sitting in the middle of the empty reservoir, as his launching pad for today's soaring Castle.

On his day of negotiations with me, MCR used the nighttime refrigerator and morning-oven baking features of the bottle house to insure my quick removal from the reservoir floor and into a completed house on the Northeast corner, known today as the Chip House. Of course, Michael's real negotiating gambit may have been to drive a sane person into quitting such foolhardy building and living attempts and move to a more normal outside world rental setting.

Living in "that bottle house," one learns quickly of tin's insulating qualities. Tin colds quickly. When surrounded by a cement reservoir and encased in a cemented and bottled oven, tin heats rapidly. Sleeping in this bottle contraption, amidst the crinkling sound of the early morning's baking and crackling tin oven, spiced with a hint of left over ketchup, serves as a quiet but effective EARLY MORNING SUFFOCATING alarm clock to anyone within.

So, the bottle house hastened phunny Pharmer's move to boots, Levis, hammers, nail pounding, hauling, lugging, and related wood butchering pursuits . . .

Several hours into a Saturday morning pounding session, a little girl rides her horse into the reservoir with her hands cupping this barely visible white pup on her saddle. Working above the reservoir in my Northeast Territory effort to homestead, I hear Pharmhands down below "Oouing and Ahhing!" about the angelic puppy.

Then, from below, I hear, "But Dwayne doesn't have a dog . . . Isn't it pretty, Dwayne? You know you really need a dog, DWAYNE . . . Why don't you come down and look at this one."

"I don't have time for a dog. I've got to have a place to live first."

"Dogs don't take any time. Anyway, he can keep you warm in the bottle house," John Cox chuckled, as he moved into his metaphysical mode. "Now get down here and look into this doggie's eyes. If you don't take him, he's incinerator ash for the dog pound . . ."

Samoan-Husky wins hearts

So with such metaphysical pontifications, pure white Kia, a Samoan -Husky mix, came into my life and grew quickly to playfully exercise Nadia's undisputed rule over the Pharm's dog pound. Kia was not really a challenge to the throne. He was, however, smart, coordinated, healthy, and horny. Kia's first three attributes often riled Nadia, making her get up from any number of comfortable rests to try to teach Kia a lesson, only to have Kia's speed and coordination keep Kia free from any doffed disciplining.

Yes, Nadia was getting tired about the time Kia was wild and fancy-free. Kia's wild and fancy-free included being daring . . . and horny. Twice, I wrote a goodbye ode to my four-legged friend who pursued the shrill wail of the coyote in heat—in studly defiance of the waiting in ambush coyote pack. Each time, however, a day and a half or so later, bedraggled and bloodied Kia limped back through the Castle walls and through our Dutch doors to collapse in sleep. After a few days of licking his wounds, Kia would return to Nadia and to resting contentedly with the other Pharm dogs at Michael's feet.

As Nadia pushed into her dogged teens, her pace slowed, intimidating became harder, and her skin became more brittle. Nadia was suffering a lot in those days. Even rambunctious Kia would tease the leader no more, but merely lay at Nadia's feet in silent homage to the proud dog that could do little more.

Nadia's mange spread over her body. She scratched and itched. She suffered stoically. When Michael went to the jeep or town, Nadia wanted to also. But her feet would no longer go. Instead, her eyes followed sadly.

Michael sprinkled and bathed her. Lifted her. Brought food to her. Treated her gently, as she could do little more than lay on the rug at his feet.

One day I asked, "Michael, do you ever think about putting Nadia to sleep."

Lion hearted

"Yes . . ." he said looking first at her, then puffing his pipe, and looking at the smoke floating upward. "But I couldn't . . . You see, I owe my life to her."

"Your life?"

"You weren't here when we had the mules, were you?"

"No."

"I was given these mules on one of my travels through Mexico. Brought them back to the Pharm, hiking through the mountains. Thought they'd be neat to have around. After awhile, I thought it wasn't such a good idea, and it would be better to take them back to someone down there who could use them. And they gave me," he paused to add a temporary little smile to his somber demeanor, "an excuse to escape a beautiful woman who was tenaciously pursuing me . . . So Nadia and I hitched the mules up and started walking them back."

Michael paused for a while to relight his pipe, which often went down when words rather than puffs filled his air.

"One night we bedded down under this big rock. Mules were tied down. It was a pretty night. Pretty soon, I was sound asleep . . .

"But then Nadia woke me. She was growling at the rock above. I didn't know why, until I saw the tensed muscles of the mountain lion about to jump.

"My rifle was several feet away. I had no chance to reach it. The mountain lion jumped, and so did Nadia . . .' Michael paused, as he rocked in his chair.

"Nadia's no match for a mountain lion. The lion had maybe one or two hundred pounds on her," he added, as he looked straight ahead.

"Collided right above me. Hit me, as I rolled for my rifle.

"Nadia was knocked out on impact. I'm sure . . . But right there beside me, she kept fighting, like on instinct . . .

"I got my rifle . . . We survived . . ."

Michael lit that pipe again. He watched the smoke, as he often did when he felt he was emptied of words. Lifting his brows, he made his big-eyed face, pouted his little pout, watched the pipe smoke roll, and said, "I owe her my life . . . I don't think I can put her to sleep . . . ."

Michael didn't go to Stanley's funeral either. He said, "I owed him so much . . . I didn't think I could stand through it . . ."

The above initially penned around September 1992 and sent to MCR and Kaia for review.

And near the end, there was another of Michael's many four-footed best friends.

Lost Master

In December 2004, after several days of vomiting and diarrhea, Michael collapsed on his bedroom floor. After Kaia got help to get him into his Castle bed, she called former Troll House resident, Dr. Steve Roberts. He prescribed some Gatorade; and Michael slept through the night. The next day, before leaving for a ski trip as most "A Team" Southern California doctors do at Christmas time, Dr. Steve convinced Michael to have some X-rays done.

Michael reluctantly agreed and went where he maintained people went to get sick. The medical experts were upset with what they discovered about Michael's ticker, explaining to him that he had had a severe heart attack. Michael assessed the information and said he just wanted to go home. With the hospital's A Team out skiing, the remaining team dithered about their liability if they let Michael go.

The dithering was settled when Michael gave a Rubelian rather than factual response to the medical team's question of, "What will you do if you go home?"

"Get my rifle and shoot myself."

So, they wouldn't let Michael leave the place where people went to get sicker. And Michael got sicker.

When the A Team returned, they and some astute nurses convinced Michael to have an angiogram, which showed the A Team that MCR's blockage was so severe that they would not attempt surgery to clear the blockages. And they estimated Michael had not long to live.

So Michael crinkled his left arm and signed all sorts of liability releasing papers, but did not return home to rock strewn, cavernous halls, and the winding stairs of the Castle strewn in and out with millions of archaic yet functioning tools, unfathomable security systems, fireplaces, horses, dogs, hogs, and pollywogs . . . Instead, he bequeathed the Castle and his beloved dog to the Glendora Historic Society. And he went to Kaia's in-law unit at her children's home about a mile from the Castle.

When Glen and I arrived, one of the strongest men I have ever know, including bigger guys on football fields, was a white, pasty, sapped man confined to a recliner chair in the small bedroom off of Kaia's compact dining area.

Michael Clarke Rubel could hardly utter a weak sounding "Hello." His wave barely lifted his hand 3 inches off of the recliner chair's arm. All of us Pharmhands were scared for the loss of the giant character and spirit that Kaia and we loved.

Throughout life, Michael has had an elite circle of nuanced and direct advice givers to whom he would listen: Odo, Stanley, Glen, Skipper were in that special group. Advice or opinions from me were usually followed with a bemused smile—and later guffaws. But, perhaps because he knew my Mom had recovered from the stroke that doctors claimed would keep her in a vegetative state for what they suggested would be a short life, MCR let me start him on an alien-to-him jock's workout program that helped my Mom recover.

With concurrence of former Troll's House resident, Dr. Steve Roberts, Michael began a three a day workout program that started with me moving and tensioning his lifeless muscles. The routine progressed enough for the King of Rubelia to entitle me as his "Physical Terrorist." In weeks, his workouts grew to small weight lifting, stretching, standing, stepping in place, baby stepping, walker walking, and then walking—all tied to a new diet that Kaia was fashioning.

Adjacent to Kaia's home is an elementary school and playground. On its distant corner is a mailbox. By the second month of workouts, MCR was allowing himself to be coerced into walking outside, then to and along the chain-linked schoolyard fence, then to the mailbox rest stop where we'd drop letters.

Being a Glendoran institution, Michael as well as his dogs were known by most neighbors and school kids. Since puppy-hood, Jasper only left the walled, wired, barbed, and gated Castle with MCR. Now, however, in his noticeably depressed state, Jasper was sneaking out from beyond the Mad Max security systems. Not to fear though, neighbors and school kids would return Jasper to the Castle from whence they knew he came.

Walking the King

As Michael recovered to the point where he could walk and care for himself, so Kaia could go back to work finding all the research students wanted at Claremont Colleges' Honnold Library, he maintained he would not revisit the Castle. Not just because it was a "past era" of his life, but also because Jasper would be "devastated if he knew I were alive and had ignored him."

One day around August 2005, Michael told Kaia that someone was knocking at the front door. Kaia twice looked out and assured Michael that no one was there. Michael, known for his ability to hear termites chewing, persisted. The third time Kaia went to check, she opened the door.

The sounds Michael heard were neither termites chewing, nor knocks on a doorframe, but a dog pawing.

That pesky dog, who evaded the impossible-to-escape Castle's electronic gates, roamed the neighborhood in search of his Master's persisting creosote laden scent. In sniffing the hood about a mile away, Jasper found a mailbox, a schoolyard fence, a sidewalk, and then a house. The house emanated the scent of his burly, overalled janitor.

And what was gentle Kaia to do with whimpering Jasper at her door?

From that day till the end, friends could find and pet the friendly growling Jasper at MCR's feet, or playing in the big yard with the house's two other dogs, Buddy and Mattie, and budding All Star Christopher and his teeny friends.

In April 1989, I lost my last adopted German shepherd best friend, Oscar. My mom sent me this Dear Abby column, which I believe I shared with Michael. If I didn't, I'm sharing it now.

A Dog's Prayer
By Beth Norman Harris

Treat me kindly, my beloved master, for no heart in all the world is more grateful for kindness than the loving heart of me.

Do not break my spirit with a stick, for though I should lick your hand between the blows, your patience and understanding will more quickly teach me the things you would have me do.

Speak to me often, for your voice is the world's sweetest music, as you must know by the fierce wagging of my tail when your footsteps falls upon my waiting ear.

When it is cold and wet, please take me inside . . . for I am now a domesticated animal no longer used to bitter elements, and I ask no greater glory than the privilege of sitting at your feet beneath the hearth . . . though had you no home, I would rather follow you through ice and snow than rest upon the softest pillow in the warmest home in all the land . . . for you are my God . . . and I am your devoted worshiper.

Keep my pan filled with fresh water, for although I should not reproach you were it dry, I cannot tell you when I suffer thirst. Feed me clean food, that I may stay well, to romp and play and do your bidding, to walk by your side, and stand ready, willing and able to protect you with my life, should your life be in danger. And, beloved master, should the great master see fit to deprive me of my health or sight, do not turn me away from you. Rather hold me gently in your arms as skillful hands grant me the merciful boon of eternal rest . . . and I will leave you knowing with the last breath I drew, my fate was ever safest in your hands.

So, it was said . . .

*"My greatest sadness is when I have to put
a dog to sleep. I cry for weeks."*

Michael responding to Jason McHann's
interview for *the glendoran magazine.*

If you want your dog run over, keep him pinned up.

*Grandfather was always saying give animals and
children freedom or they'll get run over.*

Cry alone—laugh with others.
Grandfather

Jasper

Chapter 5

Remembering Old Witches

The good witch loaded with whammies.
Mrs. Friezner was one of the wise elders, who like Grandfather, zapped Michael and all of us lucky enough to know her.

David Copperfield does magic. If we are observant, and lucky, some of us have magic people dancing in our lives. Oftentimes the magic people waltzes us through magic places as they fly by. Harry Potter also hints that people must have some magic in them in order to see magic in people and places, be they old houses or junky castles.

Only two years remained before the hip decade of the 60's would be history. Five of us with two decades of experience under our belts were living on a 2.5 acre "Pharm" where piles of rail road ties were stacked and tottering 15 and 20 feet into the air, neighbors left bags of bottles in the driveway, rocks and tunnel beams—taken from the Los Angeles Feather River project via the Pharm's rattling 22 year old flatbed truck—were strewn here and there on the acreage. We knew the "collected junk" was to build memorable stuff and Michael's dream—A Castle Made of Leftovers. Unfortunately, the ritzy suburban neighborhood didn't have the same confident vision, imagination, or sense of foolhardiness.

For the five of us, there probably never was or could be a better home for that time, or maybe any time, of our lives. For me, at least, I don't believe there could have been any better place to live. On the other hand, the expensive surrounding suburban neighbors felt our home was just a bigger than life Sanford and Son backyard that made their eyes sore and dispositions sour.

Dwayne Hunn

Today, with a lot of help from his friends, luck and the good Lord, Michael and gang have buried most of that "collected junk" and other treasures within the walls of the 7 & 1/2 storied Rubelian Castle Made of Leftovers. Some of the collected junk became windmills made of retired telephone poles. Some of the railroad ties became the walls of my old house. Some of the siding from old barns and wineries became house walls, castle ceilings, and firewood. All of the neighbors' recycled bottles sit in the walls of the castle, sometimes reflecting their varied colors to the outside world when the thirteen Pharm fireplaces work their sparkles.

Dwayne Hunn doing his job at Rubel Farms.

They say that if you put enough monkeys in front of enough typewriters long enough, you can get the Bible written. If you have enough people pile enough junk together often enough, I reckon you can build a castle. I guess that's why so much junk sticking together attracts the

Glenn Speer - He builds great places at St. John Island. (1984)

refined likes of Harry Reasoner, Barbara Walters, Governor Dukemijian, Prince Philip, Michael Landon, Alfred Hitchcock, the Washington Post, L. A. Times, etc.

The five who were part of the Castle then have scattered some, but all those not wanted by the law still return to sit and talk amidst the bound-together junk. Glen Speer has taken his craftsmanship, skills and artistry to St. John, Virgin Islands where he is a local legend.

There the beauty of his Mongoose Junction shopping center caused the tour boats to move their dock to front his center; and the Rockefellers of Caneel Bay openly seek his advice. Ralph, who believed you really only needed to make the first few monthly payments on any long-term purchase, twice has escaped from confinements and seldom uses the Pharm as a reference in his credit checks. John Cox and his brother became the first two Americans to trek from the southern tip of Baja California to the California border. In part of that journey, they devoured a much thirsted-for six-pack and a crate of fruit as it was thrown to them from a steel yacht—by a tall, rugged American screen legend who answered to "Duke" most of his life.

This chronicler, who upon arrival at the Pharm couldn't tell the difference between a pipe and a socket wrench, became the Pharm gopher for many castle building projects and in the embarrassing process learned how to build a few things. Good training for a guy who the local high school and then Jerry Brown's California Conservation Corps would try to fire—both to their chagrin.

The Castle is a magnet to many, but those who have been part of its growth come back not so much for its treasure of collected junk but because of its now portly hearted—Head Janitor, Michael. We still sit around and talk about those who lived there in those hectic, hard working years. Most of us probably worked to obtain dreams then but knew not whether those dreams would be anything other than dreams. We talk of the others who came before and after, and the friends who still partake and what they are doing today.

"All ye who enter here, remove ye shoes and wear clean socks lest a curse be hung upon you."

Mrs. Friezner's commandment
Posted on door of the Tin Palace

In 1975, John Cox (left) and Alan Ehrgott, beginning their trek from the U.S. Border through Baja, California.

Often, we touch on those who were loved and are no longer with us. The ones whose spirits we remember best are probably those whose presence somehow helped us to make some dreams real. Often, they are people who seemed in some way surreal, above the ordinary, or so wizened that their mere presence could stoke the fires that built dreams. Sometimes they didn't look the role of dream builders. They didn't seem to be driving and pushing you. They just wanted you to have a good time, "but be a good boy," in having that good time. They are the kind of people who say, "So talking about it won't get it done—go do it . . ." They are the wise and worldly ladies who say, "Why don't you call the girl rather than think about calling her, you'll never know what she's like or if she even knows you are alive, if you keep your desires to yourself." They are those who don't dampen and put out your dreams but somehow put the broom to them just enough to make you trash them or test and build on them. Mrs. Edith Friezner had one of those brooms.

Michael knew her for fifteen years, loving her more each year. She cleaned for the influential people in town. She also cleaned for him. She cleaned the main kitchen, his room, and the Tin Palace with its collection of priceless antiques. Cleaning 4,000 square feet of hard wood floors is not easy for a lady well beyond the government's mandatory retirement age. To better equalize the work burden she, like all governments, made a law. "All ye who enter here, remove ye shoes and wear clean socks lest a curse be hung upon you." The law hung beside the door of the tin palace as a *beware* for all who entered. It still does.

The Shriek

Like all effective governments, she realized that education, information, and intimidation, when properly mixed, create an atmosphere from which effective administration happens. That may be why she became founding publisher and editor of The *Shriek,* the Pharm's monthly hand-scribed newspaper. All of us robust Pharmhands soon learned she had the most pervasive and bewildering network of undercover reporters ever assembled. How she found out about the most private and quietly (well, not always totally quietly) done adventures, we still don't know. That ability and the power of her often proven "hexes" made us all contrite about removing our shoes to the Tin Palace she named and helped fame. A hex of six weeks without a date for stepping into a no-shoe zone, failing to wash your dishes, or forgetting to clean the tool shop made more than one of us believers. The Shriek's monthly 2-10 pages brought a smile to all its readers' faces with her hand-sketched imagery of Pharm flowers, peacocks, dogs, birds, and its accompanying homilies. Some of us are still waiting to learn what the back masthead *"A shrill bird is a happy bird,"* means, although we could guess what the lead masthead implied with, *"A Clean Bird is a Happy Bird!"*

As the hunched-back, chain-smoking old lady—on a Pharm where no one was allowed to smoke—she was the good witch who was also something of a mother and grandmother to each of us. She seemed to know everything about us and had fun finding out more. She never said much about herself. She asked about you, what you were doing, how you were feeling, were the ladies treating you right and, of course, were you being nice? She knew our lives, knew who we had seen, knew what we did last Thursday, knew what boiled our blood, what saddened our hearts, and she told us and her readers before we told others and even ourselves what was going on with us.

Michael cried the Wednesday in 1974 when he couldn't pick her up. He too never knew where her life had been. As the hospital attendant wheeled her by the desk on the ground floor of the hospital, the secretary said, "Is that Mrs. Friezner?"

"Yes. Did you know her?" Michael said.

"Oh, Yes. Knew her well . . . Like everyone, loved her deeply."

Then the secretary told us what none of us had been able to learn. Yes, Mrs. Friezner had been married. The husband, however, drank too much and they had problems. One day, in his drunken state, he stumbled across California Route 66 with his son in tow. In the middle of the road, that 12 year old watched his father be run down by a semi-truck. Somehow, the son blamed it on the mother and never seemed to forgive her.

"Yet she seemed to live, love, work, and save every penny for him. When she asked for cigarettes, he'd say, 'I've got my 50 cents, where's yours?' Of course, when he'd ask for cigarettes, she'd say, "One minute dear, and I'll go get some.'"

Before Mrs. Friezner left us, she proudly proclaimed that her son had become a Chinese language expert with a Ph.D. in linguistics.

A visit to her spotlessly neat house, which she rented from Michael, could find her beguiling you with a number of stories about the adventures of each of her nine cats. Each story revealed each cat's peculiar personality that she cherished dearly.

The *Shriek* often said, "A good witch is a happy witch!" Well, the only witch some of us have ever met we fondly remember as one with an awesome arsenal of goblins, warlocks, and whammies that forced us to be nice. Since the floors are still pretty clean, and the law is still obeyed, Mrs. Friezner is probably a "Happy witch." Like the seer that she was, she'd probably not be too surprised by any of our adventures, since somehow within her 78 years she probably had our stories pretty much penciled out for future editions of The *Shriek* before she winged off to kitten heaven . . . And,

Edith Friesner

should we Pharmhands get to the Pearly Gates, we won't be surprised to find our friendly witch, with her broomstick in hand, checking to see that our socks are clean and that we check our shoes before we step inside the gate upon heaven's puffily clouded floors.

Slightly edited from **the glendoran magazine** Nov/Dec 1991.

So, Mrs. Friezner said . . .

*Have a good
time boys, but be
nice . . .
Or else . . .*

*And remember to
keep your rooms
clean.
A clean bird
is a happy bird.*

Plow
Deeper

'THE SHRIEK'

A Clean

is a Happy

KARL, JOHN, DWAYNE AND KAREN
ARE BURNING THEIR CANDLES
AT BOTH ENDS AND SUMMER
HAS JUST STARTED. WATCH IT.

M.C.R., Ruler of Rubelia, isn't
BURNING CANDLES. HE IS SHOOTIN
STARS - - - - - - - WOW -

BABIES SHOULD NEVER BE LEFT
IN CARS ANY TIME. REMEMBER
THIS.

MOTORCYCLES ARE NOT GOOD
DATE VEHICLES.

TERMITES LOVE JOHN McHANN,
BEES DON'T TRUST HIM.

Jolly McH IS ONE Happy
Gal!

Happy July 4TH !

And take your shoes off.

Were you nice to the girls this weekend?

So, it was said . . .

Blessed be our imagination—it makes life a joy.

The older the tree—the rougher the bark, the more gorgeous it is.

Keep your own corner swept. Examples are contagious.

Chapter 6

Every Town Needs a Castle, Part I

Especially in the shaky 21st century.

A fortress
Towering walls sheltering those inside
Keeping intruders out

A moat.
A drawbridge.
A gate through which horses gallop in and out.

Knights.
Righting injustices or flailing at windmills.

Returning in proud or humorous rest from a foggy,
*   or was it smoggy, day's efforts . . . .*

Every town needs a castle.
Not a castle built or moved by a monied ego,
Not a relic to be dusted or curated.
Not a project fashioned from corporate largess.
Not subsidized by community development block grants

But maybe one built by those
Whose heads some would say are filled with rocks.

Yet often history has hinted
that those whose heads are hard as rocks
have moved the world . . . .

Or at least moved some neighbors,
And certainly their cousins
From forever remaining blockheads.

Maybe some of that is the life good castles breathed in days of yore. The strong arms of its granite walls were there to hug the huddled peasants and small villagers when danger sneered at them in their humble homes. The muscled shoulders of its bulging walls were there to shelter the needy from the harsh realities of the outside world. The castles' good lords raised their wine glasses often and had wonderful feasts and flings. They wrote decrees with common sense and simplicity. They could laugh, sing off key, and weep. To those who passed through their castle walls with warmth and honesty, the doors remained open. For those who blanketed good castles with the gloom of their lives or broke a bond of old world integrity, the heavy gates soon slammed closed.

It wasn't long before nuclear arms outdated hugging castle walls. Castles became relics. Museums.

Today benevolent lords live in apartments, houses, and estates, usually trying to raise a couple of okay kids. Curators dust the relics inside the towering wails that once inhaled and exhaled knights who righted wrongs or flailed at windmills.

Is this the gospel as it is and should be? Not necessarily.

That spirit that pulls kids into a patch of woods to slap together a tree fort should build a castle in every town. It need not be an elaborate, ornate, fancy, expensive centerpiece. It should be richly built from old ideas, recycled things scraped together, and sparks of creativity nourished by sweaty work.

I think I know about this need for a castle, not because I might have been Robin Hood in a previous life, but because I lived in one in this life. Now it may be hard for today's suburbanites to relate to the need for castles or to stories of its errant, childlike knights. But please try to bear with me, even if just to assure you that Robin I not be.

Married with Children may be television fare that most Americans find easier to bear than words and stories of twentieth century castles. Dungeons and Dragons may be the pastimes that young folks find more enticing than slapping together tree forts and funky castles in the remaining orchards of today's outdoors. *Survivor* television shows may be the paragon of today's tinsel-hardened adventuring.

But imagine what would happen if all the American hours spent watching Married with Children, playing Dungeons and Dragons, and vying for Survivor type TV spots were uncorked . . . The bottled, youthful, dreaming spirits, now entrapped by "Jawaba the Couch"—unleashed building junky tree houses and fields of play forts.

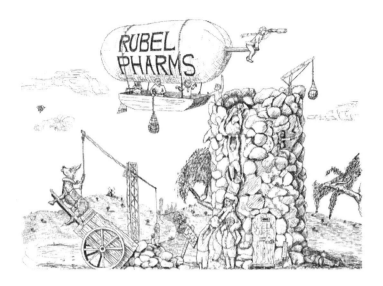

Imagine the condition of our national psyche? How many more hearty laughs and real smiles would sprout if more communities built, with their own hands, sweat, and laughable mistakes, their own brand of renaissance castles. Imagine if communities across the country traded those thousands of hours—where they mirror a couch pillow staring at a TV, or sit chasing Dungeons and Dragons—for the adventures that revolve around building a goofy bottle house, box factory, tree house, rail-road-tied hut, and majestically junky castle. Maybe your town prefers the tranquility of a televised society, but grandfather's grandson Michael magically unearthed, in a perfectly coiffured suburban community, a lot of hidden pharmers who liked recycling junk outside of society's perfectly groomed suburban rules.

It ain't easy to build a castle in every town. The spirit it takes to build a good castle probably exists in most American communities. Whether the power structure of each American community has the sagacity to allow those spirits to build castles, determines whether castles are built. And castles built by good spirits don't all look the same. What they probably have in common more than the face of a castle with its towers, turrets, gates, and moats is freedom to pursue healthy fantasies . . . To ponder realities while sheltered from the increasingly regulated, bureaucratic, regimented forces of the progressively civilized world outside.

Sometimes these castles come in the form of houses, perhaps with different gardens or uniquely hand crafted living designs. These places are inhabited by persons so different and good that people look forward to gathering there in order to nourish themselves on the tasty morsel of life the hosts always serve them. Sometimes these places may be farms—organic, communal, or otherwise where a sense of community is fashioned by honesty, integrity, and long hours of work close to the soil. Sometimes they may be storefronts, community centers, or gyms where the good fashioned from those seeking, learning, or sweating inside, offsets the scars of life surrounding them on the outside. Sometimes they may be non-traditional schools or classrooms, where the heartfelt beliefs of the teachers inside make their lessons more golden than that of the uninspired school run narrowly amidst a myopic, bitter, sick, or dangerous neighborhood outside.

Naturally high castles

Every community needs these castles. The more such castles a community has, the more its people will see, understand, and do.

Glendora has more than one of these kinds of spirited castles. There was one on Foothill in that big old house with the giant oak outside and dolls collected on its windows and mantles inside. There was one near Finkbiner Park with that backyard filled with a desert-replicated garden where kids hitting the drug scene could be listened to and turned on to more natural highs. And from Glendora's shaded valley and orchards, blessed old timers passed on insights and right living messages so wise that they had to have been learned in previous times.

Glendora also has America's answer to the real castles of yore—a real adolescent/adult built castle. Rubel's Castle, however, is a bit more rebellious than today's tamed European castles of yore.

When Harry Reasoner did his 1974 Reasoner's Reports show titled Castles in the World, he juxtaposed two European castles alongside his choice for America's castle—Rubelia. The European curators lamented that their castles were "expensive" to maintain. The head janitor of Rubella, however, responded, "No, the castle was cheap to run. When I'm hungry, I skin one of the 'Pharm' chickens and pull something from the garden . . . Burn old wood when I'm cold. When the wind blows, windmill works. Turns the washing machine and washes our old clothes Nope, ain't too expensive."

The European curators pleaded with Harry to mention the location of their castles so "tourists" would come. Rubelia's head janitor reminded Harry, "You won't say where we are if you put this place on TV, right? We got enough people riding by wanting to come in. We gotta keep the gate closed almost all the time. Can't pile rocks and railroad ties with all those people comin' by and botherin'."

The European curators showed off their old castle stuff but capitalized on the ease of using their modern conveniences at the end of a day's public relations work. When Harry asked how the castle hands got around all the old stuff, the head janitor replied, "Oh, but they use it all. It all works." Yes, from the 90-year-old cast iron, gas fired water heater that warmed water for the tin-reservoired bathroom adjoining the Big Kitchen to the wood burning stoves to the 10-gallon glass bubble top gas pump and 13 antique cars and trucks—it all worked.

It is often said that Merlin the Magician, from King Arthur's Court, retired because "rationalists" were beginning to rule the world. What do you think Merlin would say today if he were immersed in the stories of life that wash over the airwaves of our two shores? Every town needs whimsy, magic, irreverence, and the hard work that lets those wonderful ingredients of life succeed in standing the rationalists on their heads.

Rubelia has lots of the whimsy, magic, irreverence, and the hard work that turns people around or upside down. Some lose their sense or cents, when stood on their head, and seldom come back to drop more on the floor. Many get a kick out of being stood on their head and don't mind dropping dimes of their sense on the floor. Some of them enjoy continually coming back for more. Some depart the castle having untapped their hidden reservoir of whimsically flavored common sense. Hopefully, their Rubelian time levitates them from the couch into doing some sweaty work that confuses rationalists and produces real world magic.

Rubelia has stood a lot of things on its head—the Harley partially cemented almost upside down in one of its walls; to the tunnel winding upside down three levels below ground; to Crazy Bill capturing John in his string trap to hang him upside down in his dungeon bedroom. And yes, Rubella has stood quite a few upside down from the asylum directors, who after two days of visiting really believed that Rubella was a walled in "funny farm" for fairly hapless and harmless inmates, to the Zio's Pizza delivery boy who quit after his first night and first delivery to a spooked 'Pharm' guarded by helmeted soldiers carrying vintage firearms; to the Dating Game chauffeur who believed yours truly ran an international trading corporation from the Tin Palace's Round Table.

The dozen wheelbarrows that lifted rocks two, four, and seven stories high may not be needed for rocks as much anymore. Some day they could be used to cart around the chronicles of magic, whimsy, and irreverence that happened or were passed within those walls. Mrs. Friezner (see *the glendoran,* Nov/Dec. 1991 or "Witches" chapter) was one of those who helped create the magic. There were many others and if space allows a tale or three shall follow.

Why? Because you can't understand sixteenth century castles made in the twentieth century, or anything else that's made in between, unless you understand some of the characters who are foolish enough to make them and who wait until the 21st century to spin and weave about them.

Slightly edited from *the glendoran magazine*—Mar/Apr, 1992

So, it was said . . .

Concerned public officials asked grandfather, "What if an earthquake hits the Castle?" He answered,

"Why look at all the money it'll save us. Rather than go to Europe to see ruins, people can just come here."

"Michael you've taught me something . . . There's more than one way to stay single."

Grandfather

"There are talkers and there are doers. The pharm is filled with doers"

Pharmhand Doug Weakley, commenting after a Golden Years project.

Some people were walking through the packing house and they asked, "How did all this stuff happen?"
Grandpa replied, "We just forget to take things to the dump."

Chris Rubel

Chapter 7

Every Town Needs a Castle Part 2

Bock's Box Boy in the Box Factory

Clean bird's view of Rubelia

Glen Speer and Skipper Landon were two characters foolish enough to hang around building castles when they could have been doing something totally rational.

In 1959, Glen asked Michael if he could "live in the box factory." The box factory had open parking stalls for farm trucks on the ground level.

On its second floor, Al Bourne, owner of the farm and Singer Sewing Machine Company, stored boxes in which his citrus was packed.

"But Glen, there's no water, no electricity. It's just a sheet metal building with a room filled with boxes."

"Well, I'd like to fix it up and live in it."

Glen and Michael had been friends since high school. Glen's request wasn't so outlandish or foolish, when stacked against all the foolish things Michael had done and dreamed of doing.

So, of course, Michael said, "Okay."

It wasn't long before Glen's box factory had electricity, running water, a drawing table, hand-made floor to ceiling bookcases made from scrap 3"x8"'s stuffed with books, and a little gas heater. Soon thereafter, he laminated and varnished old pieces of wood into stunning kitchen and bathroom sinks with flywheel knobs and wooden water flow culverts, installed recessed floor and ceiling lighting, and cut in skylights. Although his bedroom design never advanced much beyond a large mattress on the floor, one of his bedroom walls became a majestically designed maze of exposed brass and copper piping, which on command filled his gigantic sunken self-designed and built wooden bathtub.

Sure, some nights it was cold in that uninsulated sheet metal building. Insulating was one of Glen's upcoming chores. But somehow standing around talking about the books stacked on his bookcases or about ideas, work, life—while periodically moving next to the 16" gas fire block heater, warming your back, rubbing your hands, curling you hot cup of tea—seemed to make the cold freshen and enliven the talk.

Glen never finished the insulating. Those brisk California mornings, chilly nights, and few cold days never amounted to enough discomfort to pull Glen from his other chores.

Chores? Like in work? Michael didn't make him do anything but pay a very low rent. He only worked 20 very low wage hours a week as a box boy at Glendora's Bock's Variety store. Getting to work on his Honda 350 or his rebuilt and refinished MG took less than five minutes. The words "chores and work" weren't the correct words. Glen just always had something to do and whatever it was, it always came out as some kind of artwork. He had his box factory to fix, steel spiral staircase to build, the Pharm's main kitchen to design and build, workshop to create, barbecue pit to encase, jewelry to make, paintings and drawings to do, books to read, motorbike and car to tinker with . . .

John McHann, Glen Speer, Michael

Then he also had those he always helped. Glen's mind and body and the designs and ideas it generated had always been there for Michael's beck and call.

It's a good thing Glen was shy. Had more people known how talented, caring and giving he was, his old-time friends and those of us who stumbled upon his friendship later might have been deprived of some of his special time.

In 1969, I began renting the Pharm's night watchman's house.

Twenty yards away, across the railroad tied driveway, was Glen's box factory.

Unlike his long-time friends, his new neighbor knew less than zero about building. This neighbor's first Pharm building project, imitating the design of an orange crate with a center shelf piece, and calling it a bookcase, was completed with bowed sides. With the base cut to its outside dimensions and its top cut to its inside dimensions, the nailed-on sidewalls had no choice but to bow-wow! Texturing its stain with different colored rubbed-in finger paints only added to its kindergarten-like finished quality. I always wondered what gentle inner maturity and patience made Michael and Glen stop from laughing or bow-wowing upon examining my first piece of construction. Yep! I was blessed to have stumbled into the Valley of the Glen, under the shade of the old oak tree.

Glen opened his self-built wood shop and all its valuable tools to his klutzy neighbor whose zilch knowledge of tools qualified him as tool room scary. When Michael said the staircase to the second story tree house was becoming dangerous because it was rotted and full of termites, Glen said to me, "Why don't you tear it down and build a new one. I'll help you."

From mine shafts to building materials

Recycled staircase recycles toilet

So with the 6"x8" and 2"x6" lumber that we and an old Pharm truck regularly recycled from the San Gabriel Mountain mineshafts, through which Feather River Project water was to flow, we built Glen's designed staircase. Glen would show me what needed to be done, do some of it, and leave his new neighbor to struggle and learn hours into the night and on weekends getting it assembled.

Of course, such training from good teachers always produced much more than anticipated. The old termited, crumbling stairs became a gracious and wide staircase that wound around the majestic oak tree and opened onto a new, from recycled tunnel wood, huge deck with sunken barbecue pit. The deck was about twice as big as the 400 square foot tree house, which it embraced. Soon that deck sprouted another deck that encircled the Pharm swimming/fish pool. This fashionable Los Angeles pool was designed from a farmer's tin water reservoir, which about 40 Pharm expedition friends moved from San Dimas.

Everyone who knew Glen knew he could build anything. Some of us knew he knew how to teach others gentle means to build almost anything. All of us who knew him well knew he was also humble about all the things this Berkeley Architecture School dropout knew so well.

Part of Glen's character was capsulized for me one day in 1970. Glen had been talking about leaving the Pharm, about trying "to make it in the real world." Most of his friends were making their mark in the world. In Woody Allen's most sensitive manner, Glen was defining himself as a stock boy at Bock's Variety Store. The real Glen wasn't a stock boy at Bock's. Glen loved every minute of every day on every thing he did at the Pharm. In the real world outside of the Pharm, however, Glen was starting to believe he was a stock boy at Bock's.

When the world gives only miserly rewards to a shy, sensitive artist, the world can sometimes sap that wonderful and creative artistic spirit. Glen was thinking that maybe he would have to leave the Pharm "at least for a while" and make some money in the outside world. Maybe he would accept the offer of the general contractor who had visited the Pharm and offered Glen a chance to be a framer for him on his construction crew in St. John, Virgin Islands.

A window framer?

On this day in 1970, Glen had returned from work on his Honda motorcycle with his backpack filled with a half dozen library books. Michael, Glen, and I looked at the books as Glen talked about them. All the books were about building. One even dealt with how to frame windows, showing diagrams, and pictures.

Looking at that window framing book, I asked, "Glen, what do you need this for?"

"Well, window framing is a lot more complicated then it looks . . . I figured I had better understand how it is done."

I just looked at Michael, thinking to myself, "Glen can build anything, what is he doing with these books?" Michael looked at me with that old Pharmer's hat that was punctured with holes, tarred with grease and stain spots, and reeking with the odors of soils and sweat; lifted his eye brows, puckered, opened his mouth as if to speak and then froze it shut before any words spilled out. Michael pulled his hat over his mouth and the little leprechaun, who survived in Michael's hat, often shuttered Michael's mouth like that just before he uttered.

Instead of hearing Michael speak his thoughts, my mind replayed words Michael had once said, "Glen has a gift few people have. He can look at an empty spot and visualize what could and should be there. Then he can do what even fewer people can do—he can make what should be there. When it's finished, it's always beautiful. I can build things, but I can never visualize it before hand. I can make things work, but they seldom look pretty working. Glen could always see it, build it, and make it beautiful. And it would work. He is truly gifted."

A few days after that incident, Glen was sitting in the tree house and said that the tree house could be a much nicer living pace if we knocked the walls down and redesigned it. When I asked Michael if I could do that, he said "No!"

"If Glen were doing it with me, would that be all right?"

"Well, if Glen were doing it, it would be all right."

Over the last 20 years of knowing Michael, I have never seen him not at least say "Hello" on meeting. Seldom have I seem his face go pale. The next day, upon hearing banging in the tree house, Michael climbed the stairs, opened the door to see what he believed was the tree house's bearing wall with its plaster and framing piled a foot deep on the floor, blankly stared at me, the sledge hammers, crow bars and Glen; turned pale and marched back down the stairs. Only two days later, when we had a 6"x8" beam supporting the middle of the room and Glen's supervised redesign was underway, did Michael have something to say.

As we sat around in one of the Pharm's traditional talk-a-thons over one of Michael's cheap gallons of jug wine, Michael said, "You know, the tree house was the only normal place we had on the Pharm. It had normal plaster, shower, sink, toilet, and kitchen. It was built to code for a night watchman to live in. Then, one day after I said, 'No, you couldn't mess it up,' you had it trashed on the floor. I thought the whole roof was going to cave in when I saw the bearing wall on the floor."

Everyone in that room who knew the hours I spent redoing the tree house knew that in the end nothing would go wrong. The tree house could only be better because of the quiet guy across from me who shared wine and anything else that you needed in order to be.

Glen left the Pharm that year to be a "window framer" on St. John. He was terribly lonely. He wrote and sent tapes to his friends in the hopes that they would respond. His friends' responses were his social contact with the world and a tenuous rudder on the new life he was sailing. Glen had few friends on the island. One of those was his boss's high school daughter. In time, their friendship became a deeper attraction. It became one of Glen's few but meaningful romances, the kind that he and Margaret Baird of Glendora, grew, learned from, and treasure the memories of to this day.

It wasn't very long before Glen moved from window framer to foreman. It was during that job progression, which in Glen's work ethic made his workday 16 hours long and usually seven days a week that he realized, although he never said it, that he knew more about building than anyone on the island. So Glen, along with a hip partner possessed of a much more casual work ethic who lived in the middle of the island in a large well-stocked tent, formed their own company, Lollop Construction.

Glen built the most beautiful homes on St. John for the richest people, but business was always a struggle. He paid his mostly native crews the highest wages on the island, paid them first, and himself last. His rich clients always seemed to nickel and dime him. After a few years, and going through two different partners, Glen had lots of equipment, beautifully done projects, many more headaches, but little money in the bank. He missed his friends and missed the Pharm. He had decided it was time to sell his tools, trucks, and jeep, go back to the Pharm with a little money and do things and be with people he liked.

As he was preparing to leave, the retired Chairman of the Board of Dow Chemical Corning Ware, whose St. John home Glen had built, introduced him to Dow's then Chairman of the Board. The chairman wanted Glen to build him a home. Glen, however, had decided that he could live with being a failure in some people's eyes as long as he was back around some friends and not here. Glen informed the chairman that he was quitting the construction business. The chairman persisted. After being pressed, Glen politely explained how trying it was to build when clients would make late payments, bicker over the amounts, and demand late design changes.

In writing Glen a check that night the chairman said, "Just tell me when and for how much you want the next checks, and I will send them. Design and build me a house something like this one and tell me when it is done. That's all I'll ask of you."

Glen decided to do one more, with the hope that it would provide a few dollars for returning to the Pharm. For once, Glen had a hassle free, on-time paying client. That success led to a piece of St. John land, which led to Glen doing his own project.

So while Michael was building castles out of leftovers junk and riverbed rock in California, Glen built Mongoose Junction, St. John's most beautiful shoppers' oasis, out of fine Caribbean woods and native stones.

Glen & Radha Speer's wedding

If you haven't been to St. John, you may not believe that Mongoose Junction is the finest shopping castle in the Virgin Islands. If you have been to the Caribbean, you probably noticed that every native dancer who has ever danced to the rhythms of a 55-gallon drum struts his best stuff first, when trying to close a sale on a stateside girl. Now the Governor of the Virgin Island, like Bo, knows these tenets of VI dancing. He also knows a little about marketing to tourists. That's why he moved the St. John's international cruise ships docking ramps from a mile away to front Mongoose Junction.

Most of Glendora, California knows Michael Rubel as the landmark castle builder. Heck, the Los Angeles Times, Washington Post, Harry Reasoner, Barbara Walters, Michael Landon, Alfred Hitchcock, That's Incredible, You Asked for it—all had hands or footage in memorializing Rubelia.

What the memorializers don't capture is the impact Glen has had on the funny Castle. When you know the Pharm's history, you know Glen's physical imprint—from the workshops, to the wooden sinks, to the winding staircases, to the community kitchen, to the fireplaces, to the central Castle shop, to the creatively designed tunnel and secretive but inspiring underground 4th level boy's room. Underneath that physical imprint, is something outsiders won't see or feel—as the years pile decay on the staircases, lay ash and rust on the shops and fireplaces, spread cracks on the wooden sinks' epoxy skins, and embellish the rumors and confuse the truth. You won't even find it in the innards of that magical bottle cemented 9 rows up, 12 bottles north on the east wall of the central tunnel.

By the time Glen left the Pharm in the late 60's, he had parked his impeccably restored 1948 flatbed truck, which he found rotting in a farmer's field, in the Tin Palace. Amidst the Tin Palace's priceless antiques, while giving another Tin Palace tour, some of us would casually refer to it as "Just a table." In the late 60's, 50-60 family flags, with coats of arms blazing in bright colors, hung from the rafters above that mint black and yellow truck. The flags were remains of one of those Pharm parties, where your price of admission was a family coat of arms and five bottles to cast into the Castle walls.

Coat of Arms

Glen didn't present a coat of arms to get into that party. It wasn't his style.

Over the years, however, the Castle seemed to evolve a Code of Honor, which a Coat of Arms might symbolize. It was a code, which like all strong traits was partially inherited . . . It was a code refined and built upon through the ever-present mistakes of Pharmhands growing up in a make-believe castled world surrounded by the onslaught of suburbia, overcast smog, and the politics of living . . . . Like all good guides to life, it didn't come easily. The code muscled itself by living a belief that was grounded on sweating through long hours of hard work as one of the means to worthiness . . . Part of its inherited philosophical foundation Grandpa Deuel gifted to Michael and his childhood friends with constant reminders that, "If you think about yourself, you are not working hard enough." It was a code whose foundation was built upon some footings of integrity that everyone who partook in life behind those walls seemed to have brought from their families. A code that evolved through interaction with lots of good people. A Castle Code of Honor that still evolves.

Glen's most significant impact probably lies within that unintended but Castle built Code of Honor. If an unpermitted, unallowed 20th century American Castle made of recycled bottles, railroad ties, collapsed freeways and junk needs a Coat of Arms, then a bunch of Pharmhands can take a long trip to dungeon the guy who ought to design it.

If in this interim between Henry VII and Star Trek's 23rd century, even Rubelian Phunny Castles are to have Codes of Honor and Coats of Arms, then this guy personifies the work ethic, insight, knowledge, and vision that those of us growing at the Castle were trying to take into the real world.

Sometimes the deeds of Rubelia's phunny Pharmers seemed to turn them into errant throwbacks jousting with contemporary windmills. If the

Pharm's main kitchen, designed by Glen with discarded railroad ties, to house his 10' in diameter scrap lumber table and tree trunk chairs, served as the Rubelian Knights Round Table, then the mix of life that gave Glen this culinary design vision qualifies him to design the Castle's Coat of Arms. Even if Michael colors it creosote.

Mongoose Junction, St. John, Virgin Island

Post Script: The fingerprints of Glen's handiwork are found on many of the best homes that dot St. John. His Mongoose Junction Shopping Center has more tourist footprints weaving thorough it than any other St. John Center.

Glen's Mongoose Junction at St. John, VI

Mongoose Junction is such a delight that the well-to-do Easterner who owns the adjacent parcel has had Glen build Mongoose Junction II for him. The Rockefeller owners of the posh Caneel Bay vacation site have been known to empty a room of 50+ people in order to solicit Glen's private advice . . . Not too shabby for a shy box boy from Bock's, wouldn't you say?

True wisdom lies in gathering the precious things out of each day as it goes by.
E. S. Bouton

Slightly edited from *the glendoran magazine* article of May/June 1992.

So, it was said . . .

"Something like the castle doesn't just happen. You have to have a unique and talented group of people, which doesn't come together very often."

Radha Speer, after a 2008 commemorative ceremony for Michael

Lose your dream—you die.

Things do not matter. People do.

Grandfather, and often repeated by MCR

Chapter 8

"Skipper's Always Right, You Know,"

"Skipper's always right, you know," Michael said . . .

I had lived at the Pharm for less than two weeks when we first met. He was pleasant, smiled with a twinkle in his eyes, and asked the normal, get-acquainted type questions. He seemed to like asking questions about you. They were proper questions. Skipper was "proper." They

Glen Speer, Suzanne Carpenter, & Skipper

were also smart questions—smart as in they were intended to tell Skipper how smart you were and to remind you that Skipper was smart.

In the proper sense, Frank Landon Jr. was raised "right." His dad was a successful businessman and his mother was a swell lady. Skipper was taught to get and value a good education and discipline. He did.

Skipper, however, never looked proper on his noisy 175CC Kawasaki motorbike. Pushing 6', Skipper seemed too big for that toy bike. Michael had his giant Harley, Scott had his souped up tear drop, and Glen and I had our Honda 350s. Why didn't Skipper have a real bike?

One day, when Glen and I were washing our bikes and Skipper rode onto the Pharm with his, I circuitously probed for the answer with, "Your smaller bike's a lot noisier than ours. How come?"

"Well, mine's a four banger and yours are two cycle bikes. So my four pistons are pounding up and down a lot more than yours. There are advantages and disadvantages to that which are . . .” With that opening, Skipper launched into one of his engineering educational treatises, which he delivered as often as allowed.

Ever since they were kids, Michael and he had been friends. They romped through the orchards, roamed the hills, played pranks, and built forts together. Somewhere between kidhood and formal schooling, Michael came to respect Skipper's engineering acumen. Soon after that, Michael added a couple more levels of regard to the lofty plateaus of respect, which he held on whatever Skipper had to say about engineering, government, or business.

One needed only to sit and listen to see how much Michael respected what Skipper had to say and how closely their thoughts coincided. Through the late 60's, there was plenty of opportunity to sit and listen to their thoughts.

About once a week one could mosey up to the Tin Palace, slide back the 10 foot door, walk by the wine cellar elevator, with cuckoos popping out from their clock doors and art work covering the walls and floor, step through the open 6" thick wooden refrigerator door, and take a place on the rugged floor of Michael's bedroom; a converted citrus refrigerator, big enough for a bed, couple chairs and desks, bank vault and various memorabilia. Three to 10 people from 15 to 65 years in age might be there on any given night. The Pharm's proverbial gallon of cheap wine would be passed, filling the Pharm's recycled large jelly jars or smaller shrimp cocktail wine glasses. The Vietnam War, race relations, work ethic, drugs, hippies, poverty, economic development, education, students, Glendora High School, politics, Republicans, Democrats, Black Panthers, girls, love, marriage, experiences, adventures—especially Michael's, Pharm events and more were open on any night's agenda.

Michael's room was not like most rooms. The riveting “click-clack” of the pendulum on the 1872 Seth Thomas mechanical clock, the steely stare of the Wells Fargo vault with large cloth on top, the blinking on-and-off red and green lights popping out from the conduit lining the wall near the ceiling, the little lights connected to the phone and coded black box on the wall against his bed not far from his pillow, the loaded rifles across from the Marine Corps memorabilia, the two Waldenesque solitary sitting chairs, the oriental rugs on the oak floor-filled a wooden refrigerator room bolted close by a steel handle on the 6" thick slated wooden door.

Like most rooms, it had four corners. The captivating spirit of the room came not from all its stuff. It came from the electricity that flowed on those ringside nights when spots on the oriental rugs or oak floor were at a premium.

Would people pay big dollars to sit ringside if someone zinging his ideas didn't come out from each corner? Would people have continued sprawled on the floor of that old freezer room each week for years if people didn't provide their own electricity? Believe me, Michael's cheap gallon jug wine wasn't the draw.

Guarding the Right

For those who like to see things clearly in pictures, Michael and the likes of Skipper and John McCann guarded the right corner with most of the crowd cheering them on. Glen and I danced to the left with a sparser cheering section, if any, offering support. And on any  given night, some unexpected outside Pharm hands would come with points to make and stories to tell.

Those were wonderful, challenging free-for-alls with raised voices, gestures, emotions, facts, figures, and experiences intertwined with physical, philosophical, moral, and scientific theories. No matter how heated or involved the topic or crowd became, bellowing laughter and guffaws always resounded from each and every of Michael's bedroom debate nights. No matter how noisy the night's discussion had been, there were usually so many with so much to be said that your mind always had time to be quiet, listen, and digest. Somewhere, late into the night, with Michael's rifles, family, Pharm, and Marine Corps memorabilia adorning the walls beneath the little red and green lights of the Pharm's ever-vigilant radar system, we'd also hear the click-clack of the mechanical clock. When those metallic heart beats filled larger gaps between thoughtful words, we knew it was time to go home, rest our heads, and let the talk sink in.

It didn't take much sinking in time for one to discover the profound respect with which Michael held Skipper. How Skipper gained this respect might be evident from a few examples.

For example, Skipper had something to do with preparing fortifications for Michael's 40' high childhood tower. Yes, pre-teenage Michael with friends like Skipper built a four-story fort. In looking at its picture in the *Castles by Mike* book, you immediately realize that this thing is prodigiously

Skipper and wife Phyllis

built with brilliance, planning, and vision that comes with a warped or warped speed childhood.

Early Rubelia

All the more reason, I guess, that it needed a good defense system. Skipper, knowing even as a kid that he was a masterful tactician and strategist, assumed an instrumental role in defending this bastion of freedom for kids like him and Michael from other not-so-nice kids. Trenches were laid around the fort and lined with broken glass and other sharp objects. Barbed wire lay just beyond that. Next were fences behind which working cannons filled with large carbide rocks charged by the gas from an old Hudson sprayer lay ready. Held in defensive reserve were BB guns, catapults, dogs, water hoses, and firecrackers.

(Amazingly, kid Rubel's Fortress Defense System remains essentially unchanged for Fortress Rubelia and Rubelia's Defense Budget, unlike that for Fortress America, remains steady at $7.89 per year. To the elves

of the world, Rubelia is a heart and wallet warming example of how cheaply people can thrive in a peaceful, productive community built from leftovers.)

Skipper's defense system was wonderful and Michael loved it. You may remember, however, your parents warning you that there "will always be someone tougher than you, so don't go looking for a fight." Well, their fortress and defense system advertisement brought someone tougher out of the bushes. Michael's father, like any grown-up, immediately saw how dangerous that fort could be to any neighborhood kids, so father's bulldozer plowed Skipper's defenses and the fort into an obliterated field of dreams.

I guess even the passage of years didn't erase the thought of designing a defense system for a castle from Skipper's mind. While Michael was in the Marine Corps, dispatching heavy military equipment fell into one of his areas of responsibility. Such access made these two grown kids realize how a—TANK could enhance the Rubelian Castle's safety.

Now let me stress that Camp Pendleton is not today missing a tank from years ago. But should God's video play back some days from back then, it might show that for a few days there was a tank camouflaged in bushes a lot closer to Rubelia than to Camp Pendleton.

Maturity refined Skipper's skills and turned his engineering skills to more peaceful pursuits. Guess you might even suggest it turned from harboring tanks to cleansing doves.

"Just blow it up!'

When Michael was trying to cement enough old junk together so that not even the bank would dare dismantle or plow under his grown up castle, Klaus Schilling, Ted Folley, Skipper, Glen, and Michael went riding out into the hinterlands in search of a large, ugly, out-dated engine. Miles from the Pharm, in the middle of a field on the outskirts of an unnamed city, as usual they found just what the Pharm needed. Unfortunately, this engine was ensconced in a slab of concrete that measured 10'x12' and 8" deep.

"No problem," said Skipper. "I'll just blast it out."

After speeding away for about 5 minutes, these scared young men heard a blast. A THUNDERING BLAST! Their concern with a blast much more horrendous than they had expected was reflected by the 2 weeks they waited before returning to the outskirts of this unnamed city.

"See, I told you. No problem!" Skipper said as he kicked back to "advise" Michael and gang on how to load the un-ensconced 8 ton steam engine onto a truck and take it back to the Pharm.

Today the engine brings bathing and chirping birds, cleanses doves, and rushes neighbors to their bathrooms.

The downstroke of its piston uses the neighborhood sewer line for decompression, which raises the neighbors' decibel and toilet water levels. It also sometimes raises their ire. The birds, however, are ecstatic for whenever the engine belches toilet water to its ceramic lip level—the birdbath squirts six inches of water heavenward . . . Although not documented, we think grandfather once said, "Only a bird brain would give up a bath over concern about humans' gyrating toilet bowl water levels."

> "... The "Pharm's" specially assigned Guardian Angel provided the materials at the appropriate time and price."

By the late 60's Michael's "Pharm" goals had moved well beyond riding Harleys, collecting second hand tools, installing ship engines to power bird baths, swiping Marine tanks, digging 20' deep cesspools, and filling the wine cellar with empty Gallo gallon wine jugs. Michael was more and more looking heavenward, wanting to spike cemented towers into heaven's skies. And, evidently, considering how he could re-circulate LA's then gagging smoggy air. As usual, the Pharm's specially assigned Guardian Angel provided the materials at the appropriate time and price.

Out of the smog, the phone rang. The phone company asked Michael if he would like their old telephone poles. Voila! Now Michael just needed the windmill. Guardian Angels, as you know, pay special attention to recyclers and idiots. Since Michael was supposedly one of those, God provided the windmill. As was common in those days for zany, crazy projects, a crowd of in-and-out patient "Pharmhands" gathered to help bring the windmill back from a pig farm abutting a California State Prison. About 40 fools, with nothing better to do than joust with windmills and eat pig, lined up early one weekend morning outside the Castle walls for the jaunt to Lompoc. With all the regular suspects gathered, the tools of their trade were piled in an old truck—old wrenches, acetylene torches, come-alongs, ropes, cables, sledges, crowbars, hammers, pliers, shields, and spears. After checking for old Mother Luck, the caravan of Quixotes went off again to test their pluck.

Freeing Lompoc's imprisoned windmill

The Lompoc farmer would be glad to rid himself of the windmill if we would disassemble and leave for him the 60' tower. He was so happy that a handful of city slicking fools were willing to leave him this pile of scrap steel for free that he decided to host a barbecue for us. He even invited us out to watch him shoot the master of ceremonies, the to-be barbecued pig. There weren't many squeals of delight from us city slicking fools when we watched the bullet from the farmer's rifle pork the pork.

Extrapolated soft landing site

Michael wasn't as concerned about the barbecued feast to come. Squealing, though not as badly as the pig, Michael was nervously asking, "How are we going to get that thing down in one-piece?" as he looked six stories up at the windmill, reflecting puzzled concern that often arose on Michael's face during his castle building years.

"No problem." said Skipper. "Just get me about a half dozen old mattresses."

Near to pilloried pillowed landing site

The next day, while the grunts ran around for mattresses and started torching and unbolting whatever Skipper told them to, Skipper wandered and pondered while looking up at the windmill. Finally, as the torchers and cutters were running out of tower to torch and cut, Skipper said to the mattress bearers, "Put those there and there and there."

Yes, Skipper was good in the field. Perhaps it sounded like he used a little too much dynamite to get that birdbath engine out, but he was close, and it got out. In Lompoc that day, as the ropes were pulled, the last torch cut made, and the tower followed Newton's rule to earth, we knew again that Skipper was good. He was also close. The windmill was off the tower. It was now ensconced in the earth a "close" 5' from the cushioning mattresses.

So what if Michael had to rebuild the engine. Taking the job, coming close, and getting it done is part of what brings respect. If you have never built castles out of junk and defended forts, dynamited an engine or removed a windmill, but you've worn cleats or been a sporting couch potato, you know the adage. "It's not whether you win or lose, it's how you play the game."

Big Pharm projects always became a wonderful game to play. Skipper played the game. And he played it well.

Of course, when you are new to the Pharm you neither know how much credence to put into the renowned reputation of a guy everyone calls "Skipper," nor in more recent times how much to trust suburban DC guys named "Scooter." So you just listen to the stories, watch, and beware, or wary.

"The Great Flood will come!'

After the summer forest fires of 1968, Skipper told Michael that the mountain was going to wash down the hill and destroy the Pharm. Michael listened. Then he went out to the Pharm entrance at the foot of Glencoe Heights Drive. He started digging and piling, then buried and nailed 4"x6" posts and 3"x8" planks until he had an eight-foot high wall. The Romans would have appreciated its strength.

Although Michael spent much of that summer building what we Pharmhands were certain was a wall, smarter people than us, whose smarts were reflected in the much bigger and fancier cars they drove, saw it as something else. Over and over again, one of those fancy cars would stop, the silent electronic and tinted window would slide down, and a Darth Vaderish voice from inside would ask, "Hey, Noah, how's your Ark goin? . . . Hah, Hah." Usually Michael, in his stained and holey hat, floppy and creosoted pants, would turn to look again at the wall as the car accelerated away. Then he began asking us, "What do you think?" as he'd position us to look at his work.

"Looks plenty strong, Michael."

"Ah huh. And what do you think of it?" he repeated.

"What do you mean, Michael? 'What do we think of the wall?'" we asked.

"Yeah, well, you do think it's a wall, huh?" he'd ask.

"Yeah. Well, isn't it?"

"Yeah, well, yeah it's supposed to be."

Well, Skipper's forecasting and Michael's work looked pretty silly and perhaps unbelievable until those few days in October 1969 when about 20 inches of rain flushed the mountain down. Noah's Ark didn't get up and float. It stood tall against tons of flowing mud. Sure, a garage, station wagon, boat, and tons of mud eventually broached over the wall. But the wall stood. Without Skipper's words and foolish Noah's wall, the other uncountable tons of mud wouldn't have turned "left" and the neighborhood and Pharm would have needed only lots of drying sun to become California's largest sandbox.

A few years after the flood, Michael thought the cesspool for the Tin Palace's bathroom was filled. Skipper, of course, told Michael where and how to build a new cesspool the old-fashioned way, with stacked and spaced red bricks. Michael spent many an evening digging that 20' deep by about 7' wide hole and carefully laying the red brick mosaic. When the top was approaching, Skipper explained how you bring each successive layer of red bricks to the center of the hole to close it off. Well, standing over a 15' hole, on the red bricks one is laying, while laying each additional row of bricks a little bit in from the previous row didn't look inviting. No matter how structurally safe Skipper promised it would be, it took Skipper standing on top laying those last few rows to make this doubting Thomas believe that he wouldn't fall to the bottom of a toilet flushing hole.

Nibble fingered Jesse James

Some months after *National Geographic* ran the Pharm as its October 1969 Mud Flood centerfold, Glen and I helped Michael unload an old Wells Fargo bank vault from the flat bed of one of the dilapidated Pharm trucks. This vault was so heavy, or the flat bed so worn, that we put six more holes into the truck's flatbed just rolling it off and into Michael's bedroom in the Tin Palace.

One evening, after the vault had been cleaned and prominently displayed in Michael's bedroom, Scott, another Pharmhand, came upon Skipper sitting in Michael's room. "Listen," Skipper said, with his ear pinned to the vault as he was rolling the combinations, "I can pick this."

"You're crazy, Skipper. You can't do that."

With a couple turns, the tell tale unlocking sound of the outer vault could be heard. "Holy cow!" or something cows emit, said Scott.

"Ah. It's a double lock vault. I've got to pick the next one." Skipper said as he moved on to his next mechanical challenge.

"God, Skipper, you better not."

"Ah, what's the problem? It'll be great fun."

"Well, maybe, but just in case, I don't want to be here," said Scott.

With that, Scott left and Skipper finished his fun. A few days later, Mrs. Friezner, the Pharm's good witch, keeper of the house and Editor of *The Shriek* Pharm newsletter, informed us that Skipper had shed a lot of grown up tears in the Tin Palace after performing his tumbler routine. The gnashing of teeth and shedding of tears took place shortly after Michael discovered a suffocated white mouse in the inner sanctum of his Wells Fargo vault.

Luckily, for all of us Pharmhands, a good safecracker and a vault were not enough to lock out for long Michael and Skipper's friendship. As with fine wines, their fine memories of a crackling good youth spent together have forever locked them together as friends. That . . . plus Skipper paying a locksmith to reset the tumblers and vowing never to impersonate Butch or Sundance, Clyde, or Jesse again . . .

"I had been traveling all over the world trying to find myself," MCR explained

"I had hitchhiked through Europe, Asia, and Africa. Worked as a jackeroo (cowboy) in Australia, and as a purser on a Spanish ship. The Captain (Boggs) hired me on as a paint chipper. In time, I became the purser. We sailed through the Mediterranean, the Suez Canal, to the East Indies, Japan, and Australia.

"After a couple years, I returned to California to figure out what I should do with the reservoir and packing house.

"In 1969, years after I'd sailed with the captain I was informed he had died and left me a bunch of money."

Post Script: Skipper is that top flight engineer he always knew he was. Flour Corporation kept him working on many assignments for years, until he quit to work on his Bullhead City development and Frank Landon consulting projects, none of which match up to the engineering challenges he dealt with as a Pharmer.

His wife and children have tempered his whimsical play times, but he still found time to share Glendora lunches with Michael and the ROMEOS (Real Odd Men Eating Out).

Incidentally, NASA declined Skipper's offer to have him assist them on future Moon landings. Prescient Pharmers have suggested Skipper assist the North Koreans with their soft touchdowns.

Slightly edited with some additions made from *the glendoran magazine*—July/Aug 1992

So, it was said . . .

It wouldn't be worth nothing, if it weren't for people . . . .

Michael's Very Special 1986 Party

MCR's 1986 Clock Tower Reunion. All 86 guests began by roaming downtown Glendora looking for Michael's lost charter buses to take them to dinner . . . After finding the buses and being shuttled a few cities away in the great "Dinner Hunt," the two well-dressed busloads rocked the buses, bellowing, as the drivers took them into a San Bernardino Golden Arches parking lot,

"We're eating at McDonald's?!?
We're eating at McDonald's!?!
BOOO, Michael BOOO!
BOOO! BOOO! BOOO"

Chapter 9

The Real Treasures of Life

"To love is to die a little. There is no greater joy."

One doesn't have to be a parent to know the joys and worries of raising young ones. In today's society, one can adopt or be a foster parent and learn daily of the energy and time that raising young ones takes. One can also limit one's installments of parenting to being a Big Brother or Big Sister or as a mentor.

These are wonderful ways to piece together the puzzle of life and the world. Anyone who helps mold for another a healthy perspective and respect for life and the world, leaves the world a treasure. The world seldom gauges the value of that treasure for oftentimes its riches stay quietly hidden, waiting to be discovered and treasured by others.

Curt near Warren Asa's welding shop

Sometimes, in special moments, the riches of that treasure box are opened to address worldly needs.

In what seems like a bygone era, when we were learning to be civilized, one didn't wait six years for adoption papers to be cleared, didn't apply to be a foster parent and receive state aid to help the "state" with one of its young problems, and didn't go through screening procedures to become a Big Brother or Sister or mentor. Our romantic memories of the old days had the needs of the young filled by family and friends, imagining that only a few needy sliped through the cracks.

Of course, more than just a few Orphan Annies slipped through the cracks. Nonetheless, those blessed with healthy childhood memories probably felt the grandparents, uncles, aunts, and friends of the family had a much more meaningful influence on the young than seems possible today. Making ends meet, growing up in a country and family while learning to be a citizen of a nation destined to become the world's 20th century leader, seemed to provide ample opportunity to set examples and provide perspective for the young. Today, many of those grooming hours seem lost to electronic pictures or pixels flashed on a screen.

The old way of doing things so often seems to be inherently healthy—working slowly, tempered by the sweat of the brow, building things personally, without overbearing corporate or bureaucratic snafus, sipping from warm cups and talking meaningfully without the overcast of a droning TV . . . . If as a young one you were raised amidst that, you have a treasure.

Castles of lore are supposed to be filled with treasures. The recycled Rubelian Castle in Glendora's back yard is adorned with neither shiny pieces of gold and silver nor refinements. It has, however, left many young ones with treasures.

To many, it was a sandbox of life. A life-sized erector set. A bin of junk that kids played in and loved as civilized grownups wondered why. A place where at any time of day an old rug or dirty box or antique kitchen could serve as a clubhouse where friends and strangers could sit and chat. A schoolyard with few rules—other than those learned in the kindergartens of life.

"Put the tools back where you found them . . .
"Be nice . . .
"Don't use bad words . . .
"Take your shoes off . . .
"No smoking . . .
"Be careful . . .
"Have fun . . .
"Don't take yourself too seriously . . ."

"Yes, Mrs. Friezner . . . Yes, Mr. Rubel . . . Yes, Michael . . ."

We were all young at this place. We all learned from what grew or piled up around the sandbox. The clunky cement mixer used to make the cement that would glue the castle seven stories high and Pharm hands together, hopefully for life. That's some of what Rubelia was to its first and second wave of fortress builders.

Curt, however, came later than what a Rubelian sociologist might refer to as the first and second waves. Curt came in when what might be considered, for this author's lack of a better vocabulary, the Pharm's Budding Poetic Era.

The Great Glendora Mud Flood (1969) had cascaded through the center of the Pharm. And the Pharm stood its ground.

Major political battle lines had been drawn and fought over. And the Pharm continued along on its merry, quixotic, and illegal ways.

Dreams of building some impressive, recycled, majestic castle had moved from foggy heads to toughened hands to walls of cemented riverbed rocks seasoned by thousands of bags of emptied and planted ketchup and wine bottles. The lines of the castle, built to some iambic pentameter, sounded by elevator music, played from nine ancient radios over Michael's eclectic sound system, served as lyric background from which to try one's hand at grubby poetry.

If you weren't too civilized back then, you might believe that some kind of poetry was birthing itself on this old reservoir floor.

After the Castle had grown
A story or more off the reservoir floor,

Michael often found
he needed more
   Than just himself and
resident Pharmers
   To help him pile the
junk higher.

   After hiring many
not-so-industrious
workers . . .
   To haul rock, mix
cement, lug bottles, hoist
beams, and wheel rock
laden wheelbarrows

Curt starting barn project

   To pile bed springs, junk, and steel into squishy cement walls
   To lay old beams and worn plywood for a shaky sky high walkway
   To fill worn and rickety barrows with rocks and cement;
   To hook the chain that lifts those barrels castle high . . .

Michael yearned for a worker
Who would bring music
To his ears
And a twinkle to his eyes.

   Of this, he told Pharmer
Ronald.
   Pharmhand Ronald, master
craftsman and stained glass
maker, taught his skills at a
nearby high school.
   So one day, Ronald sent a boy
Michael's way.

   A nice,
   But lightweight boy.
   How could Michael tell him
to go away?
   For most Pharm work would
be

Too heavy for him to do most
days.

   "Oh, why! Oh why!
Did—Knight Ronald
send such an underfed boy?"
Michael would say.

So Michael worked him easily
and watched in amazement,
   As the boy ran to and fro,
   For everything Michael asked
him to do.

Late in the day, grabbing this
road-runner as he sped by,
   Michael would say,
   "No need to run everywhere.
Go easier."

"Mr. Rubel, I know I am not very strong.
But what I lack in strength
I will make up in speed.
So, I would like to run for you . . .
If that's okay with you."

Michael paid the boy that day and said,
"Thank you very much. You worked very hard today."

"Shall I come back tomorrow?"

"Ah . . . let me call you.
When I have more for you to do."

That night, Michael asked Ronald
"Why did you send me such a little boy?
He's too small to use
For the work needed to build a heavy Castle."

"Michael,
He is a good boy, a good worker.
He works to help support his family.
He may be light in weight,
But not light hearted.
Why not try him for more days?"

For Ronald, Michael tried the Castle runner more.
But, worried about the boy's frail frame,
Michael added heaping plates of Pharm food
To each workday's routine.

The boy kept running
Kept answering "Yes, Mr. Rubel . . ."
Kept hauling, loading, wheel barreling,
Lifting, cutting, moving, piling,
Kept eating Pharm food and Helping the castle grow taller and heavier.

Though he never said much
And seldom stood long
enough for photos to mature,
He added music to the songs of the Castle already in its air . . .
To the crows of the Pharm's peacocks,
Quacks and cackles of its ducks,
Clucks of its chickens,
Wheezes of its horses,
And buzz of Pharm machinery . . .
The zooms of this road runner added more glee and twinkle to Pharmers'
Already twinkling eyes,
And etched more curves to their smiling furrows.

As the Castle rose,
The boy's chest and arms
Became as strong as his
jetting legs.
His heart and attitude
remained as clean
As his face seemed on that
16th birthday
That brought him through the
Pharm's gates.
And he built for himself
A tall storied home amidst the
castle walls.

Now this Castle Made of
Leftovers
Was not a normal place to
work.
No resume would record
What this work taught.
Or how it prepared one
For careers gleaned important
in the world.
But to Curt, for so long,
Living and working the Pharm
Meant more to him
Then adding to a resume
The standards the world
preferred.

Building a Castle of Junk
Without any permit is hard,
dirty, and dangerous work.
No planners approved this
Rubelian Castle's
Tentative or precise plan.
No OSHA rules were heralded
or heard.

Curt & MCR going higher

Au contraire, "Safety Third"
was
The emblazoned shield on the
1972 Pharm T-Shirt.
Old pulleys lifted steel
buggies
Filled with 800 pounds of
rock.
Up they climbed four and
seven stories from earth
To be rolled over cracked and
holed ply boards,
Supported by dilapidated
4x4's and cross laid worn 2x4's,
Balanced on dented steel
drums,
And/or on pipes protruding
From the cemented boulders
and bottles
Of the completed wall below.

Wheeling Pharm buggy loads
Across these dangerous high
roads
Was no sane, safe, or easy
chore.

Yet the dream and magic of
finishing the Castle
Pushed Michael and his
helpers.
So even though each step was
dangerous and crazy,
Another crazy, dangerous step
would be taken.
Toward the million steps, and
Millions of rocks, and
Tons of cement, and beams,
and steel . . .
That would go into building
the strong torso
Of this Junky Castle.

Enroute to building
A boy's castle
To fulfill a man's dream
This conversation was heard.

Michael,
Firmly planted on ground
below,
To the boy four stories up,
Who was about to wheel a
buggy laden with boulders
Over the patchwork of ply
boards, 4x4's, and barrels
To its next cementing spot.

"Curt, be very careful!"
"Yes, Mr. Rubel," came Curt's
reflexive reply,
As he pushed the buggy
Over its lumpy, planked, and
creaking trail.

". . . Curt, stop! Put the buggy
down."

"Yes, Mr. Rubel. Did I do
something wrong?"

"No . . .
Curt, do you understand how
important it is that you be 'very'
careful?"
"I will be careful, Mr. Rubel"

". . . Curt, do you
understand . . .
That . . . my life is in your
hands?"

". . . Huh? . . ."

"Do you understand that my
life . . . is in your hands? . . .
"You've got to understand
that my life is in your hands . . ."

While the grown man looked
up,
The boy looked down.
What seemed like minutes
passed in their gaze
As thoughts climbed and fell
From the dusty protruding
rocks, pipes, steel, and junk
Nestled between them
In the Castle Walls.

*"If you should fall and
seriously hurt yourself . . .
If anything bad happens to
you . . .*

I could not live with
myself . . .

"You see, Curt,
You must be very careful.
For my life is in your hands."

Slightly edited from *the glendoran*
magazine of March/April 1993.

So, it was said . . .

Things do not matter. People do.

The word "No" never built anything. It is simply the easiest answer.

Grandfather

Safety third. (Was it that high?)
Pharmers, tunnel diggers, and wall builders wondered aloud . . .

"I've never been very bright, but I can work hard. I'm not much of a thinker, people who think too much don't get much done. I'm not for holding onto anything that doesn't work. If it doesn't have a function . . . Although I have a lot around here that doesn't have a function . . . I'm not very consistent about everything."

Hunching his big shoulders, Michael accentuated his words with his *"I'm happily stupid"* shrug.

Stories shared around MCR's rocking chairs.

Chapter 10

Talkin' with MCR

'You've raised two very successful children.
Let's have fun with this one.'
Grandfather

"Grandfather said, 'Compared to other kids he's a hard worker and entertaining.'

"He also said to my mother one time, 'You've raised two very successful children. Let's have fun with this one.'

"My mother didn't appreciate that. She wanted me to become a teacher or a lawyer or something, so I could make money, because I was very poor. I could barely make my expenses. I had three jobs. I worked at a gas station and the National Fiber and Cushioning Company in San Dimas. They made paper sleeping bags for the forest service and the military and down at, you remember Ferris' (on Bennett and Glendora) . . . our junk shop. I worked for him at odd times. And he was very nice to me. And then I would also run the store a couple weeks in the summer, when I could, because he (the owner) wanted to go up to a place called Kuesite, (unsure spelling) a place where they had big rock shows. He would leave the store in my hands, and I was pretty successful at selling junk.

Austin (Michael's cousin) worked across the street at the gas station. So when he had to do something, I would see a car pull in—I would run across and do the windows and fill the tank and whatever. And when I had to break for a few minutes to get more junk with my old truck—when people would say if you just clean out my old garage you can just have it, you know. And so, I would take off, and if he (Austin) saw somebody stop at my store, he would cross the street to help them so we wouldn't lose a customer."

"Well, junk has been in the genes then?"

"Well, I grew up next to the dump. It was on the north side of our property. Where Goddard (School) is. We would haul stuff all the time, down the wash. My mother, every Christmas, as a Christmas gift to herself, would hire a man called Tex Gentry to come in and collect all the junk and take it back to the dump. And it always made me sad, and I hated Christmas; and she would always do it when I was in school."

"Even the junk that was in the forts?"

"They just took everything back. I was just devastated. She said, 'I have to give myself something once in a while.' (Michael chuckles). She would get rid of all the 'junk.' It was 90% 'stuff' just stacked around for future forts. And (laughs) then I had to haul it all home again. But I had a lot of friends who helped me."

"How would you haul it?"

"Just drag it. Cardboard boxes, 2x4's, and whatever we could use to build the forts with."

"Was that the start of the Pharm rule that he who uses the junk first gets it? (During Pharm building days we had a "first used" building rule that whoever had a project that used the piled railroad ties, lumber, etc. got it.)"

> **"Yes, that's right. For as grandfather said, 'If it isn't being used, it isn't worth a damn.'**

"And I've always gone by that because you can save stuff and never use it. So, it is better to be used than to plan on using it. It also speeds you up a little bit, if you know how important it is, so no one else takes it."

"But do you think that rule came from your Mom hauling stuff away?"

"I don't know. I just knew if it sat on the ground, it wasn't doing anything, wasn't good for anything. . . . . Even when other kids would ask me for stuff for their forts across the wash, I'd let them have whatever they wanted, but, generally, they would then start helping me haul stuff down from the dump. So . . . it was to my benefit too, because they could build a little fort and bring more than they needed down for me."

"Where did you get the nails, the tools?"

"Oh Skipper (Skipper Landon, one of Michael's closest childhood friends) gave them. We called them Skipper nails. Skipper gave me nails made out of aluminum because his father would bring home 50-pound kegs of nails from . . . . He was the president of Alcoa Aluminum. Skipper would bring his barrels to us. We had plenty of nails. We called them Skipper nails. And . . .

"We always seemed to have enough of everything we wanted. If we wanted 2x4's—there'd be a big stack of them at the dump . . .

"Did I ever tell you the story about . . . My grandfather one time said to me. I told him, I said, every time I go to the dump and I want something particular like a certain size of wood, or a cardboard box, I always seem to find it. It always seems to be there.

"And my grandfather says, 'Michael don't you realize by now that you're a very special person.'

"What do you mean? I said."

"Well, don't you notice how the crows always follow you to school?"

"Yeah I do."

"And don't you notice that whenever you want something someone always gives it to you?"

"I do . . ."

"And they don't follow Skipper to school."

"They don't?"

"And Skipper gets all of the things he wants from his father."

"That's right. No one gives Skipper anything. That's true."

"So isn't it about time that you understand that you are very special."

"My mother heard him talking to me. She was in the kitchen doing dishes of something, and she said, 'Harry, stop that kind of talk, it's just ridiculous. And you know it. And Michael, he's just teasing you.'"

"Mother, he's right. Everything I want has been given to me."

"'I know it, and I don't understand it,' Mother said. (Michael laughs)

"And then over Christmas, Skipper got a Marlin Pump 22 rifle and that was considered the Rolls Royce of rifles, and I said to my grandfather, 'Boy, I wish I had a rich father, so I could have a Marlin 22 . . . They sold for about $20, but that was a lot of money.'

"And grandfather said, 'Well, that's simple, Michael. Just wish for it and it'll probably be at the dump.'"

"Oh, grandfather, no one would ever throw away a Marlin 22 rifle."

"'Well, just give it a try. Concentrate.'"

"Well, it was on a Wednesday, which was a trash day, and I couldn't wait to get out of school. And what I did, I ran all the way to the dump. And I really ran hard, because I didn't want anyone else to find that Marlin rifle. And there by the gate of the dump was a brand new Marlin Pump 22 rifle. I stood and just stared at it for like five minutes. Then I walked up to it and touched it to see if it was real. And then I ran home with it and screamed, 'Grandfather! Grandfather, do you know what happened?'"

"He said, 'No.'"

"The dump gave me a brand new Marlin 22 pump action just like Skipper's."

"'I knew it would come. You know you're very special.'"

"And when I told my mother this, she said, 'Harry, damn you! You're going to warp his brain while it's . . .' (MCR laughs heavily)

"But I didn't know what that meant. I thought it was just because he told me to concentrate. But, of course, later I realized that he had put it there by the gate. But he never told me back then."

"How old were you then?"

"About 12, I think."

"He was taking a chance that you'd run from school and be there."

"He was probably watching.

"It really made me careful about what I thought, because I thought I could change things just by thinking about them."

"Michael, did the crows follow you?"

"HUH! (Laughs) They followed everybody. They were always glad to see us go to school because then they could eat oranges without being shot at.

"When you put a thought like that into your head, you begin to think they were just only following you and nobody else.

"The crows were incredibly intelligent. There was a $.25 cent bounty on a crow. And no one ever got one. I shot a crow at about 20 feet with a 410 shotgun and blew a bunch of its feathers off and ran up to get it to get my 25 cents . . . And it flew away (Laughs) . . . I couldn't believe it."

**

Eating and . . . shooting crow

"I have another wonderful story.

"The water company was owned by the farmers called the Glendora Irrigating Company, and the farmers were just being decimated with the crows and would give shells to the kids to shoot 'em with the promise that you'd only shoot their shells in their groves, you didn't go to their neighbors. So, the crows would always be gone when they saw a rifle. They (the crows) had guards and everything.

"So we would play army and shoot each other. We had to be ten trees apart. And it just kind of stung a little. It didn't hurt. We wore goggles and in those days you could buy a helmet liner. It wasn't a real steel helmet, but it was a liner that went inside of it and they were all over the place, and Mr. Ferris would give us all we wanted, so we had these helmets. We had teams, and we'd play army, and if you were less than ten trees and shot at anybody, then everybody got to have you run between everybody, and they'd hit you with a stick. So, you had to be pretty careful . . . Anyway . . .

"The farmers had the water companies use full boxes—fifty pound boxes of dynamite—up in the Eucalyptus trees, next to the pump house across from our house on Leadora. And they had the wires going down into the pump house to the plunger to set 'em all off at the same time. And the crows used to gather in those Eucalyptus trees by the thousands. I mean literally by the thousands. They'd swarm in and roost overnight.

"The first night they had a man named Sam Barnes, who worked for the water company, stay there ready for the crows and then (he) was supposed to set this dynamite off. And no crows came. (Laughs)

"And the second night, no crows came. Finally, they just gave up. They finally just left everything together, but stopped staying at the pump house and Ollie Hammer, who was head of the water company, lived just down the wash from us at the other pump house, and he asked me (that) if I saw the crows in those trees to please let him know. Well, everyday when I got home I, of course, watched the trees. And I think over a month went by and finally a whole big swarm of crows came in around dusk. And I ran down the wash, like I was dodging machine gun bullets, hoping the crows didn't see me. And I screamed, 'Ollie, Ollie, they're back. They're back!'

"Well, he got on the phone and then these men crept up the wash real sneakily, slyly. And they went into the pump house. Crows didn't fly away.

"Sam Barnes hooked up the plunger. David Wilson and myself and Charles Linthicum were in the pump house with them and . . . there's this huge, huge explosion! It shook the pump house! You could hear it all over town. And the three kids, David, Charles, and myself, we ran out to collect the dead crows, so we'd get 25 cents per crow. And there were no crows. No dead crows. There were feathers everywhere . . . I mean there were just, just . . . The ground was black with feathers . . . But the crows flew away. (Laughs)

"Everyone was just standing . . . standing around in disbelief. Couldn't comprehend it."

"All the crows that were on . . .?" I started to ask.

"All the crows that were sitting next to the dynamite, they all flew away . . . (Laughter) I know it seemed impossible."

"How many would you say were there?"

"Oh, maybe two thousand, three thousand . . . . They ate the oranges, ruined their crops. It was quite devastating, economically."

"How did they ever control it then?"

"They sold the property for houses. (Laughs) Because every year it would seem like there'd be more crows. They just couldn't control them . . . . And the crows had centuries of very, very intelligent . . . You could walk into an orchard without a rifle and the crows would be eating an orange . . . (Laughs) Twenty feet away from ya. You walk into a grove with a rifle, and you couldn't see a crow for miles."

"Well, they say birds and crows are descendents of dinosaurs with those eagle sharp eyes . . ."

"And our shotguns were limited to number 6 shot, which was tinier than sand, because a lot of us had what they called Damascus barrels which you could not use a high powered shell in because the barrels would blow up, so we were all restricted to what they called low base number 6 shot. And so, they weren't very effective. Twenty-twos were effective but we weren't allowed to use 22's without an adult around."

"You mentioned the pump house and how Glendora Mayor Joe Finkbinder was always trying to write ordinances against the farm . . ."

"The City Council was always trying to do things to me and the Pharm . . . (They passed) Nineteen hundred and twenty-three ordinances . . . (Against the Pharm) . . .

"One day, after our family came to Glendora and moved into that pump house on Leadora, they tried to pass an ordinance saying people couldn't live in tin packing houses.

"Grandfather was there and stood up and said to Mayor Finkbinder, 'Joe, it seems to me that you forgot how a lot of people got to this town. Why don't you recall how your family came to town and moved into the pump house on Leadora because they couldn't afford anything else?

"'Not all the kids could afford stucco,' grandfather said.

"Finkbinder was completely devastated by that information. (Laughs)

"They never did pass an ordinance about not living in a tin building. (Laughs) But it couldn't have affected me anyway, because I think I was told it can't be retroactive."

From 3-8-05 and 3-10-05 tapes

"Now Michael I want you to learn something. Just be quiet."
"Was your grandfather respected by the townspeople?"
"Oh, yes, he was loved. (Laughs) I don't know if he was respected, but he was loved. Everyone would talk to him. He'd go down by the hardware store, and men would just gather around him, and they'd . . . I have another wonderful story for ya . . .

"I had that 32 Ford that I still have . . . given to me when I was 14 years old. In those days, you could get your license at 14, if you lived in an agricultural area. And grandfather wanted to go down to the hardware store or something. And going down Leadora, before we got to Live Oak, grandfather said he had to pee, so I stopped, and he walked off into orchard a few paces or ten yards or whatever to pee. And the milkman, we called him Mr. McCream; his real name was Mr. McCray. He stopped and said, 'Are you having trouble, Michael?'

"And Grandfather comes out and says, 'Yeah, the car won't run.' (Laughs) I stare at my Grandfather like, What do you mean, it's just fine.

"And he says, 'Now Michael I want you to learn something. Just be quiet. We'll take care of it.'

"Stanley Baird comes down and says, 'What's going on?'

"Mr. McCream says, "Michael's car's stuck . . .' Pretty soon, Jed Stiff is there and then Mr. Vandersloth and pretty soon we had like ten men taking the air filter off, checking the spark (LAUGHS). And every time I'd begin to say something, Grandpa would say, 'Shut up and learn something here.'

"So I watched 'em and I knew about all that stuff because I was very mechanical. Anyway, they got everything put back, checked the distributor and everything.

"He said try it now and see if it works. And it started right up.

"Grandfather said, 'You know, you men put mechanics out of business all over the state. You're just absolutely wonderful. You know, only you could have fixed this car today. And they were all very proud of themselves and left.

"I said to Grandfather, when we got back into the car, 'What did you do that for?'

"He said, 'Didn't you learn something?'

"(Laughs) I learned my car runs, and they could have destroyed it (Laughs). And he said, 'No, what you learned was that when people help you or you help somebody else, it makes you feel good. And they're going to be talking about fixing your car for a week and everybody is going to be really proud of them and feel how fortunate you were to get your car fixed.

"And I said, 'OK.' So we get down to the hardware store and the first man that comes up to Grandfather and says, 'I heard that Jed Stiff fixed your grandson's car.'

"Grandfather says, 'You know, those men are geniuses. How they do all that I don't know. I've never been very good with cars, but they knew exactly what to do. And about four people, while we were down there, (came up) 'Heard the grandson's car got fixed today.' (Laughs).

"Didn't the townspeople ever catch on that grandfather was doing things like that (playing jokes, jesting for a purpose) for a deeper reason?"

"I don't think so, not on that occasion (fixing Michael's perfectly running car). My grandfather would play jokes too. One of 'em was . . . We went to Mrs. Lawton's for dinner and he had my mother put a white thread hanging out of the back of his coat. And then he had a spool of white thread on a pencil in his front pocket.

"I said, 'What's that for?'

"He said, 'It's for Mrs. Landon.'

"What does she want with that white thread in your coat?

"And he says, 'You just watch, before we sit down for dinner Mrs. Landon will try to spruce me up.'

"And sure enough — Mrs. Landon was one of these people, if you had a row of books and one of them was sticking out at one end, she'd go up and make it equal, and if there was a picture that was off a little, she'd go up and straighten it. Things like that.

"First thing she says when she walks in, she says, 'Harry come here a minute. You've got a thread hanging on the back of your coat.'

"So she takes a thread, and he takes the spool of white thread out of his pocket on the pencil and holds it in front of him.

"And she pulls and pulls (laughs) and everybody is laughing, and she says, 'What's so funny?'

"And somebody says, 'You know his coat's going to fall apart soon.'

"And she says, 'You know I think I've pulled too much thread, I think I'll just cut it off.'

"And grandfather says, 'Well, pull just a little more. It can't be that much.' (Laughs)

"Finally, she cut it off and he put what was left back in his pocket. And nobody told her what had happened. She said, 'I can't understand how there could be that much thread out of that coat, (Laughs) and it could still be hanging (Laughs) together.'

"And everybody said, 'Well, you know they made things better years ago.'"

"Did he spend much time thinking of these things?"

"I think it was things he had seen other people do . . .

"One time he had a piece of black cardboard or whatever . . . Looked like an ink spill. And he had an inkbottle, which was empty, and Mrs. Lawton always had these beautiful Damas tablecloths and napkins. She always had the best of everything. So, he goes into the dinning room when they're all buzzing around the living room. He puts the black paper down and then turns the inkbottle on its side by it, so it looks like it's been knocked over and stained the table.

(Damas is a kind of linen, but very expensive, so I'm told.)

"And he comes back in, and I watched him do this and I said, 'You know, Mrs. Lawton is not going to think that's funny.'

"He says, 'I know, (MCR laughs) but everybody else will.'

"So he joins the group. And five minutes later, or whatever, we hear this horrible scream. Mrs. Lawton just lost it. 'My God, does anybody know what's happened here?' (MCR laughs)

"My grandfather says, 'Let's go see what's happened!'"

"Everybody is devastated. You know, to ruin such a beautiful tablecloth.

"And Mrs. Lawton says, 'How did this happen? Michael, how did this happen? Michael, what did you do? Skipper what did you do?'

"And, I don't know what, but I said, 'Grandfather did it.' (Laughs)

"Mrs. Lawton looked at him incredulously. Like how is this possible? And then he went over and picked it all up and said, 'I just thought it would be funny.'

"She said, 'It wasn't funny at all.'

"And then he said, 'That's what Michael told me.' (Laughs)

"You know one time Mrs. Lawton had this great big radio. It stood about 3 foot high and 2 feet across. One of those old radios. I had some in the packinghouse. Anyway, my grandfather, when we were gathered in the living room, and there was a hush or something. And he taps the radio with his cane lightly, and he says, 'You know, I've never cottoned to talking furniture. (Laughs)

"He could always make people laugh."

"Did you follow your grandfather around?"

"Well, no . . . He did walk but . . . I mean I would listen to him when he'd talk, but I was usually out doing something.

"I enjoyed listening to him."

"Did grandfather and Stade have a lot of similar experiences?"

"I don't think so. No, but they liked each other a lot, and they'd talk about just mundane things. They didn't talk politics or religion. Primarily because neither of them was interested in all that stuff."

Papa Peck's Golden Nuggets

"When I was about ten years old, I used to go up to the Pecks to work for Papa Peck hauling rocks, for he was building his house. In his kitchen, which was finished, he had, I think it was two-quart jars of gold nuggets. Filled to the top with gold nuggets. And men would stop by once in awhile and ask him where would be the best place to pan for gold, or which canyon would be the most promising, and some of those kept starring at those bottles (Laughs). And they'd say, 'Where did you find those?'

"And he said, 'Well, I found them in Heaton Canyon near such and such a place.'

"Well, they'd be off like a shot.

"Well, one morning I got there and he sez, 'Someone came last night and stole all our gold nuggets.'"

"I said, 'Oh my goodness . . .' because there was no theft in those days and I was just, you know, devastated because I thought that was their life savings, you know.

"And he sez, 'Would you come help me, we need to make more.' (Laughs).

"And I said, 'How do you make gold?'

"He said, 'I'll show ya.'

"I said, 'Does anybody else know? Because it's so valuable.' (Laughs)

"'Well, let me show ya.'

"So we got the big Bunsen burner, which I now have in the big machine shop. And we heated up this big cast iron bowl and put this plumber's lead in it. You know, they used to use lead in drain systems. Anyway, he put a bunch of this lead in there, and we melted it, and put a bucket of water next to it, and I took a big spoon and spooned the molten lead into the water, and it would explode almost, scattering. And after we'd made a whole bunch of nuggets with the lead, he threw them out on a towel, dried 'em, and then we put some gold paint, and spread 'em around on it. Let 'em dry and then put them in the quart jars, filled the quart jars full of water, put the caps on, and put 'em back on the shelves."

From 3-10-05 tape

Canons and treasures

"Miracles just went on and on. I don't know if I can remember them chronologically, Michael said.

"We had that 1917 Krupp cannon from Germany and the American Legion owned it and it used to be in front of our City Hall. And during the Second World War, they took it up to the scrap pile, because there was a scrap drive for all metal. But because it was so big and heavy, they said it wasn't economic to melt it down. So, it sat in the scrap pile across from our house next to the wash. And there was all kinds of treasures in there—cans and gears and all kinds of stuff. Anyway, the cannon sat there for years, and when I was about seven, I guess, we used to play on it.

We could crank the barrel up and down. Then Skipper said, 'You know, we could fire this thing with carbide.' You know, (as Michael nodded at me) with acetylene and oxygen (which was how they taught this rookie about firing Castle cannons upon my arrival).

"He said, 'All you'd need to do is put a coffee can (on the cannon tip)—a coffee can sits perfect in the barrel.' Barrel was about that big around (Michael, motions with his hand).

"I said, 'Well, that wouldn't hurt anything.'

"He said, 'No, it would just flop on the ground . . . But we could turn it around and fill it full of rocks.'

"'Well, we can't shot it toward town,' I said.

"'No, we can't do that,' Skipper said.

"So, anyway, I went to the American Legion and asked them to give me the cannon. My mother dressed me all up, and they had a big meeting at the American Legion Hall, and I was just terrified. They had all these old men there, and I went down there and there were about ten of us little kids who had painted the cannon and painted the wheels yellow, and Mr. Reed, down at the hardware store, had given us all of the paint for free for fixing up the cannon.

"Anyway, I went and gave my lecture, 'It's our cannon. We painted it. We take care of it . . . We oil it. And you don't care about it. Therefore, you should give it to me . . .'

"And everybody clapped.

"And then they said, 'Okay, you can have it if you can move it within three days. And you have to pay a dollar for the bill of sales.'

"And I screamed, 'Where am I going to get a dollar!'

"And Frank Teeter said, 'I'll give you the dollar, Michael.'

"Oh, thank you, Frank. Thank you.'

"And so then I went to Loren Ward and said, 'Would you move the cannon with your tractor over to our property?'

"He said, 'No, the American Legion really doesn't want to give that cannon up. They want to put it in front of the American Legion Hall. So I went to Karl Gunn, and he said, 'No the American Legion . . .' Same story. I went to Stanley Baird, and he said, 'Michael, I'd love to do it, but I'd be blackballed in town if they lost their cannon.'

"It was a big cannon, 5 ½ tons or whatever. Krupp 1917 First World War cannon. Big story about it in *the glendoran* (magazine).

"Anyway, nobody would help me move it, and I went to about five different people with tractors, and they wouldn't do it. And I'm devastated, trying to figure how in the world are we going to do it? Well, the third day was coming and we figured, 'Well, we've just lost it.' And I was at school, and when I got home, the cannon was in our backyard.

"And I went to Stanley and said, 'Did you move the cannon for us?'

"He said, 'No.'

"'Do you know who moved the cannon for us?'

"'No.'

"And nobody would admit moving the cannon. And I told Skipper, 'I have these magic powers . . . And it's just another example of my mind making things happen . . .'

"And Skipper goes out and tries looking for the tracks because every tractor has a different size and type tread. And there's no tracks anywhere. Nothin. No truck tracks. Nothin.

"And Skipper says. 'This is a real mystery.'

"I sez, 'It's just another of those little miracles I keep telling you about.'

"So anyway . . . My grandfather is too old to run a tractor and he wouldn't have know how to run a tractor anyway . . . Anyway, for years I didn't know how that happened. And then one time Ollie Hammer was visiting me and, you see the cannon was on their property—the water company property, and he said, 'Did you ever figure out how you got that cannon moved?'

"'No' I said, 'I thought it was just one of those miracles—my mind making things happen.'

"'Well, I did it. We watched you go around and ask everybody to move it for you and we went up there to the pump house with our 1949 A frame truck (that they used for hauling pipes and stuff). We saw nobody was around (in those days it was all covered with orchards). And we then had some workers take boards and erase all the tracks.'

"So he said that's how it happened.

"I forgot to put in this little caveat. After the cannon was moved, I had these men come from the American Legion and ask, 'How did you move it?'

"I said, 'My mind. I do things with my mind.' (Michael acts this out in his childhood voice and abracadabra hands.)

"'Oh, God!' They just walked off like . . . *This poor idiot. He's the village idiot.*'

"I could see it in their faces that they didn't believe me, but . . .

"You were how old?"

"I was like seven . . .

"And then Odo Stade, when my mother gave him that half acre on the north end of our property. She gave it in the hopes that Odo and Maria would help raise me, because she was always away at work. This was when I was about eight years old. He began to build their house up there on the north end of the property, and he told me that. And he was German and had seem all the horrors of the wars, been in the revolution in Mexico . . . he sez to me, and it's a German cannon. 'You know, Michael, we have to get rid of that canon.'"

City Hall, Mom, and Singer Sewing Machine's Al Bourne
"So your mother didn't want you to live at the Pharm?"
"The city too wanted to get rid of the Pharm.

"Well, she'd say, 'But I can't stop him. I pay him rent and Grandfather lives here too. And we thought he would default in three months. He's been able to make his payments. I want this place to be subdivided, because I represent Mr. Bourne and the Episcopal church and this place will distract from the beautiful houses that have been proposed around it,' which hadn't started yet. It was a few years away but, anyway, she (mother) just premeditated the fact that it would help me. But I don't know that to be true.

"But we had so many miracles. First of all, all the people who came and got really vociferous about how I was violating all the laws. And I would complain at parties about the way the City was treating me, and these people would all of a sudden transfer to a different city. And I didn't have a clue that the people my mother associated with in Glendora were the movers and shakers in Glendora. And if I complained about somebody, they immediately told the City Council, which was usually at one of the gatherings (which his ex-actress, singer, and dancer mother would host at the Tin Palace).

"'Ya know, (Michael's voice replicates one of Dorothy's party guests) these people are bothering the Rubels . . . And you (city council) shouldn't allow it.'

"Well, then the City Council decided, 'Well, we can't approach them on that level any longer, because it creates too much static. So we'll just take him to court.' So, I get this notice of 187 violations. And in those days, they didn't provide you with an attorney or anything. And I didn't have any money. I was always broke, because my payments were $253, and in 1959 that was a fortune. Fortunately, Mr. Bourne paid my first six payments, but without that I wouldn't have made it. And my mother was furious that he did that because she wanted . . . (A knocking causes Michael to ask, 'Is there somebody out there knocking.')

"Anyway, and the developers were anxious for me to get out of there, because this place just had chain link around it with concertina wire on top, razor wire, and all that stuff and search lights that rotated and alarms systems where you tripped the wire and you honked the horn. And they were just disgusted with all those kids over there . . .

"And see, I was underage. The property had been given to the Episcopal Church, because Mr. Bourne was a very good friend of my father and my grandfather. In fact, they used to play cribbage together. I think my grandfather talked him into making my first six payments. I don't know if that's true or not, but somebody did. But I used to call Mr. Bourne and ask, 'Why in the world would you give this to the church with the provision that they'd have to sell it to me, and I don't have any money?'

"'I know, Michael, but at least it made me feel good.'

"'Oh, Mr. Bourne, you've done a terrible thing to me. I can't come up with $253 each month.'

"'I know. I'll make your first six payments.'

"But what'll I do after six months?

"'I don't know.'" (MCR laughs at repeating Mr. Bourne's response.)

"And I'd always call him collect. He lived up at Lake Tahoe. Anyway, Mr. Bourne saved my bacon. And I think my grandfather told him that after the six months I was probably going to be able to manage it. I had three jobs. I had all those little rentals. Glen Speer was paying $15 a month. My mother was paying $40. My grandfather was paying $40. With all of this stuff, I was just scrapping through."

"That's a real friend, call him collect when you need money . . ." Jack Stinson, who is also participating in the story telling session, adds.

"Oh, yes. Well, I had know Mr. Bourne all my life. He was the owner of Singer Sewing Machine Company. And was very wealthy."

☺ ☺

Barbara Walters, Harry Reasoner, and Mrs. Graham
"You didn't like Barbara Walters?" Jack Stinson asked.

"Well, I was frightened of her. See what happened is the Washington Post had an article about us, which Dwayne probably has in the scrapbook. By the way, everyone, Dwayne is in the room with us.

"When the WP article came out, they did a big article on the Castle, which wasn't there yet. I mean we just had . . . I would walk people around and say the clock tower was going to be there and this and that. It was total insanity. Well, anyway, the Washington Post sent the son or son-in-law of Mrs. Graham. And he came out because, I can't remember why . . . . But anyway he came out and asked if he could do an article about the Castle . . ."

I interject, "Wasn't that Ted Shepherd's doings?"

"Yeah, Ted Shepherd put him on to it. He lived in Washington DC. But, anyway, and I guess he told him this big castle (MCR motions with his hands) was built.

"Well, I took him into the reservoir and he said, 'Where's the Castle?'"

"Well, the clock tower will be there and . . . Well, he just started laughing.

"He says, 'Well, I was lead to believe the Castle was done.'"

"'No, we just started the foundations over here' . . . and whatever. Some of our walls were up four feet or whatever . . .

"But anyway, he said, 'Well, and I had that drawing that was on the book cover. And I gave that to him and he said, 'With that drawing and my imagination, I'll write about your castle.' (MCR LAUGHS) Well, anyway, he did that and then Harry Reasoner came. He was with 60 Minutes or something."

I interject that Harry was then doing *Reasoner's Reports*.

"She (Barbara Walters) had the Today Show when she came. But Harry Reasoner did a beautiful job with it. It was very nicely done. There was a big crew here. I liked him a lot. When I first got home from my school bus job, in the morning, he was sitting out there on the sidewalk, with his back against our wall, smoking a cigarette. And I stopped with my 1953 VW, which looked like it had been through 14 head-on collisions.

"And I said, 'Sir, may I help you?'

"He said, 'I'm trying to locate a Michael Rubel.'

"And I said, 'Well, I'm him.'"

"May I talk to you?"

"I said, 'Sure. Come on in.'

"And I hit my clicker and the big gate opened and he walked in and I yelled back, 'You're not allowed to smoke in here.'"

"'Oh, I'm sorry,' and he threw down the cigarette.

"He said, 'I'm Harry Reasoner.' I didn't have a clue who that was.

"You know, I have a television program, and I'd like to do a thing, about your Castle. I read about it in the Washington Post."

"I said, 'Well, I'll show you around. My clock tower's going to (MCR Laughs) and he started laughing. Then I took him to the Packing House. He was very impressed, of course. This was after my mother moved out. And then we had a cup of tea, and he explained that he had this TV news thing, and he wanted to do a thing about castles. He didn't just do mine, he did all over Europe, I think he did about eight castles. And then mine was the last one.

"He says, 'Now If you remember all these castles in Europe are open to the public for revenue, because they need the money to maintain their castle. And I've been told the public is not allowed in this Castle and that I can't tell where it is and I can't tell the owner's name. And I've agreed to this. So, I won't tell you where it is or this man's name. And then it goes on about showing the drawings and all that stuff, which made it look like the Castle looked like that.

"So, anyway, he did a beautiful thing on it. It was about 15 minutes, and we watched it on TV.

"And then Barbara Walters comes about six months later. She had the Today Show, which I found out later. Because when she came, I didn't know who she was either. And she came with three men that looked like thugs. Like they might rough me up, if I molested their friend. Anyway, I was in old clothes, working with cement or whatever. And she walks in and says, 'I would like to do a show with you on TV about this commune.'

"I said, 'It's not a commune.'"

"Well, I understand you have people living here."

'Yes, we live here, but we have our own quarters and kitchens and we're not living together."

"'Well, what made you start this commune?' she asked.

"I mean I got so annoyed with her. She wouldn't leave that concept. And she's very aggressive. She'd make a good drill Sargent, because she likes to put her face right next to you, and I kept backing up.

"I said, 'Mam, this isn't a commune. We're trying to build a Castle for fun and it's a lot of work and my cement mixer's running right now and I can't leave that."

"'Well, I'll just take a few minutes.'"

"And I kept backing up and backing up and she kept following me, and I went all the way to the big kitchen, which is quite a distance. And then I went clear back into the corner. And she's following me all this way, and I'm backing up all this time. And I had gloves on. And when I got into the corner in the kitchen, I couldn't go any further and began to get down on my knees.

"She said, 'What are you doing?'

"You know I've had a mental problem for years . . .

"'You stop that right now. I've seen you on Reasoner's Reports.'

"Oh, Oh, Oh yeah, I don't remember that but . . .'

"'You stop that right now,' she said.

"And she was getting very, very angry. And she said, 'I want to do a show about this place.'

"And I said, 'I understand and I don't know what to say. You have to talk to my mommy.'

"'Well, why do I have to talk to her?'

"She told me never to make any decisions."

"'Well, did Harry Reasoner have to go through her?'"

"I don't know."

"My mommy lives just down the street, 861 East Leadora."

"'Well, I'LL go down and talk with her.'"

"And I was frightened of her. I mean she really is aggressive and has no sense of tact or being polite or considerate. Whereas Harry Reasoner is very tactful, very considerate, and stuck to his promises.

"So anyway, I called my mother as fast as I could get to a phone. I said, 'Mother, mother, there's this lady coming, named Barbara something, Barbara Walters or something."

"'Oh, Barbara Walters! What an honor!'"

"But mother don't let her do a show about this place."

"'Oh, Michael it would be so wonderful to have that kind of publicity.'"

"Mother you must obey me on this issue. She thinks this is a commune. And I can't have that concept in our town. You know that we're all hippies and stuff like that."

"'Oh, Michael, you're missing a great opportunity. She has the Today Show. It has one of the highest ratings.'"

"'Mother, you must obey me on this,' I said. 'This is a serious problem we're facing.'"

"'Oh, hell, Michael, don't you have any consideration for the opportunities you get.'"

"No, none at all."

"'Oh, they're pulling in now.'"

"Oh, I told mother on the phone that I convinced her (Walters) that I have a mental problem and that I'm mentally deficient."

"'Oh, Michael, you're so. You're just . . .' and she just hung up.

"So anyway. When Barbara Walters came to the door she said, 'Are you in charge of the property on Live Oak?'

"And she said, 'Well, I do things there and.'"

"'Well, I guess your son has a problem, doesn't he?'"

"'Oh, yes.'

"And she (Mother) told that story over and over again at parties and stuff. And people were just hanging over their chairs . . . . But she (Walters) never got in again.

"I'm so thankful because 'communes' had a strange connotation in those days . . . they still do. I had enough trouble on the property without having that thrown at me too."

Tape labeled 3-10-05

Castles in the World on ABC's Reasoner's Reports,
October 13, 1974. Segment portion follows.

"Is he really strange?" asks Harry Reasoner's voiceover.

"Eccentric is the word. He is a true eccentric, and he's got the money and he can afford to be . . ." continues Harry.

"I'd like you to meet one of the most eccentric human beings I have met among California people. His name is Michael

Rubel. He's 34 years old, and he lives in an old packinghouse on 2 and 1/2 acres in the foothills of the San Gabriel Mountains. My story is not about the Packing House, which Rubel has filled with hundreds of antiques. My story is about the huge stone castle that Rubel is building in a reservoir next to the Packing House. I cannot adequately describe Rubel's property; the castle is being built of stone and concrete. But Rubel is also using bottles and chairs and bed springs and scrap metal to reinforce the walls of the castle. He's had some help from friends and neighbors, and he showed this drawing when the city council asked for his plans . . .

"And they approved construction."

"Michael, why on earth are you building a castle out here?" Reasoner asks.

"Well, it's an enjoyable project and it keeps me off of the streets, and I get depressed if I'm not dong something goofy."

"You say that you like to be building something all the time."

"Yes, right. It's been a disease since I was a small kid. We all build forts when we are young. Some of us never grow up."

"What are some of the things you have used in building the castle so far?"

"Well, some of these beams are from collapsed bridges that we continue to hear about on the news and, ah, all the stones are from the river beds in the area. And the bottles come from my neighbors who drink rather heavily. (Ha, Ha, Ha)"

"Why have you used so many strange objects to build a building like this?"

"Cause it's cheap. The economics of it is quite rational."

"How do you live, Mike? Frankly, you are not working. Where do you make your money?"

"Well, I was given a great deal of money. Well, not a great deal but enough to play with in 1969, from a sea captain who died and decided he liked this project and liked me, I guess."

"How long will it take you to build your castle?"

"Well, all my life, I guess. It'll never be finished. It can't be done, because it's too huge. It's 22,000 square feet."

"How many stories up will you go?"

"Four, if we live that long. If we don't fall off of some thing."

"Well, let's say that you take all of your life working on this. Do you hope that someone else will continue it, or does it matter to you?"

"Well, I'm hoping that the historical society will take it and perhaps keep it rather than tear it down. Similar to what happened to the Watts towers. It would be a great moment in my grave, if it would be kept rather than bulldozed down."

Prudes hide Fan Dancer Sally Rand

"And then my grandfather played strip poker with Sally Rand and our kitchen was right next to the street on the north end of the Packing House. That was before the 69 floods . . ."

"Well, she didn't wear very much, did she?" Jack Stinson asks.

"Well, she would be there at the kitchen table, and I think Dwayne remembers this, and my grandfather would pull the curtains and cars going by would stop and look in because Sally was always naked. And my grandfather, when he lost a hand would just take a cuff link off, or a stud out of his shirt. And I said to my mother . . . . When I went in, I'd always draw the curtains, and I said, 'Grandfather, having a naked girl and you playing at the table, and everybody's looking in, it's just not acceptable.'

"And he said, 'Michael, how did you get to be such a prude? Everybody loves it.'

"I said, 'Grandfather, I don't love it. I'm the one who takes all the guff from the City, and I don't want to have additional arguments against our being here.'"

"'Well, Okay,' (he'd mumble) . . . And I'd leave (the old kitchen) and he'd open the curtains.

"I mean I was furious, absolutely furious. And I almost got sick over all these antics that people were playing . . . Gad. It was just dreadful."

"Ahun, Carl . . . Ah, Your Honor . . ."

"And when they took me to court, Judge Miller was our judge at the Citrus Court in Covina. And Judge Miller, I knew all my life. And he and my mother were very close friends, but that didn't help me any at this hearing. And he said, 'Michael, we have 187, or whatever, violations against you on this property you have up there.'

"I said, 'Yes, sir . . .'

"And the bailiff said, 'You say, 'Your Honor.'"

"'Yes, sir, your honor,'"

"'How do you plead?'"

"'I'm guilty on everything there . . . I'm putting in electrical. I have a big generator that's running that's noisy and all these things are true . . . anyway.'

"He said, 'Well, Michael, I cannot let this continue. Now if you promise me to stop all these things, I will just suspend your sentence.'

"I said, 'Miller I cannot stop.'"

"Bailiff said, 'You say, 'Your Honor.'"

"I had know Carl Miller all my life, and I said, 'Ahun, ah, Carl . . . Your Honor . . . (I'm only 22 years old) I'm not going to stop. I have to do this thing, build a castle. And if I have to go to jail . . . grandfather said Benjamin Franklin went to jail, and Harrison went to jail, and Emerson went to jail, and all these people. He said if you're different, society puts you through the jail for a while. And when you get out, you just keep mixing cement. They'll get tired after 40-50 years of that.

"Miller said, 'Well, we're gonna go in and bulldoze everything. Put it on your taxes, and sentence you to some time in jail.'

"'I know, that's what I understand.'

"He said, 'You won't change your mind and start conforming to the laws?'

"I said, 'You know, your honor, there are laws against everything and if everybody abided by the laws nothing would get done.'

"'Where'd you think that one up?' said Judge Miller.

"That's what my grandfather says . . . (MCR Laughs)

"Anyway they were going to sentence me on the 20th of September 1962. And Monica Fager, who Dwayne knew, she's dead now. She had that huge house which is now a Senior Center. And she had all the rooms rented out to people that were indigent. But she would talk to everybody. She was a little short fat lady, and she loved people, and she talked to absolutely everybody.

"Well, anyway, she went to the City Council before the September 20th sentencing and she gave them _ _ _ _. I wasn't there, but my grandfather was, and he came home and he said, 'You can not believe the way that lady talked to that council.'

"And I said, 'What happened?'"

"Well, she literally told them that if they put Dorothy's son in jail for being creative, she'd have them all thrown out at the next election.

And they knew she could do it, because two years before in 1960 there was Dutch Detweiler, a real loose cannon and everybody loved him; and Ruth Crawlstreet, who opposed my project and me, being there (involved in Glendora Council race) and wanted it (the Pharm) to conform to the General Plan. And we worked really hard to get her off of the Council. But Monica was really the one who did it. And she (Ruth) got so few votes she moved out of town, and we've never seen her again. And Dutch Detweiler, who loved the project, thought it was really neat, got the most votes. And the Council remembered that.

"In those days the town was much smaller. Could never do it today. In those days, everybody who lived north of Foothill voted. And everybody loved my mother and grandfather. He was very popular. So with that combination, we were able to survive."

☺ ☺

Medellin Columbia's cliff hanging bus

"Nothing special . . . Like every day experience . . ."

"I was in Columbia, some where around Medellin, on a bus whose seats were old pews from an old church that had been nailed down in the bus. We were traveling over old roads in mountainous areas and up ahead a 50' section of the road had washed out.

"Bus driver stopped the bus and everyone had to get out. They cut a path, about this wide, (Michael shows with his hands a path not much wider than a foot) along the mountainside, and we were told to go along it to the other side. Somehow, all of us made it over that path to the other side without falling down the mountainside.

"They tied a bunch of ropes around the bus and tied them over some trees above us on the mountain side. They also tied ropes to the front fender and axles and got those ropes to the other side to a bunch of men."

"Were you helping them, Michael?"

"No. I was standing with the women. Not really understanding what was going on.

"Then they backed the bus up about fifty feet and the driver gunned the engine and hit the gas. The bus went over the edge and started falling down, like this, and the ropes above grabbed it. It swung toward the other side and the men over there kept pulling on the ropes attached to the fender and axle, and pulled and pulled and the bus came up on the other side.

"Then they just got in and continued on their way. They acted like it was just a common ever day experience. Nothing special."

So, it was said

If you do not care where you are, you can't get lost.

If you are happy with where you come from, you'll be happy where you are going.

"Experience all the emotions so you can sympathize with others."

Grandfather

Chapter 11

DB, Limo Man, Icabod, and Scott drill us.

"What memories were made here . . ."
MCR

It was not often that Pharm evenings or their stories ended on a serious note. Such chapters as this are reminders of that.

In the bottom drawer of my large black file cabinet sits about 39 pounds of large, medium, and legal sized envelopes. The backsides often have messages, such as:

BE WELL DO GOOD WORK AND KEEP IN TOUCH GARRISON KEILLOR	Zsa Zsa said, "I am happy I finally married an archeologist. The older I get the more interested he is in me."

> We look forward to your visit.
> **One man can't fix everything. If it does not work, don't fix it. Remember to fulfill your anxieties. What the hell, I'm a Rubel.**

The envelopes' front sides are postal works of art. They are covered with about 5,434 one-cent stamps, which used to be Michael's protest to postage increases. Sometimes these one-centers encase the envelope. Whatever space was left would be pretty much filled with happy faces, pictures, and sketches of castles, dragons, and insignias perched next to

BOLDED addresses and BOLDED MESSAGES free for postal persons and world to see.

Almost every envelope contained some sort of "Thank you" from Michael, along with some delightful drawings from children, photos, castle balloons, an entry pass to the Castle, or stuff that he preferred you file rather than he.

One of the many 9"x12" envelopes, with the drunken knight ensconced in his castle with his likewise inebriated Dragon filling one half of the envelope, has this bolded message filling one quarter of the envelope's remaining space:

> SKIPPER LANDON MADE THIS 20 MINUTE DVD. YOU MADE ALL THIS POSSIBLE BY BEING PART OF THIS PLACE.
>
> THANK YOU FOR BEING IN MY LIFE. WHAT MEMORIES WERE MADE HERE.

Of course, I wasn't the only blessed one to receive such a message.

Memories of living in a special community of laughter and mirth, give and take, do and learn—where each evening you gratefully rested your well used and fed body, while eagerly anticipating your next *California day*—is not an easy spirit to convey. Ever cognizant that typed words may not convey the "specialness" of Rubelia, this tunnel digger pasted several pictures and, believe me, they are not *Photo Shopped* depictions of fictitious doings, such as the *moon landing certainly was.*

After a good day's work, with old-fashioned food, and some wine, Michael could be coaxed into telling one of his magical adventures and from there he and others would revive memories of castle hijinks.

Among a growing pile of regrets as life flies by, not having *bookified* more Rubelian adventures while Michael and Kaia were around ranks high.

So before we all become too old to *forget what we already don't remember well*, and lose more special people and their wonderfully invigorating attitudes, here are a few stories that try to convey why living in a budding and building community of "Try it" Pharmers, where safety was neither first or second, was so much plain, old fashioned *phun.*

The DB, not my hometown or Doonesbury's BD

(DB is not even a cousin to Gary Trudeau's BD, aka Brian Dowling with whom cartoonist Trudeau Yale schooled. That Doonesbury BD threw oblong balls at my Cleveland St Ignatius High School, then for Yale, New England Patriots, and the Green Bay Packers. This DB QB used his pizza hut-hut to heave and deliver cheese on a crust.)

Ralph lived in the Pharm's front house before it was washed and walled away in the Great Flood of 1969. He managed Zio's Pizza Parlor down on Route 66. Whenever he got a troublesome delivery boy (DB), he had a routine that would improve the boy's manners, habits, and appreciation for the job, or divert a cheesy career path. The routine usually started with a phone call to a band of dangerous, carnivorous pizza omnivores.

"Michael would you and the boys order some extra zesty pizzas?"
"Okay, should we put extra cheese on them?" Michael would ask.
"Yes, the works would be especially good tonight," Ralph said on this particular order.
"Good. We'll let the tunnel workers come up from the damp, dark, and dank for some zesty R&R and cheesy stuff."

With the *pizzas second coming* arriving in the dark of the night as the boulder was rolled away from the tunnel gate, the unrepentant DB first faced the 8' high walled compound topped with cast iron pokers and concertina wires. Entering another walled entryway with very heavy doors framed with rough-cut 3x8 timbers and steel bars, most un-coached delivery boys were at a loss as to what to do. In this case, a speaker told the DB to pick up one of the several bewildering phone contraptions hanging from the masonry wall. After telling the voice at the other end that he was here to deliver pizzas, the voice said, "When you hear the door click, pull it and step in."

After hearing a hissing sound followed by a loud "Click," the DB pulled the heavy door and stepped in to face a bouldered pillbox with slotted windows that had a machine gun pointing directly at the heavy door in front of which he now stood. Quickly, he moved to the railroad-tied driveway that lay behind the huge, barbed in wire and hinged to cover over 20' drive-in gate to his right. He gingerly proceeded in the dark with his four pizza boxes. Even in the dark, the DB could see towers rising to his left. In front of him stood what looked like a windmill, with all sorts of weird stuff stacked around what seemed like a farm. He didn't notice the mineshaft on his left that ran downhill from the railroad-tied driveway, on which he had taken a half dozen baby steps.

"Halt! Who goes there?" shouted a voice from the mineshaft on his left that had a steel track leading downward to another heavy and barred door. From behind that door stepped a man with a flashlight taped atop his helmeted head, his hands rapped around a big rifle that pointed at the DB.

"Hands up!" was the guard's next response, which moved the DB toward juggling to avoid dumping his deliveries . . .

"I'm just delivering pizzas," blurted the DB, as he juggled boxes and nerves to obey.

"Yeah, sure . . ." the armed guard replied while chewing a stick, "Don't move one hair on your chiny-chin-chin or I'll . . ." the guard said, as he stepped back toward the tunnel with his gun still pointed at the simmering boxes. Picking up the wall phone from the railroad ties lined tunnel walls the bearded guard, in between stick chews, picked up a tunnel wall phone and called ahead.

"Oh, so pizzas been ordered? Well . . . okay . . . I'll bring 'em in."

After inspecting the DB's spread body parts, the guard pushed him down the railroad-tied path with his rifle over his forearm. The pizza boy stalled as he approached the tower, with a 20x30' gate with jagged 4x4's ominously hanging overhead. The guard lifted his rifle, pointed it, and ordered, "Through there."

Near the end of the 30'+ long tunnel lined with protruding bottles that an armored vehicle could drive through, two armed guards jumped out with their old rifles in hand. DB jumped backwards—into his back guard's rifle, causing him to jump again, and again grab for his shaky pizzas. Unphased, the trailing guard said, "S'okay. He's pizza delivery boy, and I checked the boxes, and frisked him. They're cheesy pizzas. And he's almost wet his . . ."

"Why didn't someone alert us? Geeze! We could've blown you two to the after life. And that blowing holes in people always pisses off da boss . . . Okay, go back to your post. We'll take him from here . . .," the new guards disgustedly said.

Tightly grasping his boxes, the DB couldn't help looking up at the tons of concrete towering over him, darkened beams, towers, hanging tools, ropes, clocks, pipes and protruding beams and cemented telephone poles and weird obstructions that lain along the path he was being led down. As he passed a long table made of 6-inch beams laden with grinders and pipes, he paused to stare at an anvil, coal bin, and blacksmith tools from Robin Hood's day, only to be pushed by a rifle into a tunnel only wide enough for his hunched body to move through. Bottles protruded from the walls, and there was a hanging 20-watt light bulb that barely lit his wood laid footpath. As he was pushed forward, about ten feet into the tunnel, another helmeted and pointed-gun guard jumped into the narrow exit way ordering, "Halt!"

There wasn't much up or sideways room for the DB to jump, but the armed guards thought there was enough room to wet.

"It's okay. The boss ordered some pizza," uttered the nudging guards behind the DB.

"Geeze! Someone's gonna get killed again if people don't! . . ." said the upfront, uptight new guard, as he shook his head and backed up. "Okay, leave him with us. We'll take him to da boss."

With a bewildered look, DB looked around from the slope exiting the tunnel to see an outhouse with "Ladies" on the door. A ramp ran from there into the darkness that seemed to have a metallic cylinder shaped room at its end. Before him were many feet of running plate glass with pitchforks, harnesses, and lanterns hanging from the wall it fronted. Directly in front of him was a metal rack holding about 300 shoes. While looking at the shoes and noting a ramp and tin shed to the left he was pushed forward until he stood next to a red Coke machine that had cases of those aged greened Coke bottles, which he remembered seeing around his parents' safe and secure house, for which he now longed.

Suddenly, in front of the Coke machine a 10x12' rumpled tin door slid open as another armed guard stood there motioning him to come forward into a big sheet metal building.

"Go ahead," said his other guards "go deliver your stuff."

DB followed the guard inside the Tin Palace, as the other two followed in tow. To DB that night, the tin shed he walked into seemed to be three football fields long. Flags hung from rafters fifteen feet above him. Drapes, pictures, art works, and cuckoo clocks adorned the walls around him. Antique furniture sat everywhere, including a hand made 15' long iron fireplace cut from a tank, as well as a 1927 Chevy truck with wooden spooked wheels . . . But all that quickly disappeared as the guards led him through this long room, dimly lit from old chandelier-like lights. As he tried to grasp the dark oddities around him, he passed what looked like a single woman in a nurse's outfit, rising up from the cargo elevator nearest to the sliding door. She moved not at all and looked straight ahead, as though mummified. DB followed the guards past what seemed like several refrigerator rooms (which they were) until the guard stopped at an open refrigerator door, grabbed the steel latch handle on the thick wooden door, opened it wider, and stepped aside. DB stood in a daze, as a couple cuckoo clocks popped out from their ticking wooded perches on his left and a huge picture of a lady with booming hat hung on the wall to the right.

"Go ahead. Go in. Give Michael the pizzas," urged the guards to the bewildered DB as he stood in front of a handful of people sitting on the floor.

Michael, all of the 220+ muscled pounds on his 6' frame, snapped DB out of his daze by leaping from the cushioned chair to shout and dance around like an excited 12-year-old kid juiced with ADD. "Oh, goody! Goody! Goody, the pizza has come! The pizza has come! YEAH!"

On cue, the sitting chorus joined in the cheer with similar juvenile behavior.

DB stood watching the outburst and feeling, probably, in much less danger in a room filled with cheering grown-ups acting like kids than he felt while exposed to guards who had no attention deficit disorder and carried guns in dark places. While still frozen with boxes of warm pizza in hand, the guards lifted the boxes from his hands and passed pizzas to quell the cheerily maddening crowd.

The guards then lifted DB under his arms, turned him around, and carried him out of the 6" thick wooden refrigerator door, and back into the cavernous Tin Palace. A few feet from the door, the guards let his feet again touch the floor. Only at the elevator did DB pause, turn, and stare again at the again rigid, white uniformed woman who was, this time, heading down on 2'x3' elevator pad.

After being led back through the same eerie tunnels by the same strangely armed guards, DB made one more pizza run. DB ran back to Zio's on Route 66, unbuttoned his uniform, handed it to Ralph while mumbling incoherently, and went in search of safer employment pastures.

Of course, that's something a rookie DB would do. A lingering question might be, "What would a well-coached BD, or Brian Dowling, do—who had been coached in reading crazy defenses while in the field at Ignatius, Yale, and New England, or while tattooed on a Doonesbury comic strip?"

Dating Game's Limo Man

While I was teaching, some of my high school students nudged me to audition for the Dating Game. After auditioning with about 97 other guys, and probably because of my *pharmish* responses to their sausage wrapped questions, they chose me to be one of those who went live.

I was not chosen by the long haired beauty in my first television appearance, but I was so overbearing on host and contestants that afterwards the Dating Game spent months tracking this loser down all over the world. They found me sweating amidst swarming *no-see-ems (smaller than mosquito-like pests who love biting sweaty bodies)* on sweltering St. John, Virgin Islands with Glen Speer, my patient Pharm building mentor. When I inquired on their collect call, from the only phone booth then on St. John, as to why they were asking me—the loser—to reappear, the assistant producer in charge of finding rude guests said my ratings were off the charts.

How about that, Grandfather Deuel? See, *Rudeness does pay!* And this stuff you taught MCR and us inheritable Pharm Hands about "Be quiet. Watch and listen, I want you to learn something." That must be bunko. For in the TV world, I was living proof that if you talk and talk with foolish stuff your ratings go up and you're asked back.

So, the guy who had over-talked competing contestants as well as the host—but lost the girl, was begged to return to Tinsel Town. Or, as the producer said, "As soon as you leave the sweaty U. S. Virgins, call us. We want you!"

Incidentally, that producer moved on to bigger paydays. He became the prime mover in establishing overbearing, over-talking, made-up scenarios you hear on most of today's far right wing radio, which own about 90% + of the radio talk waves. And I returned from the isle of biting virginal no-see-ems to do another Dating Game, where this Pharmer talked a little less and won the glamour date with a Hollywood babe.

After polishing my social graces for at least that night, I tried to spread my improved manners into more than an appearance on Dating Game (DG). Consequently, several times I invited the Hollywood babe, whose heart I had captured for at least a few televised minutes, to visit the Castle before we went on our prized San Francisco date. Alas, the budding starlet consistently rebuffed my invites and my attempts to practice my dated dating graces, which probably had much to do with shattering my fragile ego,

Being the slow learner that I am, I didn't see how her dust-offs of my junkyard overtures had started at our first intimate meeting. After she had chosen me as her date, we sat back stage at the DG's get-acquainted table. After a few minutes, she added a cigarette to her well-formed body and lips, ignoring the prominent "No Smoking" sign above our table. While live on air, she seemed to heed my words. Here, backstage, she ignored my healthy incantations.

After a haughty puff or two, an employee also reminded her about the sign. Flicking in my direction, she replied as a queen might, "Oh, don't worry, he'll take care of it for me," she said to the production assistant as she motioned at me. Oh, sure, thought this Pharmer, who has never been able to kiss or kiss up to an ashtray.

She was "too busy" to have a drink and chat after the show. She had little interest in whom I might be, but had plenty to say about her career and the book she was working on whose working title was something like: *Men pursuing women . . . and was it worth it to let them catch us.*

Being closer to Sanford and Sons' junkyard dogs than to Hollywood starlets, some of us Pharm Hands figured all Hollywood was jaded and pompous. So, we figured we should attempt to deflate a little of their inflated hot air. Now, if you haven't read "The DB" story, read it now, since DB's guarded Castle entry was replicated, albeit in day light hours, on the Hollywood chauffer sent to pick me up as part of The DG Prize.

This time, however, the Castle Guards did not deposit the intruder into Michael's refrigerator. Instead, they took the Limo-man to our Big Kitchen, with its rough-hewn 10' in diameter round table, whose fancy chairs were huge tree stumps, cooled by a Safari fan nosily lumbering overhead as it hung from the corrugated tin ceiling. Sitting at the head of the Knights of Rubelia's Round Table, clad in a pressed suit with a row of telephones in front, I was—answering one long distance phone call after another. My assistant, scampering around like an overgrown and demented kid, was burly Michael.

"Sir, sir, line 7 has London on it . . . And New York's still waiting on line 3 . . . Oh, my! Oh, my, what to do? What to do? Oh, golly, so busy . . . Oh, my . . ." he lamented, as he flapped his muscled arms and hands as an effeminate would.

Bewildered Limo-man stood about 15 feet from the table near the 6' in diameter cemented fireplace, encircled by quarter cut telephone poles with a 48" steely top hat chimney serving as a caged veil as well as crooked fireplace headband. Then all hell, or heck, if you are a little kid reading this, broke loose.

The WHISTLE BLEW four or five times in a row. Sirens rang. Bells went off . . . About twenty people started running out of the Packing House, up the stairs surrounding the Big Kitchen . . . The greased chain on the cargo elevator from the dungeon below started clanking and moving. One at a time, people started jumping off the elevator, while others jumped onto it on its return downward.

I maintained my executive composure, as all big bosses are supposed to, as someone yelled, "It's the third tunnel level, sir. They've had another cave in."

"Hang on," I said to Tokyo, as I asked Michael and a reporting tunnel worker, "How bad is it? Can you straighten it out?"

"Well, we're not sure yet, sir . . ."

The pandemonium went on for several more minutes, as did my commanding command performance bolstered by Michael's imbecilic antics. After several minutes of stellar performances by all—buttressed by winning sound effects and choreography, Michael and I figured out that this bewildered Limo Man was not a fatuous Hollywoodite, but just a regular Joe Good Guy. Consequently, we fixed the tunnel flooding. The wheeler-dealer phone calls were completed. And a Pharm crew found time to give Limo Man a Castle tour. After that, I apologized to the Limo Man for our emergency and for being tied up with phone calls.

Michael, acting as my solicitous assistant during the tunnel breakdown, escorted me to the limo, while cannily scanning the skies for drones that he was ready to dispose of with his laser-guided rifle. Unassuming Limo Man thanked Michael and was just plain nice, as we drove to pick up my Dating Game Gem. Pulling up at her Hollywood address, he excused himself and returned to deposit the beauty—who luckily for her had chosen me, not for life, but only for a San Franciscan night—next to me for our stretch limo ride to LA's airport.

Once Limo Man seated authoress and starlet-to-be next to me, and reseated himself, his previously quiet vocal cords ignited. After asking, "Miss, have you seen this man's Castle . . ."

After portraying the wondrous Castle and me as a powerful executive ruling from a wood splintered roundtable all the way to the plane, I had little to add, for more superlatives I could not imagine. I do, however, recall answering my glamour girl's question.

"Why," she asked with a tint of glare and just the right amount of uppity in her voice, "didn't you have me out to see your Castle?"

"But I called and asked several times," I responded in my best powerful, but humble, sounding Castle Executive's voice, which I had many opportunities to use throughout the rest of the night.

At Sam Francisco's Top of the Mark, we had the menu's most expensive meal that the cooks flamed tableside, which seemed to cause every other more cost conscious diner to stare at us with that look of "Who are you?" That was followed with entertainment by a great, big name singer, (Diana Ross, Mahalia Jackson, someone like that) which was making me feel like getting dressed up in a suit wasn't that bad after all. In the wee hours of the morning, the taxi took us to catch the last flight back to LA, where Limo Man would be waiting to take us home. At

Gough and Fillmore, I stopped our taxi, told the taxi man to make sure that our starlet got to the airport, gave him a big Dating Game supplied tip, and thanked my starlet for a great night.

With some shock and more than a little bit of awe and bite to her words, she asked, "What are you doing? Then words like, "Why didn't you tell me you were going to stay in San Francisco? I have friends here too. I could've stayed too."

"Well, I called and tried to . . . but you were too busy to talk."

I had a good SF weekend and wondered if the Limo Man talked to her anymore about the Castle. I also wonder how her book did and what became of her career. Maybe she's a star that I forgot to recognize.

Hey, Limo Man and starlet, if you read this, let me know if there is anything more to this Rubelian Limo Man Castle story.

Dating Game's Limo Man

Icabod flies into a Garden of Eden

Not 6,000,000,000 or 6,000 years ago, as some *wont ya ta believe,* but somewhere in the 1960's, God created Icabod. God said, "Icabod is good.'

God then had Icabod delivered to Rubelia. Amidst the cumquat, lemon, orange, avocado, boysenberry, Palm, Oak, etc., trees, Icabod would prance and display his array of glistening feathers that were so much more illustrious than those of mere fellow chickens, roosters, ducks, mallards, horses, rabbits, dogs, pigs, bees, termites, etc.

But, alas, for Icabod it was a lonely prance in paradise. While on one of his galactic reviews, God pulled over his clean fusion powered chariot and surrounding legion of angels for a nanosecond review of Icabod's condition. There, in front of the old tool shed, next to the staircase leading to the Big Kitchen, God found the fully plumed Icabod, waiting for someone to note and respond to his overwhelming plumage.

Being the universe's undisputed foremost social anthropologist, God immediately knew what to do.

Peering deeply, as only God can, into those beady peacock eyes, God said, "I feel your pain, Icabod. On the sixth day, I will send you an Eve. Then I shall rest, and your life and days of rest will never be the same."

Icabod heard and believed. On the sixth day, Eve, the plainly garbed peahen arrived, without even an attractive apron.

Like the tribes of Israel, the peacocks and hens multiplied. First, they kibitzed in the Pharm's trees. Then they spread to the more pedicured neighboring lawns and trees surrounding this Rubelian Garden of Eden. Soon neighboring trees and yards had flaunting peacocks adorning and prancing about their spaces.

That is when PP hit the Pharm.

With all that goes on this little corner of God's increasingly crowded, stressed, and climate challenged blue green planet, even the King of Rubelia was surprised by the PP (Peacock Problem). Here is how the King handled another momentous problem.

One smoggy California day, the confused portly Pharmer and upset Head Janitor, George Campbell, threw their heads together regarding the city's latest regulatory epistle. In the realm of city chapters, verses, commandments, and regulations, Michael and George readily admitted that even together their intellectual acuity amounted to little more than that generated by a pea brain, or feathered peacock's brain.

According to some city census, similar to one done around Noah's time, Rubelia was responsible for 18 peacocks. City codes, rules, regs, politics, or something, only allowed Rubelia to have what Noah had—two peacocks. Whether two peacocks could additionally have spousal peahens was not clearly chiseled into city code. But sexually aware

Pharmers figured two peacocks must have meant four pea brains could roam the Pharm for the sake of posterity.

Now for those of you who know the prodigious strength, girth, and clumsiness of Michael and George, you know that Tarzanically pursuing over populating peacocks, who have long camouflaged their ability to fly, whether on lawn or from tree to tree is not the forte of these two bungling, burly guys.

"What to do?" George and Michael whined as they faced off against each other well before Stephen Colbert understood the importance of formidable face-offs. For days on end, over the occasional cackle of neighboring peacocks, George and Michael agonizingly mimicked each other over morning tea and evening wining whines in dreaded anticipation of confronting their peacocked *formidable opponents.*

Their pea-brained solution?

Michael adorned himself in his best peacock chasing overalls, fresh shirt, shined shoes, including rare matching socks, and went into the neighborhood in quixotic pursuit of . . .

"Michael Rubel, what do you think you're doing to my peacock!" shouted Pharm neighbor Mrs. Crane from her patio door, as buffalo-like Michael chased a running and hopping peacock around her manicured yard.

Grateful to have a breather from chasing, Michael lifted his hat, wiped his brow, and between breaths uttered, "Sorry, Mrs. Crane, I am only following orders from the city."

"What are you talking about?"

"The city said I have to get rid of all the peacocks—but two."

"What kind of stupid order is that? You go back to your Pharm right now and leave my peacock alone, you hear?

"Yes, Mrs. Crane."

Being a law-abiding citizen as well as a reserved Reserve Marine, Michael adjusted to both instincts by pushing onto other neighboring terrain, where his peacock trapping ventures elicited similar alarms, outrages, and orders, sometimes vulgarly flavored.

"I'm so sorry, but . . ."

After his wildlife forays, Michael would follow up with profuse written and verbal apologies to the neighbors, much like our diplomatic corps does after rude invasions onto neighboring lands and living things. And the neighbors, knowing how pitifully Michael and George performed in peacock chasing and other endeavors, also followed up. Their follow-ups, however, went to those officials renowned as much smarter than a Rubelian janitor.

While a trickle of calls started going to city hall, the grapevine of gossip planted the PP story among the San Gabriel Valley's most potent lobbying group, whose independence, courage, common sense, and connections are legend.

The Union of Grade Schoolers . . .

Once the Union of Grade Schoolers learned of the PP problem, they raised their pencils and crayons and began flooding the low lying city hall with thousands of 8.5"x11" billboards depicting, in their pure minds, the fate of the peacocks, whom many of them had met for their first times on Pharm Tours.

Forsaking expensive public relations firms like California's renowned Whitaker and Baxter, the union of concerned kids blitzed city government, the mayor, and the police chief with a theme from Melissa and Albert that revolved around . . .

Deer chef Posey,

I luv peacocks. All my 4th grade fends do too,

Whie don't yu?

Sarah

Relentlessly prodded by their young, the parents of these innocents were pressed to side with city hall or with their potent little loved ones. Consequently, phones, faxes, and mail began bombarding city hall and anyone little kids thought mattered.

Now some of those parents knew people or worked themselves in media. Newspapers told the story. Then one of the LA TV channels ran with it. Not waiting to be outdone by a story of well-armored Pharmers eliminating dangerous peacocks in foreign territory for the good of democracy, other TV newscasters ran with this big news. Before too many naps had passed, a national television network picked up the story of little

David and Jessica's crayon tossings at behemoth-sized Governmental Goliaths. City hall moved from adding innocent staff and interns, to hiring private contractors from Dick Cheney's KNBR. No longer was the city merely inundated with a trickle of PPs. Now they needed protection from a droning PP carpet-bombing of their walled, not yet Green Zoned, city hall premises by little kids in Pink and Green Berets.

Finally, finding a free communications line amidst the PP phone and mail assault, Glendora's City Hall called Michael, "Michael, please have your people stop. We can't get any work done . . . We've changed the rules . . . You can keep the peacocks . . ."

As usual, in explaining this Pharm event, Michael claimed he "didn't really understand" what and why all this happened, as he tried to light his pipe, with that twinkle in his eye.

Rocking gently in his chair, he'd puff, look out from the deck at the humming birds visiting the hanging red sweet water filled canisters, and add, "Isn't life beautiful."

You may think that was a nice story. You may also think it was made up. So, here's another Pharmer's view of the peacock story for you.

> Ron Riegel's email of 1-6-09
> Happy New Year All Ye Old and New Pharm Hands,
>
> Over the holidays, I was reading the newspaper and found an article about the City of Altadena and how they are trying to expel an undisclosed number of Peacocks from their city, mostly because of the many complaints they have been receiving from residents and city workers. I guess the Peacocks are a little noisy, poop all over the dichondra and patios and live whereever they please. No S*#t Sherlock! That is exactly what Peacocks have been doing for many millennia.
>
> I wrote and sent this next poem to the Glendora City Council to voice my protest against their proposed banishment of our beautiful peacocks from the Pharm back in 1976. It must have worked because right after I sent it the Council proclaimed we could keep our "damned peacocks!"
>
> Oh, did I forget to mention that Michael went to all the neighbors within a quarter mile radius of the Pharm with these

huge gift baskets of honey, avocados, and balloons among other items to get them to write letters to the City Council in favor of the peacocks? Oh, I think I also forgot to mention that Michael orchestrated one of his largest mailings ever to people all over the country/world to get them to write letters to the City Council in favor of the peacocks. Oh yeah, one more thing I also forgot to mention was the big party we had for all of the neighbors and city employees who wanted the peacocks to remain at the Pharm. I guess I don't have to tell you who didn't receive invitations to the party, do I?

The City Council ended up begging Michael to call off his letter writing campaign as it was costing them thousands of dollars to handle and process all that mail and besides they disliked being excluded from the party list even more. Once again, Michael prevailed and the peacocks are still around, thank God!

I hope your New Year is joyous and fulfilling. Remaining an old Pharmhand, Ron . . .

~ The Peacocks Belong to us All ~
From "Pharm Phantasy"

Along the byways of Glendora we see
    Beautiful peacocks whose numbers are three
    They're as free as the winds and forever could roam
    But this is the place they have made their home.

We see a child's look of delight
    At the splendor of a peacock in flight
    'tis then we realize their value in city
    To expel them from here would be quite a pity.

From heaven above did our Father declare
    That peacocks be given to all of us here
    Not just to those who live on a Pharm
    But to EVERYONE, so that no one would harm.

Most neighborhood families, for these great birds, care
    And until their safekeeping, we will not despair
    Our lives without them would be less complete

Besides—Try to catch them, it's an impossible
feat!

R. G. Riegel
3-14-'76
Y e a r   o f   t h e
Peacock

Kid Scott Rubel

Rubelia's Sun Tzu

Like most kids around the age of 13 living around 1970, Scott Rubel had a short attention span. Unlike his dad and Uncle Michael, he sometimes seemed to like the physical part of building and destroying much less, than he liked the art of writing and arting. Nonetheless, when his uncle asked him to do something physical, he generally showed up for work, albeit sometimes late and sometimes disappeared early, or went missing for long segments of time.

For chunks of his life, Michael would consider interactions with the many governing bodies as a form of warfare although, as Icabod and his warriors can testify, he undertook warring against officialdom's official-dumb with a twinkle in his eyes and devastatingly delightful tactics that gave him a battlefield voice. While traveling the world in search of castles, Michael had also learned, probably from the likes of Sun Tzu, that the art of warfare was "deception."

One morning after exiting from the sun's early morning baking of my Bottle House rendered confinement, imposed until I could build a bigger doghouse, Michael said, "You've got about four days to finish your kitchen roof . . . That's about as long as I think I can distract the city official spying on you and your plans."

Telephone poled thingamajig

With that, Michael marched out the tunnel and down the driveway with sleepy, but always smiling, Scott in tow and started putting another of his contraptions together. Like so many of his thingamajigs, this one had come-alongs, pullies, chains, ratchets, ropes, hooks, bolts, and BIG beams. The tentacles that sprouted from this thingamajig wrapped themselves around one of the many telephone poles the telephone company unloaded upon us in their early recycling efforts, for which we were their primary tinker toying debris box.

Reacting to my leader's battle plan, behind the northwest wall that separated me from the sniping, auto-camouflaged city spy, I gathered battle materials to assault the ridgeline, capture the land below, and expand the roof of the embryonic Chip House.

Unbeknownst to the city scout and with battlefield precise timing, Michael's cannon-like thingamajig started to breach the southern skies just as I mounted the 2"x6" girded ridgeline, stealthily laid cheap 1"x5" wood roof covering, and started firing bullets, which some would refer to as nails, in a crouched position, to capture that ridge line for the rebels of Rubelia.

Before I started hammering away at the ridgeline, the city spy noted Michael's thingamajig cannon rising in the sky. Rolling his early-modeled humvee forward to obtain a clearer view, the scout left the northwest ridgeline open to hours and then days of continuous ridgeline assault.

Deception is the art of warfare

Michael, ever deliberate about when he left the main gate open, left it open on these forthcoming days. For those of you who failed at Sun Tzu Warfarenomics 101, Michael was orchestrating an economically efficient campaign of deceit, deception, and distraction so essential to winning bloody as well as political wars. And he was recycling while doing so . . . What a general!

The city official reacted with a predictable city tactical reaction to the specter of a 13-ish year old pulling ropes and chains tied to trees and buildings, under the command of this goofily dressed man who, with pliers hanging from his bib overalls, shouted commands as the first of several lined up telephone poles lurched skyward, looking like a wobbly cannon in the sky.

Hey! Early Romans built like this, not 20th century regulated Californians!

As most lower echelon spies in the field of battle are wont to do, this official reported to headquarters before making his battlefield move. Such timely indecisions allowed the Rubelians to

Where old telephones go

consolidate their northwest ridgeline gains, while also establishing the southern thingamajig fortification.

So, when the city official finally came in to demand that Michael tell him what he was doing, Michael calmly replied, as he and Scottford continued raising another telephone pole skyward, "Why, isn't it obvious? We're building a windmill."

"Ah . . . what? But . . . But you can't build a windmill here."

"Oh, sure we can. Lots of people used to build windmills for water and such. There's no code against windmills . . ."

As most victors know, from General *Maximus Decimus Meridius* to Paton and Schwartzkorpf, speed in battle is essential. By the time the city couldn't find a code prohibiting Michael's windmill, the telephoned pole framed windmill was well underway. While the heavily fortified and creosoted poles were being bolted into place, the ridgeline (aka my new kitchen roofline) of the Chip House was secured.

Scottford's ADD keeps him wandering about

Michael continued pulling Scott in to help him crane telephone poles into place without a crane, but some of us would also find the artful Scott available to help us with our projects. I have pictorial proof that Scott helped, for at least five minutes, frame the bathroom walls under the ridgeline that the city forgot about during the Northwest Frontier Thingamajig Windmill Assault.

Here, however, is how some Pharmer remembers Scott helping with framing, and other things. I say "some Pharmer" because the essay it comes from has Heinze Rubel typed in as author, who is scratched out in favor of Scott Rubel, although artful and attention delinquent Scott has little recollection of penning it. So, the question remains for those who care, was this penned by:

A. *Heinze Rubel, aka Grandfather.*
B. *Scott Rubel, still suffering ADD.*
C. *Michael Rubel, a flat out liar.*
D. *This typist, on the IBM Selectric, from which Dan Rather was accused.*
E. *Others, who Rubelians may or may not know.*
F. *Uncle Ted, as another of his post Washington Post fabricated letters.*

When Rubelia's Crazy Bill irrefutably determines the author's identity, we'll post it at both the Rubelian and the Whitehouse.gov websites.

Scott says he'll drill my wall

"Sure sounds like work," says I, when Dwayne asked me to drill a hole in his wall. Where is the drill, I thought, and went searching for it.

Going up to the barn, I noticed a water leak and thought I better fix that first, whereupon I went to the shop to get a pipe wrench to take the faucet off. The pipe wrench was gone, which made me mad, but I got out the truck to drive up to George's place and borrowed his when I noticed the right rear tire was flat. Dwayne and I put the spare tire on and let the jack down to find that the spare was flat. I walked up to George's and asked if he had a pipe wrench. He said he would drive me up to his barn to get it and drive me down to our Farm.

We were almost up the hill when his old truck ran out of gas. I said I would go to town and get some, but he said he had a fifty-gallon barrel of gas down by that well. I walked down to the barrel and found a little tiny hole had rusted through the bottom that let the gas out.

I went to Jed, a neighbor, to see if he had some gas, and we took the plug out of an old model A to drain some gas into a bottle. I thanked him and took the jug back up the hill to George. He poured the gas in and tried to start the truck. It would not start, and we found after several hours that we had poured water into the gas tank from the jug. That was the reason Jed was having trouble with the model A, we decided.

We had supper and I walked home and went to bed, after a few drinks.

The following day, Dwayne asked me if I would help him drill that hole in his wall, and I said that reminded me of a leaky faucet that had to be fixed and wondered if you would roll the tires to town and get them patched so we could get our old truck going. He said, yes, and I went out looking for our pipe wrench.

I walked up to George's and he was just getting his truck started. He had broken the drain plug out of his gas tank, when trying to get the water out of his tank and had stuck a piece of wood in the hole. I told him I would fix it if he would bring it down to our Farm. He said he would.

We drove up to his barn and looked for the pipe wrench, but found that some of the old tarpaper on the roof had blown off and George asked me if I would help him tack some other stuff on. I went up to the peak of the roof and lowered a rope to pull up the roll of tarpaper, when the wood under my feet gave way and I fell through.

George asked me if I was all right. I told him I was. He smiled. We decided to go up and take a swim in the cement reservoir in the canyon. When we got there, the reservoir was bone dry. George looked sad and said the pipeline going up into the canyon must have rusted through or something. We hiked for a long time through brush and it got pretty dusty. We found the line had broken where an old dead oak tree had fallen across it. The pipe was smashed and broken and the tree was too big to move without going down and getting an ax.

We hiked down and decided to go to my place to eat lunch. We got to my place, we had a beer, and I went to turn on the stove, but the gas had been turned off. Since the flood last year, there has been a gas leak somewhere under the ground. I started to go about digging here and there and the gas company would not help. They finally told me to get it fixed by a plumber or they would not turn the gas on again. George told me he had a wood stove that worked pretty well, but no stove pipe, so we got into the old truck to go get it when the neighbor Jed drives in and tells us about Dwayne rolling the tires to town. At the base of a hill, one of the tires had bounced right through a big picture window of one of those new subdivision houses they are building down near town. (He said Dwayne had told him about the water in his Model A and he was sure glad to figure out why it didn't run after all these years.) We told Jed we better take ourselves down and see if those people were mad about their window. Jed said hop in and we were off, with George following us in his truck. Dwayne was talking to a police officer about the tire in the house and the lady was saying something about she could have been killed.

George seemed mad, and said to me that we could all be killed every day—and that to think about what might have happened is ridiculous. Just be happy it did not hurt anybody. The window was really all broken up. Dwayne looked at me and I offered him a ride home. The lady would not let us have the tire unless we paid for the window—so we had to leave the tire. We agreed to meet up at George's place and have some lunch.

Dwayne asked me if I had found the drill about the time George drove in with his truck. I told Dwayne I had to fix George's gas tank

Scott didn't drill the hole

first. We took the gas tank lid off and ran water into it to wash most of the gas out so I could patch the hole in the bottom. I got the hole almost brazed up when something happened. I got out from underneath the truck and we all stood around and watched George's good old truck burn up.

I was sorry.

Curing ADD

After two psychologists spent two days observing how we Pharmers handled the inmates and visit-mates, they acknowledged us as certifiable medical and psychological savants. (Seriously, two psychologists did believe that we ran an effective institution after we ran a 48-hour institutional game on them while they visited. They believed Rubelia was turning troubled lives around.)

We thought some of that award might have stemmed from our discovery of the cure for ADD, which we demonstrated to them with stories we told bolstered by exposure to inmates like Scott and several others.

No matter how often we applied the Rubelian curative for ADD, Michael was never sure that our cure cured Scottford's ADD. No matter how often we loudly proclaimed it, postered it on walls, printed it in the *Shriek*, and offered it free and clear of patent infringement; it didn't seem like enough Americans were following our healthily addictive cures the national malaise of Attention Deficit Disorder, which merely required following these three prescriptions daily . . .

Thinking stops many good things from happening—just shut up and dig.

Plow deeper. Dig deeper.

Work is fun.

MCR figured the problem with just curing Scott's ADD stemmed from Scott's own Rubelian ADD immune response—**A**void **D**igging **D**eeper. Scottford's Rubelian ADD seemed to be just as powerful a response to our homeopathic ADD cure—**A**lways **D**ig **D**eeper.

So, it was said . . .

"Gossip's good. Keeps people in line when everyone's willing to know and tell their neighbor how someone else is misbehaving."

"If they would have lived in a tent, they would not have had all those problems."

Grandfather

Behind every great disaster goes a lot of work . . . Grandfather used to add.

"We spend very little on materials. People call us up and tell us an old building is being torn down, or a freeway collapses and we all roll out our trucks."

MCR

"And then Buster Keaton would say, 'Throw all those damn scripts away and just do what you want. It's better than the stuff I wrote for you.'"

MCR's mentor, Odo Stade, repeating Buster Keaton response to the work of their production crew.

Chapter 12

Ted thunders for Michael.

"What memories were made here . . ."
Little Uncle Teddy

That he was five foot twenty-one inches high may not have anything to do with the fact that he:

♦ Looked phunny on a Pharm motorbike
♦ Wasn't initially trusted by Michael (Hey, me too . . .)
♦ Gave you the impression that he looked down on you
♦ Cracked us up with his writings.

But then again, being oxygen deprived at his heighty level for so many days after birth may have had everything to do with those points and subsequent weirdities.

One day, somewhat like it happened with newscaster Harry Reasoner appearing at the Castle's front gate, this guy appeared outside the walls of the Castle. It was a move junk around day for the Pharmhands, so the gate was open. When the guy wandered in, George Campbell wandered over to him, lifted his grimy hat, wiped his brow, sniffed his hat innards, and asked, "Hi, may I help you with something?" (Michael actually seemed to know the proper time to use "may" versus "can" and often exhibited this confusing to the well-groomed hoi-poloi highbrow trait, while looking like a scavenging janitor.)

With little emotion, the stranger only glanced to his left at the pillbox, dozens of garbage cans, small and large tunnel entrances, and tower rising above the large tunnel, then responded, "I'm looking for Michael Clarke Rubel. Are you Michael Rubel?"

"No. Who are you? And why are you looking for Mr. Rubel?

"I am Eugene L. Meyer. Mr. Rubel contacted my editor about doing a story about this place and my boss sent me to talk to Mr. Rubel and do the story."

"Your boss said Mr. Rubel contacted him? Your boss is editor of what?"

"My editor is Ben Bradlee."

"And who is he?" George, a.k.a. Michael, responded.

"My boss is Ben Bradlee, editor of the Washington Post," Eugene said to the sweaty guy in shouldered denim overalls, "You do know the Washington Post, don't you?" Eugene L. Meyer queried.

"I guess so. It's like the LA Times, isn't it?"

"Ah, my boss might disagree. But, it's something like the LA Times."

"I think there has been some sort of mistake. Mr. Rubel would never write to some newspaper asking them to do a story about this place. Newspapers write stories. Stories bring visitors. Visitors bother workers. And nothing gets built. Mr. Rubel doesn't want anyone to even know about this place. So I'm sorry you came all this way for a mistake." George responded.

"I don't think there's been a mistake, Mr. Campbell. In fact," reaching into his pocket to pull out a two-page letter, he continued, "I have Mr. Rubel's letter with me."

George began reading the nicely typed, wonderfully phrased letter. It quickly brought a twinkle then smirk to his face, which caused him to quickly flip to the last page where a glance at Michael's signature brought a broad smile to his face and a guffaw into the conversation. "Oh, Mr. Rubel didn't write this."

"What makes you so sure?"

"For one, it's much too well-written. And the words are too smart. For two, that's not Mr. Rubel's happy face."

"What do you mean?"

"Well, we all have our own happy faces here, and that's not Mr. Rubel's."

"Whose happy face is it?"

"Oh, that's Ted's happy face."

"Ted? Ted who?"

"Ted Shepherd's," George responded.

After a pause and eastward look, Eugene L. Meyer responded, "Why that son of a #!&#!"

Back-story

Ted Shepherd was from back East, but before he settled into hanging out around the Chesapeake Bay he traveled, like all young men are supposed to—West. Ted came from well-stocked lineage. His dad had quite a lot to do with making that thing that Alexander Graham Bell invented into a big, prosperous company.

Michael was theatrically forced into meeting Ted through America's most renowned fan dancer, Sally Rand, who was good friends with Michael's mom. Michael didn't like theatrics, but he liked his mom very, very much, so what could one do but meet Ted. Because of the intro process and because the guy's head was so high in the sky, it took a while for Michael to get comfortable around the guy.

After slumming awhile in Michael's junkyard, Ted went back East. Ted would write the King of Rubelia who would sometimes share these mirthful scribbling with us. We consumers of Tedisms were certain about what the good Shepherd should be doing—writing funny lines for plays to which people go to laugh their wallets, warts, and worries away.

Instead, Ted spent some time writing for National Geographic and the Washington Post. We all thought that was good too. Except, the Post's style mostly made you cry. Whereas Ted's style might make you cry—but only from laughing too hard. Ted's writings made you pass high-fives. Most Washington Post writings pushed you into bloody nose-dives. Oh well, we thought, at least the Washington Post now had another great writer.

Unfortunately, whoever is in charge of passing out high fives and paychecks at the Washington Post didn't recognize Ted's ability at pulling ink, paper, and happy faces together. After being restructured out of a job, Ted wrote a letter to that Washington Post editor. Keep in mind that this is the editor that a cabal of Richard Nixon, the Plumbers, G. Gordon Liddy, and the Justice Department could not throw off his editorial game.

It took Woodward and Bernstein reams of paper, phone calls, deep throated meetings, mixed with months of pushing, cajoling, and writing before Editor Ben Bradlee gave them more than a few columns of ink.

It took one falsely signed letter from Ted Shepherd to convince Ben Bradlee to assign a reporter to devote five Washington Post (WP) pictures and about five pages to "Fortress Rubelia Rises Midst the Junk" in August of 1975.

Mr. Bradlee made a big mistake. About 81 inches of mistake. Imagine if the WP would've teamed Ted Shepherd up with a Carl Sheepstein. The insights and style of Shepherd and Sheepstein could have enticed and immersed Americans into cleaning up politics. And they probably could've done it with a bunch of ☺ ☺ faces. And the WP could have sold a lot more papers, which would have made Bradley ☺ ☺.

But at least Eugene was shepherded into doing a nice story, and the title worked then and now amidst an era mixed with Cold Warring and recycling.

Oh, yes, and almost immediately after Bradlee had assigned recalcitrant reporter Meyer to fly out West to tap his fingers around Rubelia, Eugene got a phone call that went something like this,

"Hey, Gene, what's up? Want to have lunch next week to mourn my short-lived Post sojourn?"

"Wish I could, Ted, but got to go to California next week."

"What's in California?"

"Some castle or something."

"Castle? What's that about?" Ted asked.

"Don't really know. Ain't my idea to go. Some guy wrote the boss and I gotta go."

"Well, when you get back, let's catch lunch."

"Okay," replied Eugene.

Michael was a "Show me what you can do" guy. With Michael, fanciful talk counted if it were embedded in a laughter-provoking story, and counted more if tied to the end of a productive workday. So, yes, it took a while for Michael to trust Ted. One of the means by which Michael came to trust Ted was by having Ted competently serve as his laundry boy. But there is much more to this trust-building story than clean socks, soiled underwear, laundry pick-up, etc., or so Uncle Ted tells.

Thundering Acme Thunderers
By Uncle Ted

Long ago, when there was a farmer and a farmer's mother and a farmer's brother and sister but no castle, there came to the Tin Palace a long, confused person. And with him, he brought his whistle. It was a fine whistle, made of shiny metal with a little ball inside that spun around when you puffed your cheeks and emptied your lungs. It made a Big Shrill sound. I loved it.

I got this whistle when I was working in the Poconos. I was there for the lifeguarding. All my life up to that time (at that time I was about 30), I had yearned to be a lifeguard. Not for the savings of lives but for the winning of women. I was not good at woman winning. In fact, I stunk, and I do not exaggerate when I say that. I know my stinks, but more about that later.

I had been working for the National Geographic and I was tired of that. I wanted to find myself. Not in the usual, head-scratching sense of the term, in the absolute and specific sense. I wanted to find myself high in a lifeguard chair, under a pith helmet, looking out with a serious expression, a lifeguard kind of face. And Fortune smiled upon me. I had a buddy who was very good at going to the beach and fighting (and losing to) Cassius Clay (he had not promoted himself at this time), and my friend was in charge of the pool in a large resort—and he hired me. Which was good, because I had quit the National Geographic and needed money.

I could not swim well but I was excellent at walking around in a pool. (That is why I chose to try the pool lifeguard route rather than the ocean brand, which I knew from experience was way over my head and had things that would nip and sting and even swallow you, whether you were a guard or not.)

I made one save during a month or so. The story unfolds easily. It is summer. I am in my chair, under my helmet, with my whistle around my neck. It was called an Acme Thunderer. I am daydreaming, which is where I spent most of my time then and still do, today. I can't speak highly enough of the activity. It is even better than being in denial, which is superb except when you have to come out of it.

In the midst of my daydream, I hear a voice yelling, "Guard! Guard!" This annoys me, first because it is interfering with my daydream but second because it indicates that somebody isn't doing his job, and a guard at that. After a while, I look around to see who is failing in his life-watching duties and I see, at the foot of my chair, a kid. He is looking up at me. He is saying, "Guard!"

I recognize him with a casual stare. He turns and points to the pool, to a large woman standing in water up to her large thighs. She is waving at me. She does not look like anybody I want to save. I finger my Acme Thunderer, ready to alert another guard—but there is no other guard.

I step down from my chair, walk over to the edge of the pool, the shallow end, and then over to the steps, down into the pool, and, sloshing with the kind of easy athleticism that marks the veteran lifeguard, over to the woman. "Yes?" I say.

"It's my earring," she says.

"Yes," I say. What she says makes no sense but it is not bad to be positive.

"I dropped it," she says.

These words make me sad. This is an Olympic-sized pool with fifteen or twenty thousand people in it, all creating the kind of high-energy waves that could push an earring almost anywhere.

"I'm standing on it," she says.

I can't even get out a "Yes." Why would she call a certified life-saving specialist from his high lookout to get a damn dropped jewelry? And then I see why: she's just gotten her hair done. She doesn't want to stick her fixed up head down into the mix of chlorine and urine anymore than I do.

It isn't part of my job description but I figure that in between saving lives I might as well add this complimentary service. I feel down her great leg to the pudgy foot, lift it up, grasp a hard little object, bring it to the surface, and see a well-chewed ball of gum.

"It's the other foot," she said.

I look at her hard to see if she's laughing. She's not. Not even a smirk. I go down and lift up the other leg, get the earring, gave it to her, receive thanks, think about saying, "No problem, ma'am. Danger is my business. That's what I'm here for." But she wasn't *that* thankful. So I don't.

I got out of the pool and out of the Poconos and several months later ran into Sally Rand who I had known through another guy whose specialty was getting fired from newspaper jobs and going on to bigger and better newspaper jobs. He had, after his most recent firing, gotten to know Sally Rand and introduced her to me. That was on the East Coast. Our subsequent meeting was on the West. She needed somebody to work her lights while she danced around half naked. She was much older than me but I didn't look all that bad, so I decided to take the job and wait for her to make a pass.

She never did. I didn't blame her. Anybody who was lifeguard and never saved anything better than gum and earrings, who would find that attractive?

What she did do was recommend that, as long as I was going on South to Hollywood to become a movie star within the next few months (I had shared my rough timetable), I stop off on the way to see her friend Dorothy Rubel who, Sally said, had an odd but interesting son I might enjoy meeting. I thanked her and went South.

I didn't want to be a movie star right away. I knew that that kind of thing takes serious daydreams. Be prepared—or at least have a good excuse—was my motto. Still is. You have to wait for the serious daydreams. They don't just happen haphazardly, even to a seasoned daydreamer. So I decided to stop off and see Sally's friend's son. It would give me a chance to meet somebody interesting (I have never found much time for un-interesting people) and also do some research on what people did Out West. I didn't figure that San Francisco was really Out West. It was more just Far Out.

I met Dorothy. I met Michael. He immediately distrusted me. Not so much because I was a stranger, but because I had been recommended by Sally. Michael was always leery of Sally although she always thought a lot of him and loved his mother.

Dorothy invited me to stay in the Tin Palace. This was getting on towards Christmas and she pointed out that in the room where I would sleep—it was approximately five miles long—there were 144 paper angels swinging around from the rafters. Michael pointed out how I would need to go if I wanted to go to the bathroom. This involved going outside and around and then in several directions. Because I am not good at directions (I have a one in four chance of getting them right, which does not inspire confidence unless you are at one of the poles, where you will be going only South or North) I resolved not go out until it was daylight and I could see to ask directions.

It was a long night and I couldn't hold it. I got up and walked several miles back and forth in the huge room. Then out and about and it was cold and dark. I wondered whether I would die from a fall, the cold, or a bladder explosion. I finally found relief but then got more lost trying to find my way back.

Michael had stayed awake to wait for me to try to steal the silver or something else. He followed me around, wondering whether I was casing the entire farm, which would help me to steal the whole damned thing, or I was just casing my escape route for when I snatched the silver. He told me these years later. I said I was sorry about that. He said he was, too. I asked if I had let him down by not fulfilling his expectations. He said, no, I had not fulfilled a lot of other expectations anyway. I took this as a compliment.

Not too many years after that, he decided to walk around the world with two mules named Babe and Geronimo. (It may have been Sonny and Cher though; my memory is not what it used to be but then it never was.) He was in some deserty part of California down near Mexico and  he called his mother to ask if she would take back some of the far too many clothes she had insisted he take with him. She asked me would I go get the excess haberdashery. I said I would.

I drove for a long time through the most uninteresting country I could remember. Finally, there in the middle of nowhere were the three jackasses, Michael, and the mules.

It was cold, a raw kind of weather, the kind of thing a desert will do to you when it is tired of baking your top couple of skin layers off. So we sat in my car. He gave me about twenty pounds of underwear. Now, right here, is a warning. What I talk about next is not fit to go into the ears of women, children, or men of good background. If you want to risk it, go on. Otherwise go and take a walk, a nap, maybe both.

Right there in my nice, well kept, clean, sometimes polished car, Michael Clarke Rubel committed an Ill Wind. You may think I am trying to smooth over a passing of gas or the creating of flatulence. You would be wrong. We are not talking about your average colon perfume. What he committed in my car was a Crime Against Humanity.

My life began to pass before my eyes, which were watering terribly. Between prayers, I struggled to open the door before he could fire Round Two. Finally, the door fell open and I fell out on the hard desert floor. It was cold there but at least I had gotten away from Agent Orange. I lay there, glad that God had chosen not to call me home, and I listened to sounds from inside the car that sounded like Har! Har! And Tee! Hee!

Because God had chosen not to end my new Western Life, I tried to find good in what had happened, to see if this gas attack contained any silver lining. I found one. "Getting rid of THAT," I hollered back into the car, "you have GOT to feel better."

Michael Clarke didn't answer. He was laughing too hard while he rocked back and forth on the seat, an inventor in love with his awful invention. Swinging around his great thick neck I could see my Acme Thunderer. I had given it to him to take on the trip in case he needed to save anybody. What a mistake!

I thought about taking it back but it was in the car with the poison fumes. So I stayed outside and he proceeded to warm up the car some more. Then he got out and thanked me for returning the wardrobe to his mother. I said there had to be harder ways to go south than the one he was following. He said, yeah, but he hadn't been able to find one. So, off he and his fellow travelers went, and I, after waiting around another hour or two to allow the main thrust of the toxicity to leave my car, drove his underwear and me back to Dorothy.

Later on, after Michael had gone around the world or to Panama or gone to work for Captain Ahab or whoever, he came back and I asked him about the whistle. It seemed to me that AcThun, as I had come to conceive it, might be the subject of a biographical movie someday, like a rare violin that has been passed down the generations from one genius to another. The movie might be called Whistle While You Play.

Michael said he had used the Acme Thunderer once. He was in the middle of a town in Nicaragua when someone had the impulse to rob him (or he had the impulse to just see how a North American whistle would sound in Central America; he would lie not just at the drop of a hat but even if a hat looked like it might drop.). Michael said that in order to discourage the robbery, he blew the whistle. It made things happen. The robber stopped robbing. And all sorts of soldiers came running out from all over and pointed their rifles at Michael and the reformed robber. Then the soldiers said that you were NOT to blow whistles in or around that town.

Michael said the whole episode had something to do with being frightened. Hearing that made me feel kind of guilty. I could have explained to him that this was a thing to be used ONLY when you were wearing a pith helmet—and certainly not the ugly thing he put on and usually kept on top of his head. But I kept the guilt in check because I figured the real reason the guy had threatened Michael wasn't because he wanted to rob him. I also figured that the real reason the soldier had come out and pointed their rifles wasn't because somebody had blown a whistle.

The real reason the guy threatened Michael Clarke Rubel and the soldiers came charging out with their rifles had nothing to do with robbery or a whistle. The real reason, I figured, was right in the middle of a friendly little town on a hot day, Mykee had cut one. I don't know how he made it home alive.

I sure hope that Acme Thunderer ended up with Kaia or Scott or Chris or Glen or Skipper or veteran ROMEOs or somebody else who knows how to handle a fine piece of machinery. The Chief Rubelian might have been good at castles and fire engines and clock towers and such. But as far as I'm concerned, he may have known beans about beams, but as far as I'm concerned he didn't know beans about lifeguard whistles.

(Editor's note: ROMEOs = Real Odd Men Eating Out)

This little kid's book deals with the tended and unintended consequences of being raised by wizened old timers and the resultant dreaming, goofing, learning, and building it evoked in a mature suburban community. It deals with basics. Even as basic as flatulence. It suggests how those basics address life's complexities—from community, politics, economics, and the environment. Between its lines, it is filled with a special kind of leadership instilled behind fully grouted and reinforced walls by a very benevolent dictator whose replication would generate many more healthy communities and happy faces—with or without whistles, but certainly with a lot of Rubelian balloons and happy faces.

Ted's following memories of Michael (sent to nephew Scott Rubel) dishes out similarly consequential stuff, while delving into such basics as dirt, money, business, elections, the White House, and whatever your vivid imagination creates after perusing well-intended words . . .

"Breath for . . ."
Another Uncle Ted story

As *Michael Memory Day* approaches, my mind meanders over things Rubelian. There are times when I sat in your father's long bathtub because

I had valley fever, whatever the heck that is, and my skin looked like it wouldn't find a buyer at a toad convention. And times when Kaia would do things like make a long red and white clown costume so that I could wear it while I rode around on top of a fire engine and hurled Frisbees. Good times, better times, all fallen down in the hourglass.

For me, in those long ago days, Michael was one of a troika: Skipper, Glen, and "George," as he liked to be known now and then, feeling easier as the zoo's hired man than as the proprietor.

Of the three, I spent the least time with Skipper. He was this bright guy who lived up against the hill down the road with his mother and a raccoon named Mitzi. I went up to see her one time. She was, like Skipper, an engineer. But whereas he specialized in putting things together—gate mechanisms, short wave radios, anything electric—Mitzi specialized in deconstruction: telephone, kitchen faucets.

Glen I got to know better. He was always making things, a home, things that went in it, things that went on you (he made me a motorcycle jacket and a helmet with the Wizard of Oz characters on it; I still have the helmet), things that might come in handi in or around a castle, things that would make the castle a castle.

I had names for this trio. Skipper was the Everlasting Engineer, Glen the Artful Thing Maker, Michael the Primitive Doer.

I first saw/met Michael around Christmastime of 1965 when I stayed in the great room of the tin palace while Michael waited for me to steal the silver. After Michael had watched me for days or weeks or months (my memory is not what it used to be, but then it never was), he decided I might be trustworthy—or at least not extremely un-trustworthy. We began to talk about a variety of things—one of them money. Michael said he trusted having his money in dirt. Dirt, he said, would be there when you went to sleep on it. And there was a pretty good chance it would be there when you woke up.

I was from Back East and we didn't have much dirt there, aside from what was in our ears, and most of it had been paved. Michael said yes, dirt could be lost. I asked, "Is that why you never wash your hat?" He said it was. The hat was kind of an insurance policy. If a landslide or earthquake took the rest of his dirt, he'd have a stake to get started again.

I said I liked stocks. Being made out of paper, they were easier to deal with, cleaner, too. I told him that I had my eye on a good stock. He asked what was a good stock. I said one that when you put money in it went higher. Well, he gave me some money and I put it in the stock. The stock sat there quiet, waiting for its opportunity to go up. Michael got nervous and antsy and anxious. One day the stock went up. I sold it. He got his money back and the new money, too. He was happy. I was happy. (I had gotten to having second thoughts about the stock.)

Then, sometime later, Michael said there were some houses that it might be wise to buy. I said OK. My mind really wasn't on houses. It was on a movie I wanted to see. "I guess you'll be needing some money," I said, showing that I knew a thing or two about business. He said that was exactly right. He named a figure. I can't remember what it was, maybe ten thousand dollars. My memory is not . . . well. I told him I had ten thousand dollars and asked would a check do. He looked horrified.

"You mean you're just going to give me ten thousand dollars, just like that?" he said.

"Well," I said, "If you prefer, I could give you a dollar a day for ten thousand days."

I kind of liked that reply. It was sarcastic, and I prided myself on doing some pretty fine sarcastic when I set my mind upon it. He ignored that reply.

"What would your father say," Michael asked, "if he knew you were going to just give somebody ten thousand dollars and you hadn't taken even a little time to check out the business proposition being offered?"

"He would say I was an idiot," I said. It was a true statement and I felt good being honest.

"Well?" Michael said.

"Well?" I said.

"Don't you realize I could cheat you?" Michael asked.

"This is going to be a good movie if we can get to it," I said.

It wasn't the right thing to say. Michael wanted a better answer. He was stubborn. He could do stubborn better than I could do sarcastic. I decided to do non-sarcastic.

"Let me ask you something," I asked. "If I studied this proposition carefully, up and down and sideways and even operated on the problem and looked into its insides, could you still cheat me?"

"Oh yes!" Michael said and nodded. He was one fine nodder. Sometimes when he nodded, he would get so excited that he'd smack his lips. That was a thing to see: nod smack nod smack. But time was running out.

"Then why," I said, trying hard to be logical—it has never come easy to me—"should I study this housing proposition when all it is going to do is waste valuable time and no matter what I come up with, you can cheat me anyway?"

Michael could see he was trapped. We went to the movie. I remember this because it was the one and only time I ever came out ahead in a Logic contest with Michael. But that is beside the point. The point is: what happened with this housing proposition?

Well, what happened was I got the best business partner I have ever had. I have had more dishonest business partners, several of them. There is no shortage. I can tell you that from experience. But Michael couldn't do dishonest worth a damn. That is why I gave him the money.

He never asked for anymore. This was astounding. Houses, in my experience, cost. While you are asleep, your average house lets termites in to eat your beams, water to rot your doors, bats to foul the attic, radon to poison the basement. This is in addition to forest fires, earthquakes, appliances going kaput on the day after their warranties expire, and floods. I have lived in my share of houses and every one of them was ready to take my money. But in these houses, which I did not live in, there was never a problem, or I should say there was never a problem for me.

When a toilet or a boiler or a stove or some other apparatus broke and the people called up and said, "It's broke!" Michael would go to his back-up room and get an old whatever was needed that he had gotten earlier from a dump or a ruined house. He would take the thing and a hammer or Scotch tape or whatever and bash or glue the thing into working order. And that would be that. Occasionally, I would ask in a letter what I owed and he would say I owed nothing. Let me tell young people who think getting a Love Letter is thrilling and makes you feel soft and joyous, that simply can't compare to the feeling you get when your business partner says, "It is fixed and you owe nothing."

This went on for years because whenever I offered to help him with house maintenance, he said, "No thank you." He knew what that would mean to the partnership. I don't think I had told Michael that in high school woodshop we were supposed to construct, as our first project, a ruler. Or that I was the only guy in the whole class who had a ruler none of whose inches were the same length. Or that this outcome put the teacher in a terrible mood. Michael didn't have to be told. Things like that he knew.

After a long time, the houses got to be worth more. Michael said it might be a good thing to sell the houses. I could find no reason to argue with that. The thought of making a lot of money thrilled me. If there is anything I am fond of, it is money. Simply said, it just agrees with me. Michael felt like that, too. He felt almost religious when he could get something for a dime that most people would have paid a dollar for. He would say that he felt bad because he really only wanted to give a nickel, but I could tell he felt pretty good about being Thrifty. Anyway, I said, "Yippee! Sell the houses for a lot of money!"

Well, he said that we weren't planning on selling the houses or going to sell the houses and get a lot of money. We were going to finance the houses ourselves and get a humongous amount of money, although it would take time. I said what did he plan to do. He said he had already done it. He had asked the people renting the houses if they would like to own the houses if the payment wasn't a whole lot different than the rent and if they could have forty years or so to pay the house off.

I thought it was a dumb thing, an incredibly stupid and idiotic and brainless thing. I shared these thoughts, though in a tactful way (I think I picked up a nearby hammer and began to hit myself along the part of my hair). But I was wrong, magnificently wrong. (I don't like to boast but if any of you listening think you are good at being wrong, I say that I can be wronger faster and worse than you even when I am sick and you are well.) Wrong? I KNOW wrong. I have never been so happy to be wrong.

Michael understood that many people do not think about next year or next decade or even the day after tomorrow. They think: Can I make the payment? Can I make the payment easily? Can I make the payment so easily that I think I'm living in a dream?

And Michael made the dream come true. Which made the people very happy. And us a lot of money.

I began to have this thought: If we could let this guy run the country, things would be a lot better. When Michael said he was going to run for mayor, I said I already had his campaign slogan: BREATH FOR RUBEL!

I said that his slogan should be one he said out loud. When he went before a crowd, instead of nodding and smacking his lips, he should say, "I don't need you to say right out loud that you are going to vote for me. If you could just let me know you are by breathing, then I will know. So, if you're going to vote for me, just keep breathing. If you're not, stop breathing. It's entirely your choice."

Well, he didn't get elected. I personally think that was because he didn't give my slogan a chance. But it didn't bother me all that much. I wanted to get him Back East. I thought he would have been much better suited to working in the White House. I still think that.

But, just like Life, Death happens and instead of sitting there telling lies to Michael and Kaia, I end up writing memories. Well, what is there to say? I say this: I'm not all that religious but if I should happen to meet my old business partner again, even on something as shaky as a cloud, it wouldn't bother me a bit.

Let me close my memory with a quote I stole from your magical uncle (it is worth far more than silver) and plan never to give back:

"Joy to the World!"

Ted Shepherd sent to Scott Rubel, son of Christopher, Michael's brother, October 1, 2008.

So, it was said

"Don't bore people with the truth."

"Business must be based on reputation—not trust."

"I'm like an Oxon. I like to work hard"

"My three mottos in life are:
"Work hard, enjoy life, and safety third!"

Signs are posted throughout the project,
"Safety third!—Shut up and dig!"

Chapter 13

Immaculate thank-yous.

"Cry alone—laugh with others."
Grandfather

There is something special about a letter. We all like to get one.
E-mail on the other hand, has all the charm of a freight train. When
I was growing up we all knew when the mailman was coming and
we waited for him even though we hardly ever got a letter.
Andy Rooney, 60 Minutes, October 4, 2009

Thank you letters

Old fashioned Michael didn't Twitter. Didn't call friends much. Didn't
do e-mail. He wrote letters. He wrote a lot of "Thank you" letters. Every
year he'd send all those living at the Pharm, and some others, a "Thank
you for all you do to make this wonderful place work . . ."

Sometimes, if you also read between the lines, those letters would
give a glimpse into what was being done, or no longer able to be done,
at the Pharm. Of course, to some of us, it seems that all of his letters
were "Thank-yous" and glimpses of all that could and should be done.
A couple of those follow.

Glen Speer, one of Michael's dearest friends, who was turning the Box
Factory into a wondrous place with curvy epoxied wooden sinks, shiny
exposed copper pipes, a sunken wooden bath tub, and well read books,
was dearly missed when he set sail to St. John, Virgin Islands to be a
window framer; and ended up building his renowned Mongoose Junction
Shoppers Castle. Glen was dearly missed at the Pharm in those early

years away. Glen would send solitary, lonely sounding tapes, with sounds of virginal crickets and the nighttime countryside life buffeted by ocean waves in the background. The tapes would be shared with Pharmers and Michael's response to one of those tapes went with hopes that it would cheer Glen's after work and fill some of his solitary evenings. And, of course, MCR's letter reflected some of Grandfather's advice,

"Laugh at yourself—Taking yourself seriously means you have not looked at the heavens."

What follows is from a letter Michael wrote to Glen Speer on May 27, 1970. Michael had just lost his bid for election to the Glendora City Council, defeated by standing firmly on his platform that women should not be allowed to vote and by the infamous campaign slogan, "Because you love them, protect them from Rubel." The Pharm was still recovering from the 1969 floods. Glen went on to build Mongoose Junction in the Virgin Islands, leaving Michael to continue building his 'Dream Castle.'

Dear Glen,

We have all listened to your tape recordings and we are all impressed with the amount of equipment you are purchasing. The whole project down there sounds tremendous. We are all pulling for you and we know you can do it if you decide to. Dwayne is talking about coming down to see you this summer. Karen Sue may (I'm sure she will) take Dwayne's place and live there until he returns. Eleanor Riker is enjoying your place and she is a true delight to have here. A beautiful, industrious, positive, happy girl, and we ALL literally love her. Dwayne dated her heavily, however, at this point it appears, from my tiny vantage point that Walt Wiley is moving in like the large metal war ship. It is wonderful to watch. Poor Skipper got sat on at the beginning, however, he is in possession of a most beautiful, wonderful, pleasant girl: ANN BROWN. I am so jealous I can hardly stand it. However, I keep pouring cement. Cement everywhere. The towers are going very slowly. We must gather rocks and haul them in and mix the cement and work. Well, the hammock seems to monopolize most of my time and this slows down progress. We have lots of help, however. Wonderful new people who add a lot to the Farm.

The election was a horrible failure. Even my 7 supporters wonder what happened. It was disastrous. My ego was and is, really smashed. The only solution seems to be—pour more cement. Cement everywhere. Everyone is pleased with the way it turned out, so that should make me happy.

I am driving a school bus once again, and it is going well. It is not as much fun as driving Bus #11, however, the hours and vacations and other time off pleases my attitude with working.

We finished the birdbath structure several weeks ago. It is truly a masterpiece. Much larger than the last structure and all constructed out of palm trees and eucalyptus hunks. You will be horrified, and I stand about grinning at it. We had thirty people helping to lift the logs into place. It is truly a wonder.

The Farm electrical system is so complicated that I cannot get a bit of rest. Lights, buzzers, indicators, meters, bells and flashing red and yellow and green lights make my room look like a submarine control room. It is truly a marvel. We turned it all on the other evening after we had had our fill of visitors and for the rest of the evening I sat up in bed at attention, watching the marvelous room change colour and shake. My brother was staying in the living room that evening, and he finally came in to ask if there was anything to be done about the electric room. He claims the door shakes and the relays vibrate so strangely that his bed was giving him a message. We finally turned it off, and this caused the main gates to close, lock and seal automatically, which I forgot would happen when the power was shut off, and then Scott, Eleanor and Klaus came to try and get in.

Well, this was four in the morning, and they tried to use the gate telephone, but when the power goes off it does not work. They tried to open the gates, but they were locked. Then, Scott climbed over the wall, breaking the alarm wire which runs on twelve volts and which in turn set off the horns, bells, and buzzers. I ran out into the world naked as a spider, shot gun in hand. "INVASION," I yelled, half asleep, and began methodically shooting it out with the Indians.

When all quieted down we had the culprits and everyone got up to have tea. When the main alarm system comes on the lights on the wall, drive, garages, kitchen, and living room all come on, which blew my brother's mind. He was fed up, and left at five AM.

I think Dwayne is getting tired of the gates and controls he must cope with to get out and in, however, in the Shriek, (Mrs. Friezner's Pharm newsletter), there is a cry from the Editor to turn off the whole damn thing. She was cleaning the north bathroom the other day and thought she would open the north doors. Well, since we have no use for the north doors, I put micro switches or them so when they open a bell in the north bath room and the electric room come on and stay on for twelve minutes and then goes off, and in so doing (off) turns on the drive lights and my room lights and honks the fire horn three times. Mrs. Friezner was running around and doing what any normal women would do, began to cry.

Well, we're going to shut this monster down, I guess.

Love Michael ☺

Although grandfather would say,

**"Don't tell people about the labor
pains. Show them the baby."**

Michael didn't even like taking time out to show the baby. Sometimes, during the Golden Era of high-energy building, a group might get Michael to give them a tour, but MCR usually finagled another Pharmer into doing those supposed honors. In the post Golden Era, just scheduling, allowing, and observing the tours became an imposition and drain on MCR and Kaia's energy and the serenity that the Castle's hummingbirds, towers, music, and story telling was meant to provide . . .

A RUBEL FARMS PEOPLE STORY
BY
KAIA RUBEL

MICHAEL TALKS MORE AND MORE OF TAKING UP
A MOST GENEROUS OFFER. THIS ENTAILS MOVING
TO DENMARK AND GIVING THE FARM TO OUR LOCAL

HISTORICAL SOCIETY. I DO NOT WANT TO LEAVE MY FAMILY SO THIS BOTHERS ME. I WILL GO WITH MICHAEL IF THAT IS HIS DECISION.

LET ME OUTLINE SOME OF THE CIRCUMSTANCES BEHIND THIS TALK. I'M GOING TO LIMIT THIS STORY TO THE MONTH OF MAY 2001.

STARTING ON TUESDAY, MAY 1ST, MICHAEL TOURED OVER FIFTY PEOPLE. DICK MACY WAS ON A TRIP. JIM RILEY WAS BUSY AND WARREN BOWEN WAS FACING A HIP REPLACEMENT. MAY 5TH, SATURDAY, WE HAD TO DRIVE TO LAX TO PICK UP A LADY WHO FLEW IN FROM DENMARK AT FOUR IN THE MORNING. MAY 7TH MICHAEL'S SISTER CALLED TO ASK THAT A FAMILY MIGHT STAY AT THE FARM WHO WERE COMING IN FROM TEXAS. FRIDAY, MAY 11TH, A FAMILY STAYED IN THE CABOOSE WHO ARE FRIENDS OF BILL FORMAN WHO LIVES IN TEXAS. MAY 12TH WE DROVE OUR DANISH FRIEND TO LAX AT 10 IN THE EVENING AND RETURNED BACK TO THE CASTLE AT THREE IN THE MORNING. FROM THE 13TH TO THE 17TH, WE PROBABLY HAD FIFTY (NO EXAGGERATION) PEOPLE VISIT. LA FETRA SCHOOL BROUGHT SIXTY PEOPLE AT 9:30 AM AND JIM RILEY AND DEAN DEMPSEY TOOK THE TOUR. DWAYNE HUNN HAD SOME FRIENDS VISIT ON THE 19TH, WHO WE MISSED BECAUSE WE WENT ON THE METRO LINK TO OLVERA STREET. MAY 20TH DWAYNE CAME DOWN FROM MILL VALLEY TO STAY FOR A WEEK. HE STAYED IN THE CABOOSE AND WORKED REALLY HARD ON RESTORING THE LADIES' LAVATORY BY THE OLD FARM KITCHEN. HE DID A GREAT JOB, I MIGHT ADD. CULLEN SCHOOL BROUGHT SIXTY CHILDREN INCLUDING PARENTS AND DICK MACY TOOK THAT TOUR MAY 23RD. MAY 24TH DICK MACY TOOK ANOTHER SIXTY-FIVE PEOPLE ON A TOUR FROM CULLEN AT 10:30 AM. FRIDAY, MAY 25TH, ANOTHER SIXTY PEOPLE CAME FROM CULLEN. SATURDAY, MAY 26TH AND SUNDAY MAY 27TH WE HAD PEOPLE FOR LUNCH AND DINNER. SUTHERLAND SCHOOL CAME AT 8:45 WITH FORTY SOME PEOPLE. ON TUESDAY MAY 30TH, CULLEN SCHOOL BROUGHT OVER FIFTY PEOPLE AT 10:30. MAY 30TH, THREE TOURS TOOK

PLACE; CULLEN SCHOOL, SELLERS SCHOOL AND AT 2:30 PM A GROUP OF BOY SCOUTS.

I LIM1TED THIS STORY TO THE MONTH OF MAY. SOME MONTHS ARE BUSIER AND SOME MONTHS ARE TERRIBLE. MICHAEL GETS DEPRESSED WHEN HE IS INHOSPITABLE. HE TALKS OF DENMARK MORE AND MORE. MICHAEL SENT OUT OVER TWO-HUNDRED LETTERS RECENTLY ASKING HIS FRIENDS TO STOP SENDING THEIR FRIENDS BECAUSE WE ARE SOCIALLY EXHAUSTED. THIS HAS HELPED A LOT. MICHAEL HAS TURNED DOWN FIVE CAR CLUBS IN ONE WEEK WHO WANT TO HAVE A DAY AT THE FARMS. HE HATES DOING THIS. HE HANDS THE TELEPHONE TO ME WHEN HE CAN SO THAT I CAN SCREEN WHO VISITS. WE HAVE HAND SIGNALS, WHICH THE KINGS OF ROME USED AT THE COLISEUM.

I'M WRITING THIS TO EMPHASIZE WHAT WE ARE GOING THROUGH HERE AND TO TRY AND HEIGHTEN PEOPLE'S AWARENESS ON WHAT WE FACE. MICHAEL AND I BOTH ENJOY OUR FRIENDS' VISITING, BE ASSURED!

> *"I don't live here in peace and harmony by being pleasant to everybody. Be selective."*
>
> *"The castle is a young man's dream and an old man's nightmare."*

Michael was . . .

Michael was . . . built like a 6' spark plug. Thin legs supported a chiseled hard body that churned energy all day long. He consumed food, juice, and wine and shot that energy back into rocks, cement, beams, and anything else that might build castle walls.

The spark plug was invincible for years, which is a common malady of the hardened, hard charging young, especially when supported by a team of doers who liked playing that way too. Like so many hard charging heavy-lifters, for a long time Michael just seemed to get stronger, and found more and more creative ways to move the castle higher and forward.

Maybe some of Michael's mentors, and probably his mother, told him to rest or slow down some, but at a Pharm whose mantra was "Safety Third", we Pharmhands heard little of taking R&R for body and mind therapy. (If you expressed personal problems at the Pharm, you were likely to hear some such answer as, "You gotta a problem? Work harder, dig deeper, pile higher . . . It'll go away.")

> "It will never be finished, will just go on my whole life," the Lord of Rubelia sighs and says more hopefully, "it's all a big dream but I think it's going to come true because I've got 40 years left."
> Washington Post Tuesday, August 19, 1975 by Eugene L. Meyer

So, as happens to great athletes, some parts began breaking down. After handling, lifting, moving 20,000+ tons of cement, rocks, steel, beams, and junk, (check God's computer if Goggle, Bing, or Open Secrets fails to supply the exact tonnage lifted) Michael needed a surgery. Thence forward, Michael had trouble turning, the beeping R2D2-like head atop the well chiseled spark plug that had long been conditioned to lift, push, drive, and tell stories that made us laugh.

Luckily, most of the physically demanding castle building had been done before Michael's pain drove him to fusing his disks into limited movement. Michael, always with people to his left and right, never complained about losing his unfettered ability to swivel right or left to see you. Your position didn't matter much. He already knew who you were in so many different ways that, if he chose to ask your help with work, he didn't have t o look, because he already knew what you were capable of doing. If he were encircled in conversation, he didn't need to turn your way, since listening had allowed him to know where you stood. And if the conversation were in his kitchen, he could look out from his all-encompassing chair and see you whether you were washing dishes, chopping food, sitting in a chair, or mingling with dogs on the slightly carpeted floor.

So, as Glen often says, Michael "learned to cope" with every adversity in a wonderful way. There was, however, an adversity that hurt him more than exposure to fusion power. It probably stemmed from his driving desire to get things done quickly.

Both on and within the Castle walls lie a lot of arc-welded steel, iron, and other rusting stuff. The arc-welding masks used in the Castle's early building years where pre-historic hand-me downs then. Their soiled and old eye-windows hindered arc-welding efficiency. So, in forwarding the rapid can-do spirit inherent to the Safety Third Brigades, Michael too often discarded those old, but still somewhat protective, arc-welding helmets.

Several experimental eye injections and surgeries did not help. Nonetheless, Michael had his unique way of defining his situation and coping, as he revealed in his annual letter to Pharmers in 2002.

michael rubel
844 n. live oak
glendora, california
91740

The Yearly Pharm Letter, 2002

This is a long rambling letter. You surely have better things to do with your time than to read this.

This year has been a challenge. I have a condition called **"immaculate deception"** which affects my vision. With this change comes a slow down in hosting so many people here. We are beginning to host only schools, which take up a lot of time for Dick Macy. Without his help, we could not handle the social pressures.

Rebuilding the gate this year was work that nearly defeated me. Attitude is everything in life, and mine went south with the inability to see wires. I'm so blessed with friends who volunteer to help me keep the farm going.

David Thum and Dean Dempsey help me constantly. David copes with the nightly activity that we face each night with such willingness that it amazes Kaia and me. Dean has provided the countless cords of firewood that we go through.

Slowing the farm down is a tedious process. It's like slowing the train that has run for years at full speed. We still host countless schools and turn down countless organizations.

I remember how ecstatic it was when my properties were sold. Now this emotion is again within grasp as the Farm is less chaotic. It is called retirement.

I can't remember not managing so many situations that managing properties entails. Forgive me if I dance. Perhaps my deteriorating vision is what is needed to make this retirement work. I am so fortunate to have Kaia by my side. I am so thankful that she likes me.

This book that David Traversi has written is incredible. He has captured the energy that we all had to create this amazing place. I'm in shock when walking around the Farm. How did we do this?

Thank you for supporting the Farm. Thank you for your friendship.

With love, let us remain,

Your local farmers,
Mykee and Kaia

So, it was said

Change is one guarantee we have through life.

Health is wealth.

Eliminate the "I" from your thoughts. We and you are of interest to the other person.

Notice how the Willow tree survives? It bends.

Chapter 14

Cruising into his sixth inning

"What memories were made here . . ."

In the last decade of the 20th century, my chipped Marin County mailbox hinged on my vine covered fence had several bills, a couple real estate solicitations for pricey neighboring properties, and this postcard from Mykee and Kaia.

> Hi,
> Well, Kaia gave all her property away. She is so happy. We loved Estonia. They treated us royally. ☺

Kaia gave her Estonia farmland away and returned to the Castle she already had, where she shared this letter to those she had given her family land to and some of us Pharmers.

Dear brothers and sisters,
I feel as though I am a character in a romance novel as I write these lines in my cozy room on the third level of the Pigeon Tower which Michael furnished for me with many of his treasures i.e., antique rifles complete with fixed bayonets, WW I hand grenades, battle axes from the 17th century, various knives, steam engines, collections of sheriffs badges from the Wild West, and brass camp stoves we collected on trips to Denmark. The British battle flag Prince Philip gave to Michael during one of his visits to the castle hangs above my daybed, and on my daybed I can nap snuggling under a quilt

made for me by my colleagues at the Libraries. (Claremont Colleges' Honnold Library)

I have for entertainment an extraordinary stage. My window looks down to the courtyard below. Michael dressed in his agrarian jumpsuit is tinkering with the 1930's air compressor. Warren Asa's blacksmithing class is learning the almost lost art of tempering steel. One of the students just completed a suit of armor and several jousting poles. Docent Macy lectures a gaggle of ladies in Red Hats and purple dresses who are touring the Castle/Tin Palace about the history of this place, how all this junk was acquired and who did it. Five high school girls from Orange County are filming a class project using as inspiration the Reality TV show "While You Were Out."

Every day this activity continues—different characters— different stories that are performed against the backdrop of towers, parapets, and walls built from river boulders . . . all framed by the rugged San Gabriel Mountains and softened by lovely Washingtonian Robusta palms and eucalyptus trees. The tower bells ring every half-hour and the 1870s steam engine whistle blows at noon to break for lunch and 6 PM reminding farmers it's time to put the tools away and go home.

Kaia

Shortly after getting his cruise feet wet, Michael stumbled into even cheaper ways to ply the seas in even plusher digs by merely being who he was. After booking a cruise with Holland American lines, Michael received a phone call asking whether he was "Michael Clarke Rubel, who booked an inner cabin for our upcoming cruise?"

Concerned, MCR asked, "Yes, is there something wrong?"

"No, sir. We'd just like to make a few adjustments and refunds to your booking."

As the conversation continued, MCR became a bit befuddled. He stressed that the room he had booked fit their room and budgetary needs and hoped that the changes they were doing would not impinge on those needs. The caller tried to allay his fears, but the simple Pharmer was still concerned. The always-collected Kaia wasn't as befuddled after reading on European Cruises letterhead dated 24/9/95 such lines as:

> Our Director has instructed me to extend to you and Ms. Kaia Niiler Poorbaugh a refund on your transatlantic passage with the Holland American line . . .
>
> Under separate postal cover you will receive a letter asking that you honor our Director with a visit and dinner when visiting the Netherlands . . .
>
> Our office has instructed the cursor to extend to you all available services when traveling and also extend a $500 credit for charges not covered by the Line's fare . . .
>
> As a personal note, let me say that your former employer, the notorious Boggs, was a close friend and I heard of you through this association. It would be our family's pleasure to have an opportunity to meet you if possible.

When Kaia and Michael arrived for early boarding, they were ushered up many levels above their previously booked inner rooms to the plushest of staterooms, adorned with sunken tubs, views, and comfy stuff . . .

All these comforts for a two-bit black market bookie who, in his swashbuckling years, worked his way up from Swabbee to Purser on the ships that Captain Boggs kept at sea.

Back story
How Michael became a seafarer

Decades ago, where the muggy airs of the Middle East mixes with those of Africa, a big, naive American boy sat on his bunk behind Egyptian jail bars. Patiently, he waited for his guards to appear, so they could escort him to his self-paid lunch. After serving many days behind bars, it began taking longer for his luncheon guards to appear; for instead of having his original one or two guards, he now had a half dozen. Increased security stemmed not from fearing that Michael would flee, but from his *tea party* generosity, (Oh, my! How friendly American Pharmer Michael's Tea Parties have been defiled today. Ah, for a return to MCR's Tea Parties.)

When Michael started going to jail lunch, he had one or two guards and instinctively bought them a pot of penny tea, lest Mother Dorothy scold him subconsciously . . . Word of this much appreciated American's early "Three Pots of Tea" hospitality spread quickly, which provided Michael with a friendly contingent of a half dozen happily armed guards at each of his armed forked and knifed outings.

Yes, jailed Pharmer Michael's Three Pots of Tea personal generosity was the precursor to Author Greg Mortenson's Three Cups of Tea diplomacy, which if America were better versed in the world would be the bulwark of America's 21st century Middle Eastern diplomacy. (This will be the focus of the next book in a series tentatively titled, "Castle Building for Dummies" or "What Every Town, State, and Nation Needs" series.)

How did Michael come to initiate what should be the replacement for our costly gunboat droneplomacy with cheap tealeaf diplomacy?

MCR's Tea Party Diplomacy

Here's the splintered in-field education that led aging teenager MCR to initiate a smarter, cheaper American public policy.

As a kid, Michael counted a lot. He counted birdshot, nails, lumber, rocks, etc. He counted hours till school ended and he could go build forts with his friends. This developed his head's facility for juggling numbers.

Added to these math skills was a certain sense of history spiced with a zest for life. Knowing just enough history to visualize endless adventures and immortality in his head, he set out to see the world. In other words, he set out to see the world knowing just enough history to be dangerous, which does much to add spice to one's life.

Knowing such history, he adorned his Harley with both an Algerian and French flag while buzzing through the Algerian desert during their lingering warfare. Consequently, one or both sides shot him off his bike in the middle of an Algerian desert.

Subsequently, governing officials found many different currencies in his pockets. When the officials asked why, Michael explained that he had found that exchanging them in different countries usually allowed him to stretch his food dollar further. To the officials, this sounded a lot like Black Marketeering. The sentence for working the Egyptian Black was like—death by beheading, lynching, or something like that, except maybe for young dummies from what was then the world's foremost and best-liked power.

Then again, Michael might have been jailed for being caught trying to stow away aboard a cargo ship in an Egyptian port. Anyway, whichever foreign offense MCR fessed-up to in his recollections depended on how many shrimp cocktail glasses of wine Michael had swallowed before he specified his mode of Sphinxable offense.

No matter his mode of offense, since Egyptian jails didn't budget for sustenance back then, Michael had to feed himself. So, when Michael wanted to eat lunch or dinner, he had to be escorted by a guard, or more.

On one of his six guard luncheon escapades, while Michael was simultaneously lowering his plate of piled high food and raising his cholesterol, a Dane loomed above his table, and asked, "What are you doing?"

"Eating," MCR replied, breaking for only a glance away from his feeding trough.

"I see that. Why are you eating here?"

Filling his fork and spoon again, MCR replied, "Cheap."

"Well," replied the Dane, "It's also the best food around here."

"Didn't know that," replied the well-protected prisoner.

"Why are all these soldiers with you?"

"I'm their prisoner," Michael began.

As his plate's chompable mound dwindled, Michael rambled some about his cheap travel, his facility with numbers juggling, and his hope that some money might come from home before his food allowance ran out, and added, "Who are those people with you?"

"They are some of my crew," Captain Boggs replied.

By day's end, the guards' most gracious tea provider was taken from the now chai-less guards. Bailed out by the Danish captain, Michael was now a swabbee of deck, hull, toilet, and anything else very low on the ship's totem pole that needed scrubbing.

Although commuted to a job with a short commute, Michael didn't unabashedly love his job or its community, and the First Mate didn't love Michael. After a while, responsibilities and complexities increased under the First Mate's guardianship. Then, the Purser jumped ship in some Asian port.

"Michael," said the captain, "didn't you say your mother did real estate?'

"Yes, sir."

"Did you say you kept the books for her?"

"Yes, sir. I did."

"Do you think you could keep the books for us?"

"Ah, yes, sir. I think so," responded the swabbee with visions of a better life swelling in his fertile mind.

Thus began Michael's venture into trying to balance Captain C. J. Boggs's purse strings. On the undeniably happy side of this venture—Michael got his own little cabin and forsook clutching steaming, dripping pipes while counting sheep in a bunk surrounded by sweaty, hairy-armed men. In his room, Michael immediately went about trying to balance the ship's books. After working almost a week on balancing revenues and costs, rather than sanitizing garbages, toilet bowls, and such, Michael thought he had one more full day to get the ship's finances ship-shape.

The First Mate, however, ran the ship from a different schedule and perspective. When they entered a Japanese harbor, he ordered strapping Michael to spend his day lifting cargo instead of pushing numbers.

"But I'm Purser now," replied Michael.

Those hours of fixing the numbers disappeared with the raspy sound of the First Darth Vader's utterances, "You're my crew. You'll do real work too. Get down and unload the ship!"

A few hours after leaving port, Michael, attended his first Officers' Meeting, where he was called upon to stand and deliver—the Purser's Report. With an obvious "jiggly" in his legs and voice, Michael quickly delivered a very shaky financial report, and thereupon promptly sat down.

For many seconds, silence reigned supreme over the youngster's report, until the First Mate's empathy-less words crackled and hung in the air, "Rubel, we've never been $400,000 out of balance . . ."

Banter continued, including some sympathy for the rookie expressed by the captain. The First Mate, however, seemed to deliver the prevailing sentiment, "Rubel, do you know how long you will have to scrub toilets to make up a $400,000 loss?"

After what seemed like a long silence, Michael rose again, imploring, "Ah, excuse me, sir. Sir, I guess I wasn't clear but, sir, we're not $400,000 in the red . . . We're $400,000 in the black."

Again, many seconds of stillness ensued. And again, the First Mate was the first to express disdain at this youngster's lack of knowledge and detail, "Rubel, did it ever occur to you that moving that surplus off of the books could have balanced everything?"

The embarrassed youngster rose again, "But, sir, wouldn't that have been improper?"

Deeper Back Story
For those of pure—or dubious—accounting hearts

This section is for those who are pure of heart and have no need to subscribe to the philosophy that "Greed is good!" It is for the uninitiated who are unaware that many large corporations keep two sets of books, one for regulators and the public and one for their own self-aggrandizement It is also for those who slept through the Bernie Nadoff ponzi scam and didn't see the significance of red and black numbers early enough to do something positive about it.

Once, when telling this story from the comfort of one of his rocking chairs, Michael fessed-up that the thought of moving the surplus to another account had occurred to him. It had occurred to him often during his first days on the job. No one would know, he thought. There the money could sit till someone needed it . . . Maybe even someone like him.
"It was a tempting thought," Michael said.
It was much later in their relationship that the captain said to Michael, "Michael, I want you to know something, I knew to the penny how much overage we had in those accounts."
Sometime later, in the late '60's, Captain Boggs passed on. A little later, Michael was named as one of only thirteen in the captain's will. Michael, in what he thought was a Skipper hoax, was directed to report to the Bank of Swiss, or some such named bank.
If you are having trouble getting the kids or your roommates to scrub the toilets, learn how to add, and keep honest books, have them read about the Captain Boggs here, the Captain who owned more than thirteen ships.
Yes, kids, the basics are important. So, learn how to add and subtract, to keep the toilet bowl clean, and to play games honestly.
It wasn't much after the will naming that Glen and I rolled a flat bed crunching Wells Fargo vault off of one of the old Pharm trucks and into Michael's refrigerator bedroom in the Tin Packing House . . .
But that Wells Fargo safe gets into another Rubelian story that you may have to hear in person rather than in printed word. And that story is only told when the room is cleaned of IRS agents, listening devices, and snitches. That story includes possibly forged letters, borderline destitution, safe cracking, bitter-sweet accusations and flights, romances with captain's daughters and heiress, European counts, marbled halls,

high finance, dead rats, suffocations, high walls, and rifles, as well as the innocent and stupid. In other words, it contains almost all the prerequisites of a Grade B+ movie shot at a Hoagsmithian Castle.

Phun Cruising

There in that Holland American Line's letter dated 24/9/95 was another result of Michael cruising through life, steering clear of bad words, and avoiding doing anything "terribly improper," unless, of course, the improprieties revolved around castle building.

How does that Big Clockmaker in the Sky know how to tie cruising on a Harley to running numbers to sipping tea with jailers to scrubbing toilets to mixing cement into a community that stumbles into building a wondrous recycled Castle of Junk?

The answer lies somewhere between Grandfather saying,

"My lack of knowledge is terrifying."

&

"Isn't life wonderful?"

On those wonderful days, when a bunch of Pharmhands and Michael would chew food, drink wine, and reminisce on a messy and maybe constructive day's work, Castle life was the best cruisin one could do.

Glendora or bust

Rubelian Railroad System

"Cruising" became a comfortable travel mode for Michael and Kaia, as was "Training." Sometimes, however, Michael's inherent vagabondish spirit tumbled out, and got in the way of "comfortable" training. It's a good thing "comfortable comforting" didn't matter much to Kaia.

CANADIAN TRAINS
(I WISH I WASN'T SO STUPID)
By
MYKEE

KAIA AND I WERE IN THE MOST SCENIC AREA OF THE CANADIAN ROCKIES. I SPOTTED A STEAM TRAIN AND ASKED THE CAR ATTENDANT IF WE COULD GET OFF. THE TRAIN WE WERE ON WILL STOP ANYWHERE THAT EITHER DELIVER PACKAGES OR PEOPLE OR PICK UP HIKERS OR WILDERNESS CAMPERS. HE READILY AGREED AND STOPPED THE TRAIN. WE WALKED TO A DILAPIDATED BUILDING AND KAIA SAT ON A LOG WHILE I WENT OVER TO ADMIRE THE ENGINE. THE ENGINEER WAS SHOVELING COAL AND ENJOYED TELLING ME ABOUT THIS 1922 FR GRACE ENGINE. I ASKED ABOUT THE TRIP HE WAS INTENDING AND HE SAID THAT THE ORE TRAIN TOOK ABOUT TWO HOURS. THERE IS A CREW CAR ATTACHED AND I ASKED IF MY WIFE AND I COULD RIDE ALONG. HE SAID ANYONE COULD RIDE ALONG AND THAT HE FREQUENTLY TOOK WLDERNESS PARTIES TO THE END OF THE LINE TO HELP THEM ALONG ON THEIR CAMPING TRIP. "YOU DONT LOOK LIKE A WILDERNESS PERSON," HE OBSERVED. I EXPLAINED THAT WE WEREN'T BUT THAT WE REALLY LIKED STEAM TRAINS AND THIS ONE WAS A REAL FIND. HE WAS PLEASED AND BEGAN SHOVELING COAL.

WE RODE ALONE IN A DIRTY CREW CAR AT ABOUT TEN MILES AN HOUR. WHEN WE ARRIVED ABOUT TEN IN THE MORNING AT A COPPER MINE, WE GOT OFF AND ASKED WHERE A CAFE OR RESTAURANT MIGHT BE FOUND. TWO WILD LOOKING MEN STARED AT US LIKE WE HAD JUST FALLEN OFF A TURNIP TRUCK. THEY

EXPlAINED IN COLORFUL LANGUAGE THAT THERE *WERE NO* PROVISIONS AND THAT PEOPLE NEEDED TO BRING THEIR GEAR WITH THEM. WE HAD A CAN OF BREA AND TWO APPLES, SO THAT WOULD CARRY US OVER UNTIL THE TRAIN WENT BACK.

    I WALKED UP TO THE ENGINEER AND ASKED HOW LONG HIS LAYOVER WOULD BE BEFORE HEADING BACK. HE STARED WITH THIS BLANK BEWILDERMENT AND SAID IT WOULD BE FIVE OR SIX DAYS. KAIA, WHEN I WENT BACK TO TELL HER, BEGAN TO SMILE. I ALSO EXPLAINED THAT THERE WAS NO FOOD NOR ANYWHERE TO STAY FOR TOURISTS. I APOLOGIZED AND SAT ON THE CREW CAR STEP. AFTER WHAT KAIA AND HER FAMILY WENT THROUGH DURING WWII, THIS WAS A PIECE OF CAKE FOR HER.

    THERE WAS AN OLD PICK-UP TRUCK AND WALKING OVER TO ONE OF THE WILD MEN I ASKED IF IT WAS POSSIBLE TO GET A RIDE BACK TO THE MAINLINER TRACK. THE FELLOW TOLD ME THAT HE HAD NOT DRIVEN THE TRAIL FOR SEVERAL MONTHS AND IT WOULD BE PRETTY DIFFICULT. WHEN HE WAS OFFERED A HUNDRED DOLLARS, HE SAID, "HOP IN, WE'LL MAKE IT!" HE WENT AND GOT A CHAIN SAW THAT LOOKED LIKE IT HAD BEEN RUN OVER BY THE TRAIN. HE WALKED ABOUT A LOT AND GATHERED UP STUFF LIKE GASOLINE AND AN AX. KAIA SAT IN THE MIDDLE OF THE MOST HORRIBLE CONDITIONS AS WE BOUNCED AND JERKED ALONG A TRAIL THAT LEWIS AND CLARK PROBABLY CUT. IT WAS TERRIBLE! WE STOPPED AT A SMALL STREAM AND OUR DRIVER (HIS NAME IS LEAD) IDLED NEXT TO THE WATER AND BEGAN SHAKING HIS HEAD. HIS CONVERSATION WENT LIKE THIS: "NOW IF IT WAS JUST ME I'D GIVE IT A TRY. RISKING THE TWO OF YOU IS SOMETHING I DON'T WANT TO DO. WE HAVE HAD MORE SNOW THIS YEAR THAN IN MY MEMORY AND THE WARM WEATHER MAKES THIS MIGHTY BAD. CAN YOU BOTH SWIM? THE WATER IS COLD AND WE

STILL HAVE ABOUT THREE HOURS OF DRIVING OR AT LEAST A DAY OF WALKING, THAT IS IF WE GET YOU ACROSS." WE SAT THERE FOR ABOUT A HALF HOUR TRYING TO THINK OUT OUR OPTIONS. LEAD SAID THAT THE TRUCK WOULD BE ALL RIGHT EVEN IF THE MOTOR QUIT, WHICH HE THOUGHT WAS LIKELY, AND HE COULD HAVE HELP BACK TO GET US IN ABOUT TWO DAYS. HE DIDN'T THINK WE SHOULD BAIL OUT AND TRY TO GET TO THE BANK. IT WAS A SMALL STREAM BUT KAIA AND I WERE WORRIED. WHILE WE WERE THINKING WHAT WE SHOULD DO, LEAD YELLED OUT, "O' HELL—EXCUSE ME MA'AM." AND OFF WE WENT ACROSS THE STREAM. WE HAD THREE MORE STREAMS TO CROSS (SMALLER ONES THANKFULLY) AND ABOUT SIX TREES TO CUT AND REMOVE FROM OUR PATH. KAIA SAID THAT WE SHOULD HAVE KNOWN THIS WAS A PECULIAR SERVICE SINCE NO ONE WANTED TO SELL US A TICKET. I PAID LEAD WHO SEEMED DELIGHTED IN HIS DAY'S WORK. HE RAN OVER TO A DILAPIDATED PUB. WE ASSUME HE WAS GOING TO ENJOY A PERSONAL DRINKING PROBLEM. WE STAYED IN A B&B SHED NEXT TO THE PUB AND DRANK BEER. THIS WAS IN THE SPRUCE KINGDOM OF THE WORLD ON A BEAUTIFUL DAY IN JUNE OF 1999.

More stories but . . .

There are more stories and thoughts. Some may even be worth living by, but carpel tunnel suggests that they should be saved for telling at village and town bookstores, and especially the Village Bookstore in Glendora, where some people might come to:

- Repeat some of their grandfather's sayings.
- 'Splain how those sayings routed their lives.
- Hear, refute, embellish, and add to Pharm lore.
- View power pointed pixilated pictures that add to what's here.
- See if you and your friends might be seduced into:

  - Buying some books for posterity.
  - Getting a few to Captain Bogg's family.
  - Encouraging the Rubelian Castle building spirit in your community.
  - Inspiring some readers to become unique leaders.
  - Strengthening some healthy attitudes.
  - Working to insure that your town has a Castle too for—every town could benefit from having a Castle like Michael's.

So, it was said.

ATTITUDE
By Charles Swindoll

The longer I live, the more I realize the impact of attitude on my life. Attitude, to me, is more important than facts. It is more important than the past, than education, than money, than circumstances, than failures, than successes, than what other people think or *say* or do. It is more important than appearances, giftedness, or skill. It will make or break a company . . . a church . . . a home.

The remarkable thing is we have a choice everyday regarding the attitude we will embrace for that day. We cannot change our past . . . We cannot change the fact that people will act in a certain way. We cannot change the inevitable. The only thing we can do is play on the string that we have, and that is our attitude . . . I am convinced that life is 10% what happens to me and 90% how I react to it.

And it is with you . . .

"WE ARE IN CHARGE OF OUR ATTITUDES."

On one of MCR's many mailers

Chapter 15

MCR's Civics Lessons

> **"Older I get, more I realize I was wrong on almost everything,"**
> MCR
>
> **"Keep your own corner swept—examples are your strongest gifts to others."**
> Grandfather

The more one peaceably participates in the happenings of civilization the more civil more citizens become. The more one communicates with and understands those who play public roles in building civil societies, the healthier civilization becomes.

Michael got up early every day to play hard at working, or work hard at playing. He traveled the world, as an interested, observant, ordinary citizen. An Ugly American, ordinary extraordinary Michael was not. He made friends everywhere, no matter your nomenclature. He was civil to all, and they to him. He mostly followed the rules of civil society, if they meshed with his sense of common sense. He recycled junk into a wondrous stop-and-stare, not a gimmicky stop-and-shop.

He even ran for mayor, without any of the customary political snares. Nonetheless, he planted the shakes in the incumbent mayor's handshake by introducing his well-known self to voters with none of the typical phony political fanfare.

On those rare occasions, when Michael would leave rock piling to participate in a Candidates Night, Michael's self-aggrandizing political introduction would run something like, "I don't belong to any clubs. I haven't chaired any boards. I just pile rocks, cement, and bottles and drive a school bus. And I'd like you to vote for me." He'd then shrug, lightly puff those cheeks, enlarge those eyes, and sit down.

> The election was a horrible failure. Even my 7 supporters wonder what happened. It was disastrous. My ego was and is, really smashed. The only solution seems to be—pour more cement. Cement everywhere. Everyone is pleased with the way it turned out, so that should make me happy.
>
> Letter to Glen Speer

When his body was strong and stronger, he used it to roam, lift, and build. When it became worn, he used it for reading, listening, story telling, and napping in his rocking chair, so he could live, laugh, and wander again from the comfort of one of his many discarded and reupholstered leather chairs.

Rocking in his chair, Michael had become an evolving and evolved Civics Lesson, whose classes too much of America has dropped from its curriculum. Where he stood politically as a young man was a long leap from where he landed decades later. But wherever he stood and whatever he stood for on any particular day or era in his evolution, he practiced civics in his own colorful Rubelian way.

If you fill too much time with gimmickry and are failing to participate in building a smarter world, take a cue from Rock Star MCR, and hammer louder, pile higher, and sing louder to your own friendly village idiot's music. In doing so, remember to travel, work hard, learn, and teach, as Rocker MCR did, so that you have something sensible but phun to say that is based on sweaty, experienced, observed truths. Unfortunately, too much of today's America does not base their beliefs on sweaty, experienced truths. Instead, they fill their heads with illogical rants from those who have never done the extraordinary travel and work that the extraordinary Michaels have done in building a sustainable and happy world. We need a lot more Americans living grandfather's words:

"Experience all the emotions, so you
can sympathize with others,"

so that, hopefully, every town can have its Rubelian castles and the spirits they exhume.

Michael participated civically through his words, actions, and deeds. Since he always tried to keep everyone happy, he did not push his civic beliefs in gatherings, unless the conversation drew him there naturally. More comfortable was he in conveying his beliefs via his working actions and embedded between the lines of pen, paper, stories, and its related progeny. May more of us develop MCR's learning and teaching techniques, even as we add gadgets and technologies to advertise niches, twitter microscopic beliefs, and swallow time.

Is the Pen mightier than the Twitter?

More importantly than debating the consequences of moving from thoughtful letters to immediate twitters, MCR's life left one considering whether the clunky messy cement mixer was an even more important communications point than a silently precise computer chip.

Does one's, and a nation's, character grow more from laboriously building something with one's hands and sweat, rather than buying ready made plastics from far away?

Does one's, and the world's, community flourish by buying and plopping down expensive, corporatized, sanitized designs, or by having friends and neighbors share in the figuring, lifting, and pounding involved in getting a phunny looking barn up and working?

Does your, mine, and the world's understanding, and consequent public policies, grow smarter by having many more MCRs bumping along the world's dirt roads and river beds, rather than leaving those public policy decisions in the smooth hands of a few deciding from corporate jets the lives of those below?

Michael was raised by a generation of old timers who knew how to work hard and how to make things work. That generation made MCR grow to love and live his motto "Love to work. Work is fun," which made it easy for him to appreciate the likes of Ross Perot, even when MCR disagreed with him.

So, as Perot warned of "Jobs being sucked out of the country . . ." MCR probably sensed that being lost with the jobs was the unique "Can-do" character that Grandfather's generation had cast as a spell upon Kid Michael.

29th of September, 1993

Mr. Ross Perot
c/- United We Stand America
P.O. Box 516087, Dallas
Texas 75251

Dear Ross,

Please adjust your thinking concerning NAFTA. Your free trade zone in Texas benefits you as a NAFTA free trade treaty would benefit our Country.

It is incomprehensible to me how you can oppose this treaty unless you feel we can not compete. We can compete and we do. Free trade creates wealth for those envolved. Witness Japan and the U.S.A. Without trade, countries become isolated and poor. An example is China in the 1900s and Russia still today, with incredible resources at their disposal.

Please wise up. Your stance on this issue is very distructive. It may appeal to the sweat shops in this country but that is not our future that you so frequently portray.

Sincerely yours,

COPY

Michael C. Rubel
(818- 335-5226

The Perot was a simple talking maverick who brought simplified clipboard education to presidential campaigning. Straightforward, hard working, Marine types heard him loud and clear. So, it wasn't a surprise to often hear MCR wax on, lobby for, and even pen about *The Perot*.

RUBEL FARMS—JANITORIAL ADVOCACY DEPARTMENT

PLEASE VOTE FOR PEROT, HE IS OUR LAST CHANCE FOR RESPONSIBLE GOVERNMENT. REPUBLICAN AND DEMOCRAT ADMINISTRATIONS HAVE BANKRUPTED OUR COUNTRY. SEND A MESSAGE FOR CHANGE. VOTE FOR ROSS PEROT.

VOTING FOR BOXER OR FEINSTEIN IS A VOTE FOR CORRUPTION. FEINSTEIN IS INDICTED ON AN EIGHT MILLION DOLLAR TAX FRAUD CASE, WHICH WILL DRAG THROUGH THE COURTS STARTING NEXT YEAR. BOXER IS ONE OF THE WORST PEOPLE FOR ABUSE WITH THE HOUSE—BANKING SCANDAL. NO MATTER HOW MUCH YOU DISLIKE THEIR OPPONENTS, PLEASE, DO NOT VOTE FOR CORRUPTION BY GIVING THESE TWO HORRORS YOUR VOTE.

REMEMBER HOW I BEGGED EVERYONE NOT TO VOTE FOR CRANSTON???? WELL, IF YOU DID YOU OWE ME ONE.

OF COURSE, FEINSTEIN AND BOXER AND CLINTON WILL WIN. CRANSTON ALWAYS WON TOO. MAY GOD BLESS AMERICA AND PLEASE HURRY.

FROM YOUR LOCAL FARMER, ☺

The good King of Rubelia didn't like dishonesty, as well as swearing, smoking, rudeness, etc. He also didn't like property taxes.

**michael rubel
844 n. live oak
glendora, california
91740**

19TH OF JUNE, 1992
THE JUSTICES OF THE UNITED STATES
SUPREME COURT OF THE UNITED STATES
DC, ONE FIRST STREET N.E.
WASHINGTON, D.C.
20543

DEAR SUPREME COURT JUSTICES,

THANK YOU !   THANK YOU !   THANK YOU !

FOR UPHOLDING CALIFORNIA'S PROPOSITION 13.

YOU HAVE SAVED OUR HOMES FOR US.

WITH GREAT APPRECIATION, I REMAIN,

SINCERELY YOURS,

MICHAEL C. RUBEL

What would you expect from a King and Castle proprietor who didn't collect the taxes and never treated those around him as indentured servants upon which he could build a fiefdom? To a young property holder and King on his way to building castles in the Republic of Rubelia, limiting tax increases to those young 'uns who lived outside his paradise initially seemed fine to him.

But for those who didn't run good kingdoms where its inhabitants could save and build, Michael developed clear feelings.

michael rubel
844 n. live oak
glendora, california
91740

10th of June, 1993

President Bill Clinton
c/- The White House
Washington, D.C.
205" - - "

Sir,

Please show resolve in dealing with the Iraq
challenges going on right now. Give General
Colin Powell the authority to deal with this
small fire before it escalates.

Your propensity for talk and Warren Christopher's
love of negotiation rather than action is a sign
of weakness when dealing with Saddam Hussein.

Please, do not procratinate on this issue!!

Thank you for bringing in David Gergen - - listen
to him please.

Sincerely,

COPY

Michael C. Rubel

What would you expect of a Marine Pharmer who started as a Vietnam War hawk and who seemed to believe, for a while, that the Commies really were coming. During the "Commies are coming!" period, Michael felt his West Coast bastion needed canons on Castle towers, concertina and trip wires on perimeter walls, radar eyes on the perimeter that were hooked into numerous control rooms, and rifles by most every bed.

In the era of despised Sadhams and admired Colins, Rubelia's Head Janitor, who was also a Union Steward, had grown accustomed to wisely advising Presidents. So, Michael wisely advised many *Prezes*.

The advice seem to be going well, until the 43rd President set up what MCR's union, the Amalgamated Union of Janitorial Employed

Savants—Northern Organization (AUJES-NO) [pronounced "Aw, Jez, No!] concluded that George W. Bush's dumpster dumped a fetid haul on their admired Colin.

Michael also sent President Clinton more than a few letters and was happy how Clinton's actions reflected MCR's civic advice. Once Michael thought something through, which sometimes took awhile since he spent so much time tinkering or thinking with his clunky cement mixer, he didn't hesitate to criticize hypocrisy, knowingly confess man's foibles, and recognize how those weaknesses still had to work within a bigger picture. So, Michael wrote the 42nd Prez the following letter.

11th of December, 1998

President Bill Clinton
Mrs. Hillary Clinton
THE WHITE HOUSE
Washington, D.C. 20—"

Dear President Clinton & Hillary,

THANK YOU for all you do. The jackals snarling around your tent have always been in Government. Roman history is an example.

As Mandela tried to convey, the world is appalled at the wasted resources devoted to this investigation.

It must drive your opponents crazy that you are the most popular world leader today.

Thank you again for serving our country.

Yours sincerely,

Michael C. Rubel

cc/ The Judiciary Committee

BE WELL
DO GOOD WORK
AND KEEP IN TOUCH
By Garrison Keillor

MCR's letter inspired the column that follows (which MCR liked), and caused him to repeat one of his worn phrases,

"If it weren't for sex, none of us would be here."

Marin Independent Journal
Marin Voice of 12-11-98

"God knows the truth . . . and He . . . will play out the hand of judgment"

Each fall, marking man's fall, Gabriel and Lucifer gather under puffy clouds around a poker table next to a barbecue pit's molten flames. With a wry smile, God often watches.

With a fiery look under his cocked eyebrow and voicing glee, Lucifer: "We're going to get that sleaze-bag of a lying, adulterous President, aren't we?"

Gabriel: "On our celestial computer, lying gets an awfully high number of hits. And for earthlings, sex has been an attraction since the Garden of Eden. Do you think that will cause Big G to give a Big Willie to you?"

Lucifer: "He's wavered outside his marriage numerous times!"

Gabriel: "Some religions have and condone more than one wife. Should they be condemned?"

Lucifer: "He took advantage of a young thing under his powerful sway!"

Rolling his eyes, Gabriel smiles: "Luc, are you saying this young woman was not sexually sophisticated, and her heavenly arm was twisted?"

Lucifer: "The power of his office was the twist!"

Gabriel: "Power is an aphrodisiac to many juvenile earthlings . . . So should God lump a Willy with those despotic leaders who take whatever women they want, try to rape whole countries, and kill and starve innocents with ease?"

Lucifer: "Course not, give them to me! But flog The Big Dog, and give me him too."

Pausing and looking pensive, Gabriel: "God is wondering how long the flogging should go on."

Lucifer: "Let it go on a long time . . . scares the be-jeezus out of sinners and potential sinners, no?"

Gabriel: "You still think God is about scaring and punishing, not loving, eh? If casting stones at Big Dog's sins goes on much longer, the pious stone throwers may learn how much glass they live behind."

Lucifer: "Then let the castigating go on, and I'll have room for the self-righteous too."

Gabriel: "Perhaps. But God is concerned about what happens to the world's poor and struggling classes, what the terrorists are planning, and what despots are doing with vile and deadly weapons—while the leader of Caesar's world is distracted by having lied about sex."

Lucifer: "God should let the world economy go to hell. Prosperity brings materialism and those comforts cause people to forget your sanctimonious tenets . . . Let the terrorists and despots rain down death and pestilence. Fear and privation makes people behave."

Gabriel: "Perhaps God's view of how earthlings should grow and progress is broader than yours."

Lucifer: "Don't hardships cleanse the soul? Pile the adversity on Clinton. Impeach him. Then let me have the Big Dawg . . ."

Gabriel: Isn't the American impeachment process for 'high crimes and misdemeanors'? Like sabotaging the electoral process, revealing national secrets, selling drugs for guns, and shooting up poor people in another nation without Congressional consent? Well, maybe that last example, like lying and adultery, falls more in God's realm of judgment and concern."

With that remark, Lucifer throws down four Kings. Gabriel responds. "You've had 8 of the last 9 Kings, are you cheating again Lucifer?"

"Course not. Just trying to make some kingly points."

"A point possibly being that 8 of the last 9 American Kings have allegedly had affairs?" Gabriel asks.

As his horns get hornier, Lucifer replies, "It might be that too. And how much hot flesh do I have to show for it?"

"God knows the truth, circumstances, and consequences of those allegations and He, not you or the hubris of earthlings, will play out the hand of judgment . . . ."

As Gabriel rises, "And Lucifer, next fall I'll bring the cards. And the Jokers won't have pitchforks."

The Mill Valley author swears he has never lied, lifted poker cards, or cheated at sex—but prays Ken Starr not spend $50 million checking on him.
(Slightly edited from Marin IJ column of 12-11-98)

So often in the Bush 43 Presidency, you could hear Michael say, "Oh, how we miss Bill Clinton . . . What a mess this Bush has made . . ."

Secretary-General Kofi Annan & Newsman Jim Lehrer

In March of 1998, the UN negotiated, under Kofi Annan an agreement with Iraq that in U.N. Secretary-General Kofi Annan's words:

> "Offers full and unrestricted access for the U.N. inspectors. And we are also being given access and entry into the presidential palaces."

Secretary-General Kofi Annan's competence led to a peaceful deal with Iraqi President Saddam Hussein that averted the kind of war that later contributed mightily to breaking America's economy, bleeding its shrinking middle class, and anguish throughout the world.

On March 4, 1998, Kofi Annan explained the details of the agreement to Margret Warner of The News Hour with Jim Lehrer, one of Michael's favorite news sources.

Near the end of the show, Margret Warner asked:

> *"Finally, as you know, your deal has been criticized by some Republicans in Congress, and you personally. Trent Lott, the Senate Majority Leader, said—he was describing your dealings with Saddam Hussein, and he said you were someone bent on appeasement and someone devoted to building a human relationship with a mass murderer. How do you answer critics like that?"*

"Well, these are rather strong and harsh words. And I'm not even sure if I can comment because I don't know what is behind those statements, because I think what I did was to try to save lives, to try and get Iraq to comply in accordance with the Security Council resolutions. And I think if this effort, which was not an easy one, which entailed quite a lot of risks, to try and get Iraq to comply, to save lives, and to prevent explosion in the Middle East—is going to be described in those terms, then of course we have different objectives. I know that some people on the Hill have a different idea as to how Iraq and President Saddam Hussein should be handled. That is not my concern. I am guided by Security Council resolutions. Yesterday, on the Larry King Show I was asked: Some people say the President must be taken out. And I explained, quite candidly, that the U.N. is not in the business of taking out any president, this or that president out. In our organization that is illegal. And I have no mandate from the Council. And so for those who think that should be the objective, whatever you do short of that is failure, is appeasement, and is weakness. And so I don't think there is anything else I can say."
http://www.pbs.org/newshour/bb/middle_east/jan-june98/annan_3-4.html

The next day, Michael C. Rubel sent his Happy Dragon and Castle letterhead, along with his Rubelian coat of arms with two simple declarative sentences:

5th of March 1998

Dear Mr. Annan,

Your clarity in communicating is truly remarkable.
Thank you very much for serving the world!!

Very truly yours,

Michael C. Rubel

Republican Leader Dick Army

Remember Dick Army? If you don't remember him from the Bush II years then maybe you know him from the 21st century Tea Parties, or as chief puppeteer for those who yell and scream at health reform public meetings. Well, Michael also wrote *The Dick* some time back.

Several Rubelian tunnel diggers, who mostly dig the tunnels that go left, saluted Michael's Army letter. Those same hardly paid tunnel blasters, who also believe in unionizing when above ground working on non-Rubelian projects, believe that MCR's letter was the resounding blast that hurt Bush II's House Republican Majority Leader enough for him to resign in 2002. For awhile, some of the younger, minimum wage, left-turn tunnel diggers cheered the collapse of The Dick. Then, the older and wiser diggers showed the younger workers where to dig in newspapers, magazines, and internets, so they could better understand whether such seeming victories would bring light, darkness, or haze at the end of their phun-filled tunnel digging soujourn.

> "Politicians are not deep thinkers and are not bothered by facts."
> Dick Armey, **The Economist,** August 2009

Here's what they unzipped about Dick and how much his shift from Congressional life might shine or darken tunnel diggers' top side lives:

- Almost immediately upon resignation, Dick became one of DC's approximately 13,000+ comfy, registered lobbyists. Dick now cashes big checks for implementing big interests' interests, among his former army of legislation makers. Dick zipped into a senior advisor position with DLA Piper and then left them to arm his own lobbying firm, Freedom Works, which helped organize Fox's blackboarding evangelist Glen Beck's August 28, 2010 Washington, DC rally.

  > "Politics is about 97% fiction and 3% imagination."
  > Dick Armey,
  > **The Economist,**
  > August 2009

- Being specialists in pranks themselves, the tunnel diggers initially chuckled at how Dick's Freedom Works. Dick's Freedom Works organized the "spontaneous" Tea Parties, where people yelled and sreamed against economic and tax policies that would benefit them—but might bother the ranks of the uber rich. Then he parlayed the outfoxed Tea Baggers into crowds—yelling and screamings against health security that would benefit them—but would bother the CEO's of a broad range of health insurance and disability companies. In 2008, these CEO middle men money shufflers had average salaries of about $7 million sans other perks. Of course, the bigger health insurance CEO's had salaries in the $20+ million dollar range.
- The young tunnel diggers thought Dick must be cool. Scare the unknowing folks, get them running, and send them home confused. "Wow, that's what we do to folks who stumble into our lair and don't understand how this Castling sfuff works. And this guy gets paid big bucks and has fun for scaring the unknowing, lost, and confused! Cool!"

Cooler, more seasoned diggers had to explain to the young that such endeavors by lobbyists shaft tunnelers when they surface from phunny Rubelian tunneling to the serious blastings of upper earth.

One world-traveled digger even taught tunnelers about impoverished Ethiopia, Eritrea, and comfortale Dick Army over a caving break for lunch.

"Where is Ethiopia and Eritrea?" asked the helmeted tunnel digger, as he unwrapped his balloney and cheese sandwich wrapped in an old Orwo bread bag.

"On the southeast coast of Africa. Both countries are mired in poverty and for too long have been wasting money on a war with each other."

"So what does that have to do with the cool Dick, who just scares and riles people up at meetings and gets paid big bucks?" asked another young bandanaed digger as he leaned up against a beam with his peeled banana.

"In 2000 the majority Ethiopian government, the one elected by a majority of the voters, established peace with Eritrea, so both nations could instead spend war money on helping their poor peoples."

Removing the banana from his mouth, the digger continued, "Yeah, so what does that have to do with Mr. Army?"

The old timer continued, "Well, Mr. Army enters the scene because Meles Zenawi, the leader of the minority regime in Ethiopia, hires him to disrupt the fragile peace established between the two countries in 2000. Ethiopians and Eritreans alike refer to Dick Army as the million dollar lobbyist for Meles Zenawi's minority regime."

"He makes money lobbying to destroy the peace finally established between two little poor African nations?" asks one of the diggers.

"Yeah, that's how some report Dick Army's lobbying works."

"Not cool," says another after masticating his baloney.

"Remember," said the greying, wrinkled digger, "it takes a thousand people to build a bridge—or a tunnel or a peace—and only one to destroy it."

"Yeah," replied another young tunnel worker, who then repeated one of Grandfather's sayings, "And no lie is more corroborated than the lie that causes a person pain."

Laughter then reverberated through the tunnel as the baloney guy uttered, "What the hell does 'corroborated' mean anyway?"

On hearing all this on the tunnel intercom, Michael just shrugged and mumbled, Grandfather said,

"You can lead a man to Congress,
but you can't make him think."

15th of April, 1998

Representative Richard ARMY
House of Representatives
Washington, D.C.   20"--"

Dear Representative Army,

The outburst over people having affairs bothers me. None
of us would be here if our ancestors did not enjoy themselves;
some of whom behaved secretively.

Rather than condemn people who enjoy themsevles why
not ask for people to resign who have had **NO** affairs.
Relaxed and contented people make much better company
than uptight and tense souls.

We really do need term limits.

Sincerely,

Michael C. Rubel

cc/ The White House

Ignore those boots on the ground

To learn the truth about the trumped-up, economies-wrecking Iraq War, it helps to have time for public television—from C Span Radio to C Span TV—and to be -married to a Claremont Universities Honnold Library librarian. That injection of RLTVL (Radio, Live TV and Librarian) gave the guy with the hurting eyes a fast lane advantage when traveling the bumpy road to truthful, high-minded, smiley-faced civic participation.

So, one day, the guy who once proclaimed himself to be "To the right of Attila the Hun, or Hunn" used his free time, comfortable chair, and C

Span to invite UN Weapons Inspector and fellow Marine Scott Ritter to use his truth-skewering oratorical knife to deepen MCR's civic outlook.

As Michael settled into his chair, Ritter told stories that revolved around how:

- In April 2001, the Republican Congressional Theme Team (TT) invited him to Washington, DC. The Republican TT, responsible for monitoring the ideological pulse of America, was upset that a Republican, former Marine officer, and former Chief UN Weapons Inspector was trashing Bush's evolving Iraq policy.
- He told the Republican TT that the Weapons of Mass Destruction (WMD) case being made against Saddam Hussein and Iraq was made up and did not hold water.
- If Republicans invaded Iraq over a "trumped-up" WMD allegation, they would involve America in a win-less war, destroy the Republican Party's credibility, and turn Congress Democratic.
- Both the House and the Senate should hold truth-seeking hearings on Iraq.
- The Democrats had to do better than the "mealy-mouthed" Joe Biden-led hearings held on Iraq in July-August 2002, where fellow Congressional reps rubber-stamped the President's case for war.
- All the President's men and women should be summoned and grilled on every phrase and word uttered about the Iraqi threat, WMDs, and the need for war.
- The media should be demanding facts to back up the rhetoric that pushes Americans toward trumped-up wars in which Marines needlessly die.

After listening to his fellow Marine, Michael picked up his mighty, incisive, and sometimes phunny pen.

M. C. R.

Michael Clarke Rubel

9-16-2002 Monday

COPY

Mr. Scott Ritterr
c/- C-SPAN RADIO & T.V.
Washington, D.C. 200 " - - "

Dear Scott Ritter,

Listening to you Monday night made so much sense. It always seems harder to wage peace and solutions than to talk war. Your message is so clear, "Allow unconditional U.N. inspection of Iraq or face certain destruction.

Colin Powell has tried to lead everyone in this direction with the administration discounting his effort. Your assessment of using our collective fear towards approving a war is right on the mark.

With Iraq's approval today of unfettered inspection with no conditions is a direct result, I think, of your work. The international community obviously respects you or your meetings in South Africa could not have taken place.

Thank you and hopefully someday the world will thank you.

Sincerely,

Michael C. Rubel

Copies sent to: G. W. Bush; Kofi Annan; Colon Powell; Madeline Albright et all

Michael's sense of civic responsibility came from the sense of right and wrong instilled by old timers, military academy, family, friends, and travels that were mixed and distilled by logical thoughts and conversations. He was blessed playing amidst the riches of California's peaceful great outdoors, where excess wood, junk, and guns could be turned into sometimes less than simple and sensible forts . . . and phun. He played in the world, maybe because his travels taught him how blessed his life was compared to how so many others had to live.

Michael's sense of right and wrong, when merged with his extraordinary capacity to work, travel, converse, and think in a commonsensical way, attracted people. His simple and magnetic attraction built a healthy and phun Pharm community.

Pharmers lived exposed to a mix of beliefs from Grandfather Deuel, Odo Stade, Stanley Baird, Mother Dorothy, George Richards, Lorne Ward, Carl Gunn, Bill Graham, and a cast of San Gabriel Valley and worldly old and younger-timers tweaked by the likes of Emerson, Thoreau, and Don Quixote. The riches of Golden Southern California surrounded them. By day, they worked and recycled aside a Don Quixotic workaholic in a Sanford and Sons junkyard. By night, they often merrily hunkered down under blue-blacked smoggy skies for Walden Pondish story telling.

In a world pushing 7 billion that is proliferating WMDs, gaping disparities, and crazies, how wonderfully healthy it would be to sprout a bunch of these whimsical communities, where people tread lightly on Mother Earth, work hard, are honest, learn from mistakes, and don't take greed or themselves too seriously.

Since such communities wouldn't look like another Camelot, maybe they could be called Rubelots, (Not Rubbishlots, which is closer to what many initially said Rubelia would be.)

The older, exasperated side of MCR could often be heard uttering, "It's hopeless." He'd utter this in reference to maintaining Rubelia, overcoming physical maladies, or dealing with the world's ills. Nonetheless, he still exuded HOPE in his actions, words, stories, and dinner gatherings.

And in the depth of his heart, he saw in children, in the examples set for them, and in their fresh spirit, the answer to so much that ails all of us. In order for children to grow up with a still fresh, young, and innocent spirit, MCR, whether he espoused it or not, lived chunks of his life as though he believed in the power of myths, as well as in Pete Seeger's and Grandfather's words:

"Participation, that's the salvation of the human race."

and

Give animals and children freedom or they'll get run over.

So, it was said

The greatest sin is to hurt someone.

Getting rich quickly has to be hurting someone. It's wrong.

Man is only as big as the things that bother him.

The truth surfaces every 20 years.

Grandfather

Chapter 16

"Children are fragile flowers— don't step on them."

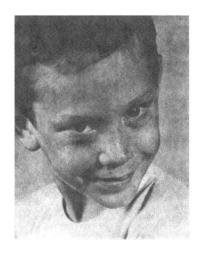

"I'm Mike. I build castles. I'm 9 . . . Everybody dreams of castles now and then, but I build 'em. I'd like the chance to be your General Contractor when you decide you really want to build one."

Their squeaky, innocent, happy voices squeal with delight whether they spill and clean up hot chocolate on a Starbuck's floor, build and knock down their tinker toyed designs, chase balloons, or run around in circles—just because they can. You can spin them cat and mice stories, and they run with them. You can create a Jurassic Park children's book filled with friendly dinosaurs, and they learn a little of what was long ago—and even think dinosaurs are nice pets. You can watch *ET* with them, and they are reminded that even friendly aliens should call home. You can read to them about castles, witches, magicians, good and bad kings, white and black knights, and hope that they grow into good-doers.

All that mostly imaginary stuff, when done with love, will, we hope, form them into wonderful grownup characters.

Imagine then what touring, touching, kicking, and hearing how a real castle was built can do to about 14,286 classrooms of these still purely wonderful little kids. Imagine when they see a whole room filled with trains running through villages, and then find the flat bed of a 1937 truck filled with more trains and villages. Imagine the good stories that can be spun, which goes beyond those supported by mere books and film mimicry.

Whether you be kid Robby, Suzy, Danny, Tammy, Jimmy, Bobby, or . . . exposure to Rubelian Castle building lit and continues to light some wonderful young lights. That's why Michael loved to see classes of kids tour the Castle—especially when led by Pharmhands, docents, or someone other than the tiring Head Janitor. You can see the flicker cast by some of those jolly light and enlightened tours in some of the thank-yous that came Michael's way.

Thank You!!!

June

Dear Mrs. Burbel

Thank you for giving
us a tour around the castle. It is
better then any house I seen. It is
the biggest house I been in. It is the
funest house in been in.

your friend
Nathaniel Paredes

984 Auburn Rd.
Sandimas, CA. 91773
November 4, 1997

Dear Mr Pelel,
I want to thank you for letting us visit you
and your castle last week I had lots of fun
so here is a drawing to show you how much
I appreciate you for letting us visit. Oh yah
I forgot to tell you that my grandma
Wilma Lobb says hi to, and if you
want to call her and talk to her just
call (909)593-2871 thankyou so much I enjoyed
our visit. the best part was the motor cycle
but I liked it all just the same.

~~the~~ your
best,
John Lobb

By Jessica Galindo

I'm a 3rd grade student at Williams School. I have light brown hair and brown eye's. I am nine years old. I bet everyone who has been to your castle has had a very nice time. In my humble opinion your castle was the best! Oh! by the way my name is Jessica Ann Galindo. as you know I'm in Mrs. Bollinger's class. Do you know that I'm doing very good in reading? Well I am.

I love all of your animals too. Your bottle house was great! I mostly liked your printing press. The clock was nice too. I just want to say Thank you very much!

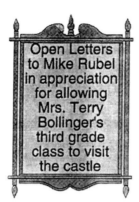

Open Letters to Mike Rubel in appreciation for allowing Mrs. Terry Bollinger's third grade class to visit the castle

By Westley Potter

Thank you for showing us the castle. I like your door and your dogs.

I would like to live there some day. It was funny that you put that stuff in the walls. I like your little house that you had to get away from your mom. I got to go now.

By Kyle Kerr

I liked Catsle, it was awesome. I liked the booby traps like the wire next to the pond and the glass on the wall. My second favorite things were the stuff in the wall. I got two things to say. one is my favorite thing was the bell. the other one is that I appreciate what you let us see because my mom and I always wanted to see what was in there, but now we know. It was fun.

By Therese Montoya

Thank you for letting all of the class come. Well, you're probley wondering who I am. I'm Therese Montoya. I'm in Mrs. Bollinger's class. I think your castle is so neat. I like all the funny things you say. I think your really nice for letting our class come.

Mrs. Bollinger told us all about you. She said, "If we ask a question, sometimes you might have a funny answer." Everybody liked the story that you wrote. Thank you for everything.

By Rita Chavez

Thank you for all the things you showed us. I hope you like living in that house you showed us. I hope my mom takes me there it is a wonderful place. We just finished studying about fairy tales. There ar lots of castles there that's why we went to Rubel farms. I like the bottles and things that were stuck to the walls and I liked the dog's but I was a little afraid of them. And I liked the caboose And I saw the bathtub and the men's bathroom. I saw where they ate and a doll was sitting there.

For children's health, every kid ought to have lots of milk. For everyone's health, every town ought to have at least one castle . . . Ought to have a castle builder . . . Ought to have kids playing at castle building . . . Ought to have growing up grown-ups still trying to stay young.

Got enough milk?

Got enough castles?

Then, you and your community will likely have good health.

> *"You've raised two very successful children.*
> *Let's have fun with this one."*
> Grandfather to Michael's mother on kid Michael

Proof? You want some contemporary proof that even today's kids have some Michael in them?

Sometime in 2010, a mother and her daughter stopped at my Starbucks table where many recognize me as that guy punching letters with his index fingers and said:

> Remember us? You gave the little Castle book to my daughter and Abel. Now my son won't let me throw anything away. He takes everything, even stuff I've thrown away, even the toilet roll, and he piles up stuff and he builds with it . . . I didn't know the book you gave them would do that to him. Now he builds everything with stuff . . . And she (daughter) is cutting out dresses and making things . . . That's how I grew up—building things with Popsicle sticks and just sticks, so I don't want them to forget that . . . Your book has them making things . . . Keep pushing your book. It will click with someone and they'll publish it . . .
>
> Mom with her daughter at Starbucks

So, it was said . . .

My mother was the wisest person.

If she said it once, she must have said it a thousand times—'Harry! Go out and play.'

Grandfather on his mom

If you want your dog run over, keep him pinned up.

Grandfather was always saying give animals and children freedom, or they'll get run over.

Chapter 17

Santa Claus in bib overalls

Throwing Frisbees

Long after plastic gifts once hugged by ribbons and shiny paper are tossed, taught gifts wondrously continue springing back to useful life. Whenever those gifts of teaching are picked up for play or show, grateful and sometimes tearful sentiments arise from the recipient's soul.

Back in his day, grandfather was probably not considered much of an iconoclast. Back then, young, wide-eyed, and wide-open America was filled with a higher percentage of iconoclasts. Grandfather's sayings weren't all originals. Many older hands had passed such insights down in their own craggy and mischievous ways.

Grandfather, along with other admired old-timers, made Michael into a "conservative" Pharmer and benevolent castle ruler, in the most benevolent sense of the "conservative" word. Grandfather Deuel's clan of grandfathers saw a fancy world coming that they probably didn't like much, which grandfather could sum up with . . .

"If you want to worry, buy something shiny."

It would be a dull and tiny book that listed shiny stuff purchased by Michael from marketing gurus designing today's world of fancifully wrapped junk, made for meager pay in a polluted town far away.

Michael traveled the world, learned of its joys and sufferings, and, as Grandfather recommended, let his empathy grow. He worked hard and expected you to do likewise. He lived long and hard enough to mix hundreds of private tears with a billion public laughs and about the same number of shovels of cement, so that his Rubelian Castle walls, its plumbing, and his philosophy would hold water and, knock on wood, withstand earthquakes while echoing *phun stories.*

Michael didn't lose the healthy sense of true conservatism inculcated by Grandfather. Michael hated wastefulness, loved old-fashioned, honest, hard work. He respected the wisdom of the ages and those who taught him to hold those wisdoms near. He liked clean talk, especially if an interesting adventure could be woven through it, at which weaving he was the humble master.

Blathering, ranting right-wingers dominating the media killed the Conservatism Michael believed in. One on one, a smiling Michael would engage in the thoughtful, open, public policy debates crowds of Pharmers would spark decades ago. But amidst crowds who had not thought, worked, and learned the healthy foundations of what came to be MCR's iconoclastic, liberal conservatism, Michael politely remained quieter than he was in the Castle building, healthier, debatable days of yore. In that earlier Golden Era, at the end of a heavy lifting workday, Pharm workers would gather to exercise budding thoughts and vocal cords.

In later recent years, Michael was comfortable being quieter. Much of that stemmed from Michael's desire to keep people happy, which came from Grandfather reminding Michael that:

"Wisdom is depressing. It alters happy perceptions."

Oh, how the country's discourse could use what the Castle had in its Golden Era, and the kind of benevolent Rubelian Ruler that we Pharmers had before in Rubelia's Golden Building Era.

Wisdom may be depressing, but when wisdom isn't used to rebut false "happy perceptions," a community and country can go downhill quickly. The wisdom lacking belief that we are always #1 and leave it to our vested leaders to keep us #1 can leave depressing conditions for the young, as 2008 began teaching more than just our young. Ah, how wonderful it would be if communities across the nation revived healthy Golden Building Eras, where dreams can be built out of recycled junk and healthy debate can commence among builders after a day of sweat where something real was built.

For many, Christmas is a wondrous time of year. My 2007 Christmas letter paid tribute to a creosote stained bib-overalled Santa Claus who gave taught-gifts, inspirations, and phun thoughts that for thinking humanoids are never trashed.

Christmas Letter 2007

Best wishes to you and yours,

Although I didn't know it then, one of my best Christmas gifts arrived after moving into a 400 square foot night watchman's room decades ago as a high school teacher. Walking up and down a termited, rotting, rickety stair case for five months before Christmas arrived, I reflected on being a tool-less, clueless Cleveland St. Ignatius High guy, who was never exposed to shop classes; son of a super hard working dad, who since thirteen cared for his polio stricken father, delivered newspapers, and had little time for hobbies or other skill building; a Peace Corps Volunteer, who was saddened by how poorly so much of the world had to live; a rookie teacher, who had only a single, deadly boring college class on teaching, but who figured that theory stuff didn't matter as much as delivering feelings and real world experiences in a classroom.

My little Rubelian rental, formerly a night watchman's room, was skinned and roofed in creosoted sheet metal. Beneath it, in open and closed garages, were Model T's, as well as a Hudson, Packard and about eight old trucks from the 1920-40's.

Across the way, more old trucks sat underneath Glen's Box Factory and next to a pristine carpenter's shop, where Glen toyed making something handsome everyday.

Sheet metal buildings were about all the 2.5 acre Rubel Pharm had to live in back then, which had been bought from Al Bourne, owner of Singer Sewing Machine, by a kid whose life experiences hinged on building forts and traveling the world a dozen plus times chasing Castles and falling into adventures.

John Steinbeck could have used what had been Al Bourne's Lemon and Citrus Packing factory to depict scenes from Grapes of Wrath. He could have used Michael's adventures to pen captivating adventures.

Every day we five guys, who lived on this tinny Phunny Pharm, would cross paths amidst the tools, antiques, piled railroad ties, stacked lumber, free-range chickens, dogs, peacocks, goldfish, etc. But two giants defined the Pharm back then. One, barrel-chested and usually encased in overalls, served as Head Janitor and King. The other, plain shirted, unassuming, and quiet, served as Chief Architect.

Michael was a perfectly sized Santa. His Pharm was filled with ancient tools—that could make happy toys. In the Big Kitchen's rafters, he even had all the harnesses, straps, and buckles to strap the reindeers to Santa's wagon.

Michael, like Santa, was an old world gift giver. To those willing to work hard and be good, he gave and gave.

Michael didn't give you fancily wrapped stuff that goaded the Jones to buy more. He gave things that counted in life—skills that lasted, feelings that warmed your heart, views often forgotten. Michael would not have fit in Vance Packard's "buy more junk" books. He was a lot different from what much of America was being marketed to become.

Even on his dressy days, Michael's clothes came via Salvation Army. Properly so, since he seemed to be teaching and building his own Salvation Army out of those who came to help him build forts and castles.

This Santa Claus, usually disguised under a stinky, creosoted hat, flannel shirts, non-matching socks, and often mismatched shoes, gave us the joys of his unending stories from his reindeerish world travels. He gave us tool sheds full of tool-toys to play with, a fort to build in an uncorked reservoir from whose dry state sprouted a seven story castle made by Pharmers of wine bottles and recycled junk, which even princely Prince Philip loved.

This Don Quixote rode us through a time warp back into childhood. And to the hundreds who worked, ate, drank, swapped stories, and shared some lies with Michael Clark Rubel, none of us ever heard another ever utter anything but heart-warming words about Kaia's Mykee.

Whoever makes the amazing universe that Hubble photos marvels our eyes with makes too few MyKees. Those of us blessed with rubbing shoulders, piling rocks, using decrepit tools, climbing OSHA-failing scaffolds, lifting wine jars, eating steaks . . . with him are bigger, stronger, wiser, funnier, and hopefully more considerate for having been blessed with a sprinkle of his time.

In his own phunny way, he mentored us on how our hands could work with our hearts, heads, and funny bones. He taught us how to temper or erase mean words. He lectured us against using bad words. He showed us the meaning of living and singing like a soused and happy Fox after a hard day's work. He grew fortress pilings into Happy Phunny Castle buildings. When the real world said such dreams were dumb and not allowed, he'd just plough ahead with that little kid's twinkle and attitude.

Don Quixote may have inspired him, but he was also a real Santa Claus, a giver of true gifts.

The Big Clock Maker in the Sky gave me great parents who from my first Christmas on scrimped, worked, and saved to send my sister and me to great schools, to play on great teams, and allowed us to add

inspiring stories to each successive Christmas. Mom wondered why, with degrees Piled Higher and Deeper, I loved living on a phunny Pharm more cluttered than Sanford and Sons' junk yard, in a house framed out of used rail road ties, dismantled barns, and recycled beams, rather than in a fancy complex. But long before they went to heaven, mom and dad realized that what Michael and the Rubelian Pharm &

Castle Crew taught kids like me was much more important than what degrees and pedigreed living generally bestowed. High school graduate Michael's spirit taught us that zestfully using one's hands, head, heart, and imagination was a bigger key to opening heavy doors than any degree or pedigree.

Without a price tag attached, but often with some sweat and muscle, every day Michael gave all of us treasured Christmas gifts and Yule Tide stories we could keep, as long as we can remember. Only a giant of a man was big enough to give such gifts away every day. Many of us will selfishly try to shine, embellish, and keep those gifts from rusting, for we so liked Mykee's way.

On October 15 2007, Michael's energy went into the cosmos. Where he figured you went and spun around, "Something like electricity."

Hey, Mykee, keep checking on us. Make sure we return our tools, and zap us with some of your boundlessly good energy, especially when we need it to measure up or spread laughs around.

May you all have treasured Santa Clauses like Michael in your lives.

May Christmas and the New Year be healthy for you and yours.

Dwayne . . . :>)

If for phun in heaven . . .

Grownups and kids come by to play with you mixing cement in clunky mixers, piling rocks real high, and shielding everything with what lots of people think is junk . . .

If for phun in heaven . . .

Visitors come by just to be with you, and you give them jars, shrimp cocktail glasses, and chipped vials in which you serve them lots of orange juice, wine, milk, and Bombay Tea—flavored with lots of honey, milk, and bottom laying tea leaves, next to a plate with sliced Pharm avocados juiced with lemons and salted with peppers . . .

If for phun in heaven . . .

Friends and strangers drop in goading you to tell a few stories about your myriad earthly vagabondings . . .

If for phun in heaven . . .

All these people come by for your parties and ply you with wine in hopes you will drink enough to sing "The Fox-Oh . . ." And if on some of those nights the puffy clouds of heaven bounce in cadence with you're out-of-rhythm dangling hands and arms swinging from your barreled torso, while joyously bellowing your voice to the escapades of an animated Fox . . .

> The Fox went out on a chilly night,
> He prayed for them to give him light,
> For he'd many a mile to go that night,
> Before he reached the town-o, town-o, town-o,
> He'd many a mile to go that night,
> Before he reached the town-o,
>
> He ran till he came to a great big pen,
> Where the ducks and geese were put therein,
> "A couple of you will grease my chin,
> Before I leave this town-o, town-o, town-o.
> A couple of you will grease my chin,
> Before I leave this town-o."
>
> He grabbed a Grey goose by the neck,
> Throwed a duck across his back,
> He didn't mind her quack, quack, quack,
> And their legs dangling down-o, down-o, down-o,
> He didn't mind their quack, quack, quack,
> And their legs a-dangling down-o . . .

If for phun—or real . . .

There is a heaven, one of its phunnest inmates to hang with, the one to whom its souls and angels gravitate, will be Glendora's portly creosoted Pharmer singing—The Fox-Oh, Fox-Oh . . . It will be for him for whom the Castle Tower chimes toll . . . For him for whom those bells roll.

With God being what He/She must be, I reckon that He has designed a huge, green, recycled, buggy-driven subdivision, wherein MCR's jovial castling, bemusing story telling, happy partying, conversational drinking, and hearty eating . . . goes on all day amidst happy dogs lying and playing as geese, peacocks, chickens, ducks, and horses meander about . . . around a heavenly castle whose stones are fluffy clouds and concertina free . . .

Thanks, God, for sending into the lives of so many of us an arc-welding Archangel Michael to preview for some of us mere Rubelians earthlings a little bit of what heaven can be.

So, it was said . . .

Ho! Ho! Ho . . . Merry Christmas, kids!
Repeated Santa Claus (aka Michael) from atop the Glendora Fire
Truck for so many Christmases, as he tossed balloons and frisbees,
embossed with "Rubel Pharms," to kids along Glendora Avenue.

The greatest joy is the joy that I have given.

The greatest pain is the pain that I have caused.

*Offending others is stupid—don't
bother people with the truth.*

*Don't bore people with the truth—
laughter is the song of men.*

*"Now, Michael, I want you to learn
something, just be quiet."*

Grandfather

Chapter 18

Moving up

**Life is difficult. If it were easy—everyone
would still be alive.**
Grandfather

Yes, Grandfather Deuel used to say that. But "Life is difficult" was not an expression often used by MCR, probably because it was overwhelmed by "Work is fun," which often made "Safety Third" and MCR so much phun to work, eat, drink, and just hang with.

Of course, its limited quoted use may have also had something to do with how Marine Rubel's body replicated a Humvee's design.

His well-armed and armored torso—topped with a battle-scarred Pharm hat, twitching fingers held in the air acting like radars, synchronized with his darting, smiling headlights, pushed by Sally's Army shoes—seemed to make heavy load carrying easier, especially when you had to help MCR move cement, rocks, beams, or telephone poles.

But alas, whoever designed our bodily machines didn't exempt Michael's hard charging engine and parts from wearing down.

Yes, Grandfather also used to say,

"The final journey is death—a great adventure."
Grandfather

Instead, when he was pushed into talking about the after life, MCR reluctantly theorized that the after life might be a place where, "Maybe we . . ." post mortem mortals zing around like "electricity . . ." in the cosmos.

Twitching and playing his fingers as though there was an invisible piano sitting shoulder high in front of him, he once said, "Maybe our energy goes back up somewhere, circling around . . ." and touching his fingers together, he then made a gentle ignition-like clap explosion. "Poof! And then it zooms around until it comes back down, and someone else gets zapped with that energy . . . But what do I know?" he'd add with a laugh and roll of his eyes, "I hardly know anything about anything. And I've been wrong on just about everything."

Both Grandfather and Michael had a Twainish take on the world. When they spoke, people listened.

When Twain spoke, much of the world listened, including Grandfather. When Grandfather spoke, Michael listened. When Michael spoke, many Pharmers listened. Ipso facto, if zapping from space has something to do with the after and present life, maybe Mark Twain, Grandfather Deuel, and Michael Rubel were jolted by some good, lively, quixotic souls who soared years before them into the cosmos.

If Michael's post mortal theory is anywhere near correct, then our little crowded 21st century Earth could use lots of zapping from the likes of Twain, Grandfather, and Michael. May such healthy electrical zapping dramatically outnumber the charging of the crazy souls doing little good and evil down here. Lately, there seem to be too many of those crazies on our crowded little globe. For, as Grandfather said,

**"It takes a thousand people to build a bridge
and only one to destroy it."**

Certainly, Twain's words,

*"Let us endeavor to live so that when we die
even the undertaker is sorry,"*

applied to all those who rubbed shoulders with Michael's earthy and eccentric electricity.

So often, sitting on the deck with the humming birds, old chairs, orange crate stools, sipping orange juice from glass jars, listening to the Castle's elevator music from a 1940's radio, priming MCR for yarn telling with a bevy of questions, MCR would sum up his years of lifting with . . .

"The castle is a young man's dream and an old man's nightmare."

So often, you could be discussing politics, greed, and sad happenings, and MCR would change the course of the conversation to something lighter and funnier. It would remind you of the attitude implanted in MCR's little black notebook filled with Grandfather's words . . .

"Laugh at yourself—Taking yourself seriously means you have not looked at the heavens."

No matter where one roamed around the Pharm, one could find cause to laugh, be it in looking through a tunnel lined with cemented bottles encasing pictures of Hollywood starlets to the . . .

- Harley cemented in the Castle wall,
- Tin-reservoired swimming pool stocked with gargantuan gold fish and connected to the,
- Neighbor's swimming pool and Pharm's wooden washing machines rollickingly powered by a windmill,
- Ship engines powering birdbaths to the Tin Palace's Coo-coo Clocks of old doubling as radar devices . . .

Rubelia's chiseled spirit

Even on Rubelia's Cemetery grounds, Michael's spirit gave pause and cause to laugh. On such hallowed ground, under the shade of sometimes thirsty orange and avocado trees, Grandfather's words and spirit was chiseled onto tombstones in the Pharm cemetery.

"4 slugs from a 44 . . . no less, no more."
Lester Moore's tombstone

"I told them I was sick."
Maude "Auntie" Baxter's tombstone

Yes, even the cemetery, perched behind the Red Caboose, which cleared entry through the massive Pharm gate with just 3 inches to spare, reminded us to approach life with Michael's twinkle, smile, and attitude. But for his best friend, it was still a wrenching loss to bear . . .

"You know, when you were a kid in the school yard and all your friends and your boyfriend left you? You felt like you were ditched. That's the way I feel without my best friend being here. Feel ditched."
Kaia Rubel 12-1-07

Even in moving on and upward, ever polite but jolly Michael's spirit still manages to produce ☺ ☺, as the polite shriek from the lady, standing aside our red caboose reminded us on MCR's 2008 Memorial Day.

Looking down to see why her red high heels felt so solidly grounded in a Rubelian Cemetery, she shrieked. With celebrants and Pharmers coming to her rescue, they all peered down to the marbled stage beneath her patent leathered high-heeled feet, standing where a Scottford designed top stone would soon sit.

Beneath her toes were Ted's Shepherd's words chiseled on Michael Clarke Rubel's tombstone, recycled onto a once used stone from Valley Monuments.

"Please move over! You're standing on my stomach."

**Confessions pried from the Rubelian author
appear in following Appendix.**

APPENDIX . . . or AFTERWORD, according to Dr. Tom King

So, why does this APPENDIX, or Chapter 19, contain a long-winded AFTERWORD? Well, it started with Dr. Tom King saying,

"I would suggest at least one place where you 'come away from the castle' and tell stories more about yourself . . . It could do with a transition leading into a separate chapter—something like:

> 'The reader might like to have a taste of what the Castle Rubelia
> ended up producing in the guy presently writing about it [or
> what he was like separate and apart from his castle identity]
> so here's a tale or two in way of sampling . . .'

So, who is Tom King and why should I listen to him and pen more words herein?

Tom retired from American River College as a Ph.D. Professor of American Literature. Shortly after retirement, he formed a Peace Pyramid group and became a regular contributor at Teach Peace meetings in the Sacramento area. He's authored:

- *TOUCHING: A Study of the Nerve-Ends of the Imagination; BLESSED RAGE FOR ORDER: A Marshalling of Rhetorical Strategies;*
- *THE VERY THING YOUR HEART CRAVES: Essays Aimed at the Realization of Rare Friendship.*

We met at one of David Dionisi's Teach Peace Meetings, to which Gold Star Mom Nadia McCaffrey of the Patrick McCaffrey Foundation had invited me. For a few minutes at that meeting, I spoke of People's

Lobby's work to have Congress introduce and implement its *American World Service Corps (AWSC) Congressional Proposals*. Afterwards, Tom suggested I come to one of his Peace Pyramid meetings. So, during Iraq War II, I drove from the Bay Area to one of his Peace Pyramid gatherings around Sacramento.

I wasn't very diplomatic during our first meeting. My dissipating diplomacy stemmed from a humane rule used at every Peace Pyramid meeting. This rule gave every attendee two minutes to express their frustrations with what's wrong with America. When over an hour of griping was added atop two hours of driving, this Pharmer forgot,

"Laugh at yourself—Taking yourself seriously
means you have not looked at the heavens.

So, well into the meeting, I spiritedly expressed my growing frustration to Tom in the kitchen, outside of participants' earshot.

Shortly thereafter, I got to speak, about the working answer to almost all the Peace Pyramid groups' gripes and frustrations about country and world. Two minutes, however, was not near the amount of time such a wonderful buildable AWSC solution deserves. Maybe one can say how fielding twenty-one million Americans volunteers over the ensuing twenty-seven years in their choice of such governmental and non-governmental organizations as the Peace Corps, AmeriCorps, Habitat for Humanity, Head Start, Doctors Without Borders, Red Cross, International Rescue Committee, Oxfam, Mercy Corps, and State Conservation Corps solves the group's gripes; but two minutes is not likely to involve them in helping implement the citizen-initiated legislation that would make it happen.

In a simplified way, the AWSC was just a cost effective way to send 21 million Pharmers to build castles and spread good will and healthy phun throughout the world as well as at home. But it takes more than two minutes to get even Rubelian Pharm volunteers to understand that philosophy, When it is that hard to recruit right leaning Rubelian Pharmers, builders, and doers to help implement the AWSC, imagine how hard it is to move TV watchers, bloggers, and credit carders to become activists, doers, and shovel lifters.

After that initial Peace Pyramid meeting, I was invited to make a keynote address to one of Tom's Peace Pyramids sessions, and to introduce Gold Star Mom Nadia McCaffrey at another. At each of these meetings, Tom seemed immersed in intensely measuring my words. Then one evening, Tom offered to help with People's Lobby's *AWSC Congressional Proposals*. Tom did some writing, editing, spreading of the word, and even got President Bill Clinton to pen supportive words for PLI's effort to introduce and enact the *AWSC Congressional Proposals*. During our phone updates, Tom would sometimes hear me ramble on about the Castle. After burning out on the sluggishness of Congress in enacting a much-needed AWSC, Tom offered instead to proof read the Castle book I had too long delayed while tilting at Congressional and other windmills.

Upon traipsing into the word and picture filled bear trap of *Every Town Needs a Castle,* Tom has probably uttered a few groans. For hiding his hidden groans and providing immense help, I am very grateful.

So, when Tom King spoke . . . I listened and wrote over 20 pages before I decided to stop and send it to Tom. He edited the Afterword and sent it back. I took his edits and did some rewrites and sent it back to Tom, and he responded . . .

> Now for general appraisal. First of all, this thing is really well written, surprising me. By well written I don't mean in terms of prose style, though that is perfectly okay, but in wit, charm, inventiveness, and a sense of what in your experience will entertain a reader—all rare commodities.
>
> Here's a final problem to ponder. In your wrap-up you mention that your afterword has become a bit long in the tooth. That's obvious. But I'm not counseling shortening it. It's all too good to cut. What to do then?
>
> It would be much more reader-friendly if it were chopped up into a series of shorter chapters. But I know—you're thinking, how could I justify a number of chapters about myself when it's only supposed to be an afterword?
>
> One possibility: you could set the afterword apart under the designation APPENDIX after your conclusion. In an appendix, of course, an author can park anything he damn well pleases.
>
> Just an idea. Don't act on this suggestion unless it feels right to you.

So, because Tom King has taught me "In an appendix, of course . . . An author can park anything he damn well pleases!" I am again listening to Tom and parking this AFTERWORD. Now I will try to fulfill some of Tom's September of 2009 emailed words of advice:

> "The reader might like to have a taste of what the Castle Rubelia ended up producing in the guy presently writing about it [or what he was like separate and apart from his castle identity], so here's a tale or two in way of sampling . . ."

Stumbling on MCR's Rubel Pharms

After college, I chose to serve as a Peace Corps (PC) volunteer in Mumbai, India. A few days before leaving to serve, Pete Shimrack, a friend of my folks, Croatian Lodge member, and CEO of a Cleveland bank, planted a few words in my head that stuck.

"Keep your eyes and ears open, maybe you'll learn something."

The slums of Mumbai (Bombay) became an eye and empathy provoking experience and merged with Grandfather Deuel's words:

> *"Experience all the emotions so you can sympathize with others."*

After PC service, I lucked into a Lincoln School Fellowship to attend Claremont Graduate University (CGU) for a Master's Degree and then Ph.D. in Public Finance and Administration.

CGU offered a contrasting eye opening experience. Instead of losing 40 pounds surrounded by teeming masses whose bodies were etched by malnutrition, numbing hunger, and dying, I ate meals in stainless cafeterias teeming with thrown-away food, surrounded by fancy cars, and comfy, pretty female students, who complained about lumpy mashed potatoes.

My Peace Corps education included pondering omnipresent masses of people and Worli Chawls tenement rats scurrying to the blaring cacophony of Indian music amidst 6' high mounds of garbage piled every 20 yards. My first year of Mastering academia exposed me to the tranquility of seeing and hearing grass grow amidst soothing breezes buffeted by the drone of television shows wafting from the porches of professorial looking homes.

Amidst this setting, I received my fourth of five Vietnam War draft notices.

Bingo, went my memory, replaying a CGU seminar class conversation. Mrs. Jeanne Welles, a Board Member of the Glendora Unified School District, was taking the class, and during a break, she asked what I was doing after finishing this Master's degree. I told her I was hoping to vagabond and work around the world some, since the Peace Corps had whetted that appetite. She responded that if I ever felt like teaching, I should consider applying in Glendora, California.

Serving your country . . . in Vietnam

That fourth draft notice brought Mrs. Welles to mind. With summer quickly approaching, I met with Glendora's Assistant Superintendent of Education. He was a very big man, who offered me a chocolate across his large, shiny, unmarred by anything desk, which later reminded me of Grandfather Deuel's observation:

"A clean shop means nothing is being done."

One of his first comments was something like, "You look like you could handle a classroom. Ever play football?"

"Yes," I replied, "in high school and college," as I wondered if Glendora needed an offense or defense run in their classrooms.

He commented that all their appointments had been made, "But maybe something could be done." Then, somehow, he offered me a teaching contract. He seemed surprised when I asked if I could have a few weeks to think about it. Nonetheless, he gave me the contract, stipulating that he needed to know within that time.

Soon I was back in my hometown of Cleveland on mom and dad's phone setting a meeting with the director of my draft board. She said, "Yes, you may come down to discuss your draft notice."

My wonderful mom and dad were second generation, hard working, mostly of Croatian and Serbian vintage, and striving to usher my sister and me into the middle class. I seldom remember them telling me, "Do this . . . or don't do that . . ." In fact, I remember the opposite. Asking mom what she thought I should do about something, she responded, "You are the first in the family to graduate from college. You've got more education than any of us. We can't tell you what to do. You've got to figure it out."

So, my wonderful mom and dad, without a parenting course syllabus, didn't tell me as much as they showed me in their simple, magical, and maybe even unknowing way, what to do. Like so many other sons of wonderful parents, I wish I had not missed so many of their cues.

A few hours after the phone call, I entered a big Selective Service room filled with about 40 desks. Most were laden with typewriters, trays, and papers. In the far left corner was the biggest desk. Behind it sat an officious bespectacled lady. Filing papers in a long row of cabinets behind her was a very good-looking assistant, a babe. No one else seemed to be there on what may have been a Saturday.

For several minutes, I stood in front of the boss lady's desk, behind which sat my image of a well-manicured Mrs. Bartleby the Scrivener. With her coiffed hair piled high, she ignored me in favor of the papers she peered at through her tip-of-the-nose perched glasses. The babe glanced at me several times, as I remained at attention, front, and center. Then the babe flashed an endearing smile, turned her back and, in front of the long row of file cabinets backing the boss lady, soundly slammed close the file cabinet directly behind her boss and then scurried several feet away to another file cabinet. The exploding slam was enough to bounce up the boss lady, so she had no excuse for ignoring me.

"Yes?" she said, looking over the bridge of her glasses.

"I'm the fellow you spoke with on the phone about an hour ago. You told me to come in and talk to you about my draft notice."

Her cold, "Yes," with her return to peering at her paper pile seemed to indicate that I should quickly state what little case I might have.

I told Mrs. Scribner that I had served in the Peace Corps, gone to grad school, and hoped to do something Peace Corps like this year.

She returned to looking at her pile of papers, remained quiet, and finally said, "Or . . . you could serve your country."

I correctly figured she meant in Vietnam.

She continued talking about her one son serving on a ship off Vietnam and the other dropping bombs, or maintaining the jets that do so, or something. At the conclusion of her dissertation about patriotism, it was clear that, unlike mom and dad, she was telling me what I was going to do.

As I readied my salute-less about face with visions of the wild blue yonder in my mind, and she was preparing to lower her spectacles back into another batch of papers, I asked, "What if I were to teach?"

Smugly, she responded, "You would have to have a signed, valid teaching contract to be exempt from the draft for this year."

I thanked her, stepped back, and as Mrs. Scrivener looked down at her papers, nodded my thanks at the beautiful one.

The Battle of the Bulge, God, and Vietnam

Only a few minutes walk from the Federal Selective Service building was a World War II Memorial Fountain dedicated to Cleveland's soldiers who had died defending America. As a kid, my parents had taken me there to show me the chiseled name of Daniel Donoskovic. Around the Battle of the Bulge, Mom and her four sisters had lost their admired brother. My saintly gram and tough, old world grandfather lost their only son. Handsome, smiling pictures, and some treasured letters were all they had to share with us grandkids about their D.R.

At the conclusion of Peace Corps service at the end of the 1960's on the way back to comfortable grad school, I flew into Vietnam. In my crew cut and t-shirt, entering Saigon posed no entry problem. Anyway, I had youthful reasons to go there. I had played college football at Indiana's St. Joseph's College with a crazy tough guy who called himself "The Bear." For some reason, which only God understands, we were on campus during our last senior student days taking our final, final exam.

A omniscient subject, "God and Creation," was a big final exam for me. Without these three religious credits, one couldn't graduate from this Catholic college. Into the final exam, I carried a failing grade. To climb from Dante's abyss, I spent two solid days reading and re-reading the course's pamphlets on said divine subject, as well as kneeling in church a lot. The words of those man-written pamphlets were chiseled onto the tableau of my brain, rubbed into my rosary beads, and primed for regurgitation.

In the classroom on Blue Book judgment day, as some footballers often learn to do, my peripheral vision noted that the nearby sitting Bear peered around quite a bit scouting for answers. The Bear passed (with a B, I think) and enlisted for blocking, tackling, and providing back side protection on Vietnam's unmarked fields, which had no visible goalines.

The Hunn, destined for Peace Corps work, failed. As the last student standing awaiting judgment on my last Blue Book day, Father B. proclaimed that one of my problems was that I thought I was "A BMOC," which to unknowing me he had to explain as what he believed was my self-perceived size as a Man On Campus. He further explained my Blue Book answers suffered from "Malapropisms," which he explained to this vocabulary-challenged student via a story about pirate Madam Malaprop, who butchered the English language by misusing the meaning of words.

He then damningly concluded "You don't understand God!"

This finite BMOC, perhaps a little tired of being belittled to a TMOC as in "Tiny," responded with "Do you think you understand God. Fr. B?"

With that, the 6'6" Fr. B. stood and glared down at me, began his stormy march out the room, down the stairs, and at the double doors tried slamming them toward my following face. Then he flunked me.

While home for several days before my class's graduation ceremonies, I explained my failing grade in "God and Creation" to the person who created me. My Mom's initial gentle response was "Well, it's only one course so don't worry about it."

After explaining the school's rules, her responses grew to:

"You got good grades for four years, went to Mass and Communion four and five times a week, and they aren't going to let you graduate?!"

"All those years we sent money to the Catholic Church and schools and they do this! #!!*#!! (Which was the only time I remember mom string such words together.) That's the last time the Catholic Church will see a dime out of me!"

Discourses on Kant, Descartes, and Spinoza

At St. Joe's Fr. Mazzola was considered one of those brainy priests. Once a year he'd offer his Honors Course to a select crew of upper classmen. Probably in the solitude of prayer, I remembered brainy Fr. Mazzola's Honor's Course, where his discourses on Kant, Descartes, and Spinoza flew way over the heads of most of us bewildered note-taking students. However, what I retained from that class was that it was substitutable for any course on campus. So, as even failed Boy Scouts learn, I prepared for the worst and talked to the college registrar about earthly Honors filling in for my inability to understand God and Creation. With an angry, wounded, and loving mom listening from her table, I made a reconfirming phone call to Fr. Robbins from the phone hanging on her knotty-pined kitchen wall.

Consequently, on Graduation Day, with faculty robed, garmented, and assembled according to height, I watched a livid and bellicose 6'6" Fr. B attack the front of the faculty line only to be talked down by a few chirps from the 5'3" Registrar Fr. Robbins. From a priestly perspective, it might have been the battle of BPOC vs. LPOC.

Perhaps, it was an unconscious attempt to understand God that led me to join the Peace Corps upon graduation. Certainly serving among the poor and hurting forced this LMOE (Little Man on Earth) to readily admit he didn't understand God. And I still don't.

Doing Vietnam—My Way

Going to Vietnam after Peace Corps service gave me an excuse to check up on my best backside practice field protection from what had been some Dark Side thuggish Chicago teammates, whom "The Bear" took on from Day One of his sophomore year transfer to our college football team.

Although Saigon's American KP (food shop) knew of Dick Beiringer, they also knew he was out in the jungle boonies somewhere. The Bear was still scouting for answers and protecting his guys from what he was told was the Dark Side. So, I had to settle for learning about the war from roaming the streets of Vietnam.

While in India, soft-tissued Time Magazine, which accompanied me to all bathroom sit-downs, had taught me some complicated stuff about Vietnam. Time had learned words from LBJ, McNamara, Westmoreland, Clifford, Ball, Fulbright, McCarthy, RFK, etc., and scary theories about Ho Chi Minh winning, Dominoes falling, the world being painted red, etc.

I learned simpler stuff on Saigon's streets and alleys.

Stuff like—Saigon's war is great for prostituting women of all ages, selling American military supplies and other stuff anywhere, being rolled in alleys, manufacturing sandbags, building barricades, structuring walled and bomb proof embassies, bivouacing armed guard all around town, etc. All good stuff, if your goal is to build a wretched, hellish economy.

So, with such stuff rolling around in my head, I walked back into that big Cleveland military employment agency, again stood at attention, and told the chief recruiter, "I've decided to teach this year."

Unmoved, unimpressed, and unflinching, Mrs. Scrivener simply retorted, "You need a valid, signed contract."

I pulled out my Glendora High School contract, signed it, gave it to her, and should have asked that aide to dinner.

So, instead of killing Viet Cong, fighting the Dark Sided Dominoes that fell nowhere, and dealing with the trauma and waste of war, I was soon in sunny and smoggy Glendora looking for a cheap place to live, so I could save that teacher's pay for traveling the world in search of The Force . . . and, oh yeah, understanding God.

Football's Field of Dreams

So, there I was searching for rental housing in Glendora. Listening to my desire for cheap rent, Mr. Fenwick Warner of Warner's Realty, running out of a 400 square foot play house on Glendora Ave near the old post office, suggested a caretaker's cottage (taken) on the hill, his sister Monica Fager's Boarding House (all rooms filled) on East Foothill, and Rubel Pharms.

Elsewhere in this book, I relate how a girlfriend's disdain for a Pharm filled with junk and stained in creosote forced her residing boyfriend to choose between her perfume or barnyard aromas. Consequently, he abandoned the Pharm's night watchman's studio. His choice of the feminine mystique over that of a little creosoted tin shed raised 15" above ground gave me a cheap and *crazy place* to live. Also elsewhere in this book, I mention how Michael didn't want to rent to a guy he figured was, "A commie pinko teacher."

Entrapped by his own set of lived-by, not just talked about, principles, ardent right-winger Michael rented to me after some semi-treacherous laddered testing of my resolve. Forthwith, some in the community tried to prove I was "A commie pinko teacher."

On the other hand, maybe all this "dangerous image and ism" stuff started with that Assistant Superintendent asking, "You look like you could handle a classroom. Ever play any football?"

In that first year, I was also one of a couple coaches helping the Varsity team and coaching the Bee (Sophomore) team. It was fun bringing Cleveland St. Ignatius's (record setting 10 state championship) winning football fundamentals to California kids, and they seemed to like it.

What I also brought to the football field was a fresh goatee. Several weeks into coaching, I was surprised to learn that Glendora High's 21 coaches had taken a vote as to whether coaches should have goatees.

I was told the vote was 20-0. I guess I was told this so I could invest in Gillette blades, but instead I thought like a disturbed teacher, or upset linebacker.

First, I asked some coaches why, since I was a coach, I wasn't invited to this electoral smack down. No satisfactory answer was given.

It's a Matter of Principle,
Glendora Press , September 21, 1969

Is my face the most important factor in judging whether I am a good American, good teacher, or good coach?

Many long-haired and bearded wonders are stereotyped by many Americans as lazy punks, dopers, and rebels. For those long-haired and bearded wonders who are hard working, moralistic, and idealistic, the world soon becomes a prejudiced and hypocritical place.

Most American history teachers have tried to present our nation as one that judges the individual on his efforts not on his "race, color, or creed." Unfortunately, this textbook approach has not always been true, and we must guard against the further spreading of our prejudices.

The fact that I know my football and worked hard to convey it while molding young characters in doing so, in my estimation, means I am a football coach. However, community pressures and a subsequent all-high school coaches voting said a coach does not look the way I do. Coaches do not wear well-kept goatees. The community "image" will not allow it.

The goatee has aided my rapport and ability to communicate to the so-called "hoods" at the high school and has not hindered any other teaching or coaching I have been called upon to do. So on September 11th, I resigned as Assistant Bee football coach, not because I am a rebel looking for trouble or to hurt a football program.

I resigned for a principle. I have been the clean-cut all-American boy who played three sports, was successful in high school and college, served in the Peace Corps, and received a master's degree. I'm not a hippie or a commie, and I am trying to judge others on what I like to be judged on—the effort I put into my job.

Second, some of my classes were asked to describe how Jesus, and several other historical luminaries, was depicted.

Third, in a couple Letters to the Editor in the local papers, readers were asked if they would endorse denying coaching rights to any of those historical luminaries, such as Jesus, because they were hirsute.

This rookie teacher tried to make the case that what I knew about winning football and how I could coach kids had nothing to do with whether I had or didn't have a well-kept goatee. To me, it may have been a teachable moment, but some in the community, administration, and staff weren't ready to learn it.

So, I resigned as football coach.

Unbeknownst at the time, MCR posted his own letter to the school principal, who replied;

"If Mr. Hunn had chosen to remain a coach, very conceivably we would have been left with a one man staff as the others (20) would have quit."

Then the varsity basketball coach asked if I would consider shaving before basketball season started in order to coach the Sophomore Basketball Team.

Then a bunch of my players came to tell me of their teachable and learning moments. "Coach Hunn, we've decided we're going to quit in protest."

I was keen on these kids. I WAS NOT keen on these kids, who filled my classes over the years, giving up their high school football dreams. They listened and remained chasing oblong balls and rainbows on those halcyon fields of high school football green. At season's end, they implored that I come to their banquet where they surprised me with a wood and gold plated Coach's Plaque, which still sits on a wall at home. Thanks guys, if any of you are reading this.

To Glendora High School 9-15-1969

Dear Gentlemen:

Hearing of Mr. Dwayne Hunn and his being disqualified from coaching is serious news.

It is my hope that the administration will take a new look at how to qualify personnel when they select people to instruct our children. Having a beard should not be a consideration.

Sincerely yours,
Michael C. Rubel

Some serendipity came into my last Bee Football game. The bus driver who brought the visiting team happened to be my landlord, Head Janitor Michael Clarke Rubel, who knew next to nothing about football, but who I hoped knew I was not clipping on the football field. And guess what the opposing coach from Alta Loma, Azusa, Covina, or whatever wore on his face? Yeah, and the foreign coach's team with the goatee drubbed Glendora convincingly.

Ain't life ironic? And picturesque. And hairy.

Now the conservative, clean-shaved, part-time bus driver, and Head Janitor of an un-walled 2.5 acre junk yard sitting in the middle of Glendora's most pricey community had another headache—me. And all he really wanted to do was pile walls of rocks and wine bottles in peace, building his little Rubelian dream. Little did the Head Janitor know that more headaches were gathering.

Emerging Nations

In my second year, with great fanfare, Glendora High School (GHS) decided to initiate a new team-taught required course, "Emerging Nations." GHS students were now to learn about "The real world."

Who better to include on the teaching team than a Peace Corps volunteer who had served and traveled in emerging nations, especially when he's got a bevy of slides and stories to share? It was a good three-man team that had 100+ students per class. In exchange for doing the brunt of the presentations, which I loved, my partners did much of the stuff I liked much less—testing, roll taking, assignment checking, etc.

Excerpt from: **Glendora Girl Speaks Out in Favor of Course**, Glendora Press, 4-22-70, Joanne Kelley

I am writing a reply to your article on the controversy over a comparative theories of government course intended to be part of GHS's curriculum next year.

It is high time the school board, not only at the community level, but also at the state level, realizes that high school students are not ignorant of world affairs, political problems or differences between political institutions.

For too long our elders have seemed to think that they are protecting us from some sort of evil demons by keeping our textbooks free of controversial issues or any historical events which may reflect unfavorably on the United States.

The comfortable, conservative, and almost all white GHS students loved learning about emerging nations. The class had a lot of student interaction that revolved around stories, slides, innovative assignments, and Peace Corpsish (PC) insights.

Around this time, I also started writing a series of lengthy articles featured in the Glendora Press about life in India from a PC perspective. For some, however, the PC perspective was not "Politically Correct." For me, they were GD Correct, or Grandfather Deuelishly Correct, for they tried to tap students into the sound old timer's rule:

"Experience all the emotions so you can sympathize with others."

John Birchers hunt commie pinkos

Unfortunately, the powerful San Gabriel Valley John Birch chapter loved neither the writings about life in India, PC insights, nor students' deductions.

After awhile the Glendora Press editor told me he was going to have to close out the popular PC series.

Although Emerging Nations was a very popular class with students, it was cut after one year, which led me back to solo teaching. A proposal to introduce a required course, "Comparative Theories of Government," found a similarly short-lived career, as one of my students pointed out in her Letter to the Editor of the Glendora Press.

Why would some powers in the community power structure want to expose students to Comparative Theories of Government, when a RPCV exposing them to the realities of emerging nations upset their simplistic, pristine view of the world so much?

The last paragraph of the Glendora Press Editorial "Glendora Pushing Backward" tartly warned what an ostrich's approach to world affairs will do. Thirty years later, at the dawning of the 21st century, the world's once undisputed economic and moral power is paying for an ostrich's ignorance of world and domestic needs in trillion dollar spades and with too many lost lives and limbs.

If fingers and time allow, my next book will delve more deeply into how we could recover from this backward approach and peacefully *surge* forward by instead building homespun castles everywhere.

Upon my return to solo teaching, each of my classes was oversubscribed. Luckily,

> **Glendora Pushing Back**, Editorial, San Gabriel Valley Tribune
> *Teachers and administrators who spent all that time in research, in studies, in preparing this "Comparative Theories of Government" course should have known by now that the board wouldn't buy their ideas or recommendations. For the best way to fail is to move backwards. The board seems to be meeting that requirement.*

I had four or more teacher's aides (TAs) per class to cover the roll taking, scoring, handout making, extra coaching, etc. jammed classes required.

Those classes also included lots of reading, discussions, and guest speakers. One of those speakers was the charismatic founder of People's Lobby, Edwin Koupal, who was using the grassroots initiative process to take on the big oil, auto, pesticide, nuclear, and lobbying industries to clean California's environment and reform its political and campaign system (For more information, click to **www.PeoplesLobby.us**). Several times he mesmerized my students, so that my students and I volunteered time in People's Lobby's crusading brand of healthy politics to try to pass the Clean Environment Initiative of 1972 and successfully pass the Political Reform Act of 1974. (For more information on California's

Political Reform Act of 1974 and the Fair Political Practices Commission it established, click to *http://www.fppc.ca.gov/index.html?id=51*)

The Koupal's inculcated People's Lobby's working steering board of 40, of which I was privileged to be one, with such philosophies as:

> *"Complaining, demonstrating, marching, etc., doesn't accomplish much."*

> *"This country runs on laws. If you want to change the country, write its laws."*

> *"Final responsibility rests with the People. Therefore, never is final authority delegated."*

Those philosophies sounded a lot like Grandfather's inculcated Rubelia philosophies:

> *"Don't tell people about the labor pains. Show them the baby."*

> *"You can lead a man to Congress, but you can't make him think."*

> *"If you want a house—build one."*

Some of my guest speakers and the discussions engendered did not sit well with the John Birch Society (JBS). Although I was never invited to attend a JBS meeting, I was told that I was often referred to at their meetings as, "We've got to get rid of that commie pinko teacher at Glendora High who writes articles . . ." For years, I was often told I was #1 on the San Gabriel Valley JBS Hit List.

Flunk 'em all

While the community buzz was growing, my excitable solo class students were not measuring up to the class and home work standards indelibly impressed upon me by Jesuit educators.

My students and visiting students were engaged with the class discussions and guest speakers, but my students were not doing enough reading and writing. So, I flunked what I thought was about 60% of my students at the nine week grading period during my third year, or tenure year, of teaching. In later charges, the administration would correct my flunking estimate.

Students' arguments such as:

"You ask us to do too much work . . ."
"But Mr. Hunn, I did 65% of my work. In Mr. Smith's class that's a C- . . ."

Were answered with:

"How do you expect to get smarter and stronger if you don't read and write?

"At my high school, 71% got you a D-."

"When a contractor builds a house for your family, will you be satisfied to know that he put in just 70% of the needed nails?"

Upon giving my students their flunking notices, I also gave them a long Extra Credit Book Report reading list, which upset Glendora High's administration and the Birchers. I also sent my students home with a letter for them and their parents, which you'll see in a few pages.

Bad Books

Shortly after issuing the Extra Credit Book Reading List to my attentive classes filled with popular "Socs," talented "Jocks," interested "Students," and hilarious Mountain View "Gang" types, I was summoned to talk to the Head Librarian. The talk went something like this:

"Hi, what's ups?"

"It's about your book list," she says.

"What about it?"

"You need to remove some books from it."

"What?"

"Just a few," she says.

"Which few?"

The books were:

- *Up the Organization Ladder*, the story about what families need to do to climb the corporate ladder to success.

- *Soul on Ice*, the story about Black Panther Eldridge Cleaver's take on how America's white man's land was run, which included some bad words and plenty of anger.
- *The Last Temptation of Christ*, the story of a loving, compassionate, and human Christ written by a man steeped in religious training.

I asked this very competent and influential administrator if she had read those books. I believe she said she had. I asked her what she thought of *Last Tempttion of Christ*, which I read more than once and was one of my all time favorites. Even as a convert to Christianity, she thought it was a wonderful book.

Dutifully, I went back to my classrooms and did what was best for God, country, students, and little bookstores.

Each class then heard something like this:

"Pull out your Extra Credit Book List.

"There are three books on the list that you are not allowed to read. You CAN NOT read these books! Scratch them from your lists and don't dare read them!"

Yep, my unusual authoritarian and doctrinaire air got plenty of attention. Even got some questions, which were fun to answer in early flippant and flappable versions of Robert Colbert or Jon Stewart. Certainly, I reminded them that there were people smarter than me who knew exactly what they should and shouldn't read. Certainly, I reminded them that they had been saved from hellish brim fire and damnation by avoiding such readings.

Glendora's Village Book Store

I often stopped by the Village Book Store to kibbutz with Dick Look, an avid desert hiker and well-versed guy, who ran the store. Nonetheless, a cold call at home from him might have been unanticipated. Dick's cold call went something like this:

"Dwayne, if you have your student assignments on a deadline, I hope you'll give them a little extra time. We've never had such a run on books as we got from your students today. We've had to back order three of the books you've assigned. It shouldn't take too long to get them in, . . ."

"No problem, Dick. They have plenty of time to read 'em after you get them in. But thanks for telling me."

Of course, Michael, with his antennae throughout the community, heard of this book banning and discussion ensued with the Head Janitor who read and loved such early dangerous writers as Emerson and Thoreau.

What did a junk yard janitor, who wore bib overalls 93.2% of the time and whose fashionable clothes came from Salvation Army, know about following rules to dress fashionably, marry properly, and party correctly in order to climb *Up the Organization Ladder*? Not much.

What critique would a Benevolent Castle Ruler who developed, without seeking, a band of Rubelian apostles, have to cast upon a humane human Jesus? Nothing.

What would Michael say about an angry and profane *Soul on Ice*? Well, there Michael had something to say. With ardent and often expressed disdain for profanity, Michael had expressed his disgust for the four lettered words often used in the book. At that stage in his life, Michael also derided the abilities of those tanned with darker pigments.

Oh, how life, love, marriage, grand children, and time so dramatically changed that perspective. Ain't life ironic? And picturesque? And full of color?

Michael said, "Kids will read what they want to," and chuckled about how the book banning spiked village book sales, something like peacock banning spiked village citizen politicking to ensure peacocks' freedom of assembly.

After awhile, when the headaches of my bungling building efforts inside Rubelia's walls were added to those caused by my out-of-the-box coaching, PC insights, classroom teachings, book bannings, etc., Michael reverted to Grandfather's words.

"Notice how the Willow tree survives? It bends."

In other words, Michael became inured to what some might consider my bothersome antics. Instead of viewing me as a persistent headache to him and his castle vision, with a shrug and accepting smile, Michael tagged me as the "Pharm's Crusader Rabbit."

He let the rabbit dig his own holes. It was one of the wisdoms Michael had learned from Grandfather. It was one of the reasons MCR was both Head Janitor and King of Rubelia. Smart thinking by the King, for I was about to roll some bigger headaches onto the Janitor, Landlord, and King of Rubelia's papyrus rolls,

Sometimes Michael would wonder aloud if Crusader Rabbit had dug too many deep holes. Thankfully, such expressions would usually be followed with chuckles, jokes, stories, or laughter.

One of those bigger headaches happened during March of 1972, the year in which I was to receive tenure as a teacher. Although a very popular teacher backed with a file of stellar teaching evaluations, I knew I had stirred some political bees in the community's power hives. That's what I was thinking about after slipping home on my Honda 350, lying on my waterbed, staring at the recycled tar stained ceiling prior to my 4:30 evaluation appointment with the principal. Even though there were plenty of early signs that some wanted to silence or get rid of me, I was probably too dumb or having too much fun to notice. However, with a sympathetic mind, I figured that for the principal, like the King of Rubelia, I had caused a few extra headaches. So, shortly after climbing back on my Honda, I was sitting in the principal's office where, after some formalities, the early version of Donald Trump's show was born.

Local Board No. 230-B   March 5, 1970
Selective Service System
769 Federal Office Building
1240 Eat 9th Street   570
Cleveland, Ohio 44199

Gentlemen:

Please note copy of contract enclosed for September 1, 1969-June 30, 1970. We have not as yet awarded Mr. Hunn a contract for 1970-71.

I cannot in good conscience request a deferment. There is no shortage of social studies teachers in California.

Sincerely yours,

Richard H. Brautigam, Ed. D.
Assistant Superintendent—Personnel

P.S. We would prefer not to lose him this spring, but have no recommendation for the fall. RHB/mfb

---

"You're Fired!"
(Which would be heard again)

My laughter seemed to bewilder the principal, so I related how I had come down here to tell him how I was going to work at causing him fewer headaches, reducing community pressures he must be feeling from my teaching, my People's Lobby's work on their Clean Environment Initiatives and Political Reform Act, my anti-Vietnam War leadership in the San Gabriel Valley, etc.

"And you tell me, 'I'm fired.' It's ironic and funny."

He sat there as though he just got up from a blindsided quarterback sack and didn't know which huddle to join.

"Just what are my charges?" which was a question I would repeat a few years later, while bumping heads with similarly helmeted administrators with my work as an early hire to start up the California Conservation Corps (CCC).

He responded that since I was a non-tenured teacher he'd rather not get into that. He added something

> **NOTICE OF ACCUSATION,**
> March 23, 1972
>
> On November 14, 1969, the Respondent failed to leave a seating chart and lesson plans for his sixth period class. Said failure placed undue hardship upon the class and the substitute teacher assigned.

about how by leaving quietly I could go with a clean record that would not harm my future chances of teaching, which was a similar mantra slipped out by the CCC's Human Resource Director years later.

My laughter, smiles, and handshake seemed to stun not only the Principal but his assistant, who seemed glued to the wall, as I opened the principal's door to pick up my helmet and ride back through the breeze into the zany security of Fortress Rubelia.

My March 13, 1972 *NOTICE OF RECOMMENDATION NOT TO REEMPLOY PROBATIONARY TEACHER* listed reasons such as:

- Lack of proper organization of work and presentation to pupils of subject matter . . .
- Failure to comply with rules and regulations and to submit records and reports as required . . .

> **NOTICE OF ACCUSATION,**
> March 23, 1972
>
> On December in 17, 1969, Respondent arrived on campus in cut-off trousers and T-shirt and in a dirty and in a rumpled condition.

- Lack of courtesy in contacts with pupils, co-workers, and community and lack of personal cleanliness and poor grooming . . .

These reasons evolved into courtroom bantered charges revolving around:

- Ineffective teacher.
- Pro-black god, anti-white Jesus Christ.
- Typographical errors.
- Bad odor.
- Cuss words.
- Lack of proper patriotism.

> **NOTICE OF ACCUSATION,**
> March 23, 1972
>
> On January 26, 1970, Respondent arrived at a faculty meeting and remained there dressed in dirty physical education clothes. His personal cleanliness was deficient as evidenced by a strong body odor.

To some the dismissal might be explained like this.

Mr. Hunn, although extremely popular with naive students, is an incompetent because he flunked 46% of his students at a nine week grading cycle, failed to fill out forms properly, came to a faculty meeting after playing basketball with students where we're positive he stunk both in the cavernous faculty/band room as well as on the court; had typographical errors and cuss words in his stack of handouts copied from books; and because he exposed his students to published concepts questioning white and Christian superiority, and talked too much about poverty and the cost of warfare; we are damn sure he's an evil commie and must be fired.

> **Former student letter to Glendora Press Letter to Editor**
>
> Mr. Hunn is just a professional killjoy. Off with his head, I say, he is smashing up my rose-colored glasses. After all, we have enough trouble in our own lives without knowing about everybody else's problems, right, Mr. (Principal).

Some of my artful, ironic, and stealthfull students (acquiring the principal's official stationery, distributing an underground student newspaper, etc.) further developed their creative writing and poetry abilities, without any coaching by me, during the year of firing.

When these teaching travails were brought up around Pharm discussions, Michael occasionally responded about how difficult or impossible it was "To fight City Hall." At least once that led Michael to suggesting, or was it urging, "Why don't you just leave and do something else?'

Superman or . . .

It wasn't long before I got to know some wonderful, stellar, non-Pharm characters that one needs in *fighting City Hall* or scaling outside world walls.

- John Muraski, President of the American Federation of Teachers Union (AFT).
- GHS Counselor David Christensen and fellow teacher Chuck Scherf, who were un-intimidated in standing beside me against the administration.
- A raft of students who never wavered and some who cut school and a couple who even took the witness stand at my Hearing Dismissal, such as David McElwee and Diana O'Brien.
- And an LA version of Attorney Clarence Darrow.

Glendora Unified School District
352 North Wabash Ave * Glendora, California
Tel. (213) 963-1611

Office of the Principal
Glendora High School
1600 East Foothill Blvd.
Glendora, CA 91740

Memo: <u>To all teachers</u>

Dear Staff:

In view of the fact that Mr. Hunn has proven himself to be a disruptive influence on the processes of education, I wish to urge you to consider the consequences of such a disruption. Please note the fact that he is out of a job at the end of this school year and it is also unlikely that he will be able to obtain another teaching position elsewhere.

I also wish to remind you that you are indeed judged by the company that you keep and it would be wise not to expose yourself to comment by the administration concerning a friendly relationship between yourself and this man.

So, I urge you, in the name of your job, to drop all association with Mr. Hunn, as his foolish vagaries and wild ways have shown us that he is indeed unfit to teach.

Tris E. Windbag, your boss
TEW/sd

John Muraski urged, and my Clarence Darrow required me, to write responses to everything in my personnel file, which I did in what I thought was a tart, cutting, and witty style. Of course, some of those writings had typographical errors.

With some of these writings in hand, John and I had a 30 minute meeting with a young attorney from the firm of Levy and Van Bourg, whom the AFT retained for their legal work.

As weeks went by, I also met with Paul Conforti, former Glendora High teacher turned attorney, who said, "If you want to win this trial, your attorney should be doing about 500 hours of discovery, interviewing a bunch of people, prepping for the trial . . ."

Part of the lack of such prep stemmed from the fact that this particular year was a heavy year for firing teachers. That probably had much to do with a freshly minted state law, which according to administrators, required teachers to teach to specifically quantified goals. That kind of teaching gears teachers to rote memory work and inspiring kids to choose A, B, C, D, or E, after you've proved your ability to guess between T and F on a paper test; but inspired students to learn little about deciphering between True and False in the Real World.

I wouldn't be a standardized teacher.

My attorney, Jack Levine, was backed up trying to be public defender to a bigger batch than usual of evil, conspiratorial teachers who perceived teaching similarly. Such was the discussion Chuck Scherf and I were having in an empty teachers lounge when the phone rang for me. The caller introduced himself, and something like the following ensued.

"I've been reading your responses to the charges against you. Find your case very interesting. Jack Levine has been swamped with cases and I wonder, Mr. Hunn, if you would mind if I picked up this case instead?"

"Excuse me, did you say your name was Abe Levy?"

"Yes, Abe Levy."

"Abe Levy, as in Levy and Van Bourg?"

"Yes, this is my firm. I have 40 attorneys working for me and . . ."

". . . I don't mind at all, Mr. Levy."

Shortly, thereafter I recall meeting for about 30 minutes in Mr. Levy's office, which had a couple pictures of the star of the then popular Billy Jack movies prominently displayed. After discussing issues around my trial, we talked of his friendship with writer, director, and actor Tom Laughlin who played Billy Jack in the same named movie, which in the 1970's was the highest-grossing independent film of all time. Maybe that's what inspired me to see the Billy Jack movies, the star of which remains a social and political activist to this day.

Weeks went by. With the trial date just a couple weeks away, Chuck Scherf and I were again sitting in an empty teachers lounge, I called Mr. Levy. I brought up what Attorney Conforti had said about the need to do 500 hours of legal discovery. I stressed that finding another job wasn't my primary concern. Losing to phonies on phony charges was.

Mr. Levy politely listened. After I cooled down, there was a pause. Mr. Levy replied, "Dwayne, let me tell you something. I've been doing this for 30 years. I could go into that courtroom without knowing one God-damn thing and get the job done . . .

"I'll see you Tuesday morning. Bring the stuff I asked you to do."

When I hung up, Chuck noticed my stare into space and asked, "What's wrong?"

"Well, either I'm screwed . . . or I got Superman for an attorney."

Mr. Hunn, do you have representation?

The accusations filed against me were heard by Hearing Officer Helen T. Gallagher of the Office of Administrative Hearings in Los Angeles on May 30, 31, and June 1, 1972.

On May 30th, Officer Gallagher twice entered the hearing room after 9:00 a.m. from the door behind her presiding judge's seat. She noted that Deputy County Counsel, David Brier, and their administrative witnesses were ready to go. She also noted that AFT President John Muraski and I sat alone on the defendants side, with a few students seated in the back. After her second entry, Judge Gallagher asked,

"Mr. Hunn, do you have legal representation?"

"Yes, your honor."

"Perhaps you had better call to make sure."

Borrowing change from John, I went down the hall in search of a phone booth and around the corner came the diminutive Mr. Levy, talking as though a cigar was dangling from his mouth. In fact, he may have had an unlit cigar dangling from there.

"Hiya, Dwayne. How're ya? . . . Good, good . . . Did you write up that stuff? . . . . Good, Good . . . Where is it? . . . Good. I'll take a look at it when we get in there . . ."

Judge Gallagher was happy to see my late attorney, and seemed to recognize him.

The hearing began with the County promising to prove the incompetency of this bungling Pharmer. The DA then commenced to present the outstanding resumes and credentials of Principal, Assistant

Superintendent, Vice Principal, etc., who were well prepped and dressed to prove my incompetence.

While the accusers' learned presentations went on, Abe Levy read my pages of accusation rebuttals. Seemingly oblivious to their opening remarks, periodically he'd lean against me after reading something I had written to whisper, "That's funny . . ."

After their long and learned opening, Mr. Levy's driven and determined opening went something like this.

"Your Honor, as you know, it's a very warm LA day. We could be in for a very long day, so I wonder if you would mind if . . . I removed my suit coat?'

A smiling judge said, "That would be fine, Mr. Levy."

And as Mr. Levy draped his coat over a chair and patiently rolled up the sleeves of his white shirt, he began etching himself as my Clarence Darrow.

As that first day ended, and John and I walked down the hall with Mr. Levy, he informed us that his wife wanted "To go to the opera tonight," and I needed to write up some answers to some of the things that were said today.

"See you tomorrow morning," said my Clarence, as he sauntered off to ponder winning concertos.

So, I went back to my twelve foot long, sculpted, butcher block glued desk at the Pharm, plugged in my portable electric typewriter, looked at my 8' cemented, circular fire place encased by 20" high rail road ties, looked at the chimney rising through the roof made of welded and stacked 70 and 35 gallon barrels, gazed at the recycled redwood boards lining my walls holding pictures of the Peace Corps, Pharm, Kennedy brothers, sunsets, oceans, mountains, etc., and tapped out the answers that came from embedding in such a Pharmer's bunker.

"Do you like to gamble?"

The next days started much as Day 1. The other side picked on me. Abe chuckled some while reading my typings, and then he got up and did his Clarence Darrow thing.

Then, during an afternoon session while the other side was complaining about my lack of a seating chart, cursory lesson plan for period 6, guest lecture request filed days rather than a week in advance, typos, bad odor, high 9 week failure rate, or sumptin . . . Abe leaned over and asked, "Do you gamble?"

Gamble? What is he thinking, I'm thinking.

"Ah, what do you mean?"

"Do you like to gamble?" was his clarification.

"Ah, I hardly ever bet money on anything," said the kid whose dad, between driving a Cleveland Plain Dealer newspaper delivery truck full time, carried this little pad from which he freelanced as a small time phone bookie to help fill mom's shoebox of envelopes labeled for monthly bill paying.

"I mean," Abe said as he turned toward the back of the hearing room and nodded at a few of my students, who somehow found a way to attend these hearings, "Do you like to take chances?"

"Like what?"

"In two days, I don't think the other side has hurt you much. But this isn't simple American justice. You are a probationary dismissal. You are assumed guilty, not presumed innocent. You have to "prove" your innocence."

Abe paused and let sink in what we already knew. Probationary dismissals hearings are geared to lose. You are supposed to lose.

"Those kids in the back of the room. We could put them on the witness stand . . . But if the other side punches a hole in anything they say, they'll rip that hole apart and you'll be finished . . . So . . . do you gamble?"

Diana and David

I recall Diana Fleetwood going on the witness stand first. How propitious for those who want to rip holes in a defendant's defense.

Shy, introverted, scared Diana was in my first classes, and it seemed every other class. She participated in People's Lobby's campaigns, worked for McGovern some when I ran his San Gabriel Valley Presidential Campaign Office. She was a wonderful and often funny writer. When I read unnamed samples of interesting student writings back to my classes, hers was usually one of them.

The first time I did that scared Diana waited till the class left to plead that I not do that again. I had to convince her that her writings were good. I had to promise not to mention her name. I had to cajole a scared kid.

Later, I had to smile when in college she became editor, or something like that, of her school paper and even wrote some for LA Magazine.

She grew a lot over her high school years, but she still was visibly scared on the witness stand.

Clarence Darrow handled her with velvet gloves. The opposition attorney, however, sensed he might be able to rip something apart here. As he began to bear down on this petite girl, the other woman of proven stature in the room straightened her back, leaned forward, and seemed to focus her glare from her presiding chair. If the DA thought he could rip a hole in Diana's story, he was aware enough to know he might be doing so in front of an especially attentive Helen of Troy to whom he would lose the war.

At the end of that day, an almost tearful Diana expressed how she "Had lost the trial for us."

We thought she had done fine, and her presence and courage probably said even more, especially to the other woman sitting above overseeing the Trojan War.

Dave McElwee brought a polar opposite presence to the witness chair. Dave had been one of the stellar players exposed to my short-lived football coaching career, a student in all my classes, a teacher's aide, class officer, Honors Student, and around a lot as a student and, I think, teacher's aide (TA) too. Confidence was not hard for him to find.

It didn't take Clarence long to take Dave to the heart of the "incompetent, ineffective teacher' charge. Abe asked Dave what he got out of Mr. Hunn's classes, TA work, coaching experiences, etc. Dave said many nice things.

Then Abe used Dave's qualities and work ethic to address one of the red hued subliminal charges against me. The exchange went something like:

"So, Mr. McElwee, have you decided what you will do after graduation?"

"No, sir, I haven't."

"You're not going to college?" Attorney Levy asked.

"Oh, I'll go to college, sir, I just haven't decided where."

"Where are you hoping to go?"

"Well, sir, I've been accepted at West Point, Army, and the Air Force Academy. I just haven't decided where to go yet."

Then Abe followed up with a series of questions that revolved around what Dave felt "About Mr. Hunn as a person . . . as an American . . . as to his patriotism?"

Anyone whose lives were exposed to Senator McCarthy's Un-American Activities Hearings would have loved hearing this high school kid's words uttered on their behalf. If that "un-patriotic, un-America, commie pinko" junk was still floating around the noose above my head in the court room, Dave shot it down like a Top Gun fighter pilot.

My files remind me that we were prepared to put on a dozen or more students, but after Dave's testimony the Los Angeles County's attorney moved to end the parade by some legal "stipulation" that said something like: "We are willing to stipulate that all the students will stipulate that Mr. Hunn is an excellent . . ."

Well, I don't remember the exact words that finished the prosecuting attorney's stipulation, but the words had something to do with me being pretty good or damn good at something.

Incidentally, an Air Force Academy graduate, fighter pilot, and fighter pilot trainer, and now commercial pilot is what Dave McElwee became. Diana Fleetwood became a teacher.

And those students who liked coming to see how my trial worked provided me with a lesson plan for the following year. In 1973 I would take a bus load of thigh school students to a bigger Los Angeles court room. For a full day they watched the well groomed and pressed suits of the attorneys from our government take on the disheveled and wrinkled suits representing Daniel Ellsberg and Anthony Russo in the Pentagon Papers Trial. On that day, they also got to see Jane Fonda, or was she there in just my imagination.

Most of the perceptions that busload of high school kids took home probably also bothered the John Birchers.

What about some of these charges?
Incompetent teacher

> **NOTICE OF ACCUSATION,** March 23, 1972
>
> The Respondent gave 46% of his students in his U.S. History classes failing grades after the first nine weeks of the 1971-72 school year.

Did this prove I was incompetent? Or was it just part of what Grandfather Deuel asks of all of those who get involved . . .

"How do we prove we are not crazy?"

Well, the letter I had all my students carry home with their nine-week grades addressed some of that charge and maybe some of why I was probably crazy.

Excerpt from **Grading Policy letter** sent to students and parents . . .

Seventy percent is the lowest passing mark in my history classes. This is higher, I was surprised to learn, than most class standards (for passing). I didn't realize that the standards I was raised on were of such ancient vintage.

My grading is done on a point system. In the first nine weeks, approximately 170 points of test, book report, and homework were possible. Those with totals below 119 failed.

Aside from my high grading standards, part of the reason for many failures may have stemmed from the belief that Mr. Hunn's classes were a "good time," which seems to often translate into "little work." A terrible score on "Good time's" first test put many in the hole, and a subsequently undone book report by more sealed some bad grades. At this point, the classroom resounded with the cry, "You grade on a curve, don't you?"

I do not. However, I do provide outlets for gaining extra credit such as book reports, movie productions, topical research, oral presentations, etc.

One, with some work to atone for past mistakes, can gain 60, 80, 100 extra credit points while turning his study habits around in the second nine weeks and be able to pull an F to a B or A.

Things that are given cheaply are usually forgotten. Education can't give knowledge away. Schools shouldn't give grades away. Students shouldn't expect to be pampered this way. I hope all my students come away a little richer and have worked to get that way.

Merry Christmas . . . May the love of the baby Jesus be with you.

Christmas break is a good time to get your kid to read an extra credit book.

Then, we entered Glendora High's Semester Grade Analysis as a Defense Exhibit, which the administration conveniently failed to enter into evidence:

Grades	A	B	C	D	F	I
D. Hunn	31.8	17.1	15.5	2.3	0	2.3
Department	14.9	21.6	27.3	13.5	6.7	4.0

The administration compiled these figures, so don't blame Clarence and team if their figures fail to compute on a couple levels.

Pro-black God, anti-white Jesus Christ?

> **NOTICE OF ACCUSATION,** March 23, 1972
>
> In January 1970, Respondent distributed to his pupils a typed page containing numerous spelling and typographical errors, as well as the vulgar words "bullshitted" and "shit." The article also attacks religion.

Somewhere in three days of hearings, the insinuation that I was "Pro-black God and anti-white Jesus Christ" started floating. I guess it floated off of the above charge. It was probably aired because I had my lily white students (in five years of teaching I had less than five students of distinctive color) read excerpts and books from angry writers exposed to color such as Eldridge Cleaver (Soul on Ice), Claude Brown (Manchild in the Promised Land), Ralph Ellison (Invisible Man), Gene Marine (Black Panthers), Dorothy Sterling (Tear Down the Walls: A History of the American Civil Rights Movement), Langston Hughes, (Black Misery), Piri Thomas (Down These Mean Streets), Michael Harrington (The Other America) . . .

Perhaps this charge didn't stick because the next charge, although true, didn't weigh heavily enough.

Typographical errors

I pled guilty. I distributed handouts that contained typographical errors.

Back in that teaching day, if a teacher wanted to excerpt writings from books to use as handouts, they weren't goggled, copied, and pasted. The words usually had to be typed on TYPEWRITERS and often MIMEOGRAPHED (remember that?) NOT COPIED. That, however, was why I welcomed having 3-5 volunteering student TAs per class. They did such chores, so I had more time to play live with students' thoughts, discussions, and growth.

Often, my TAs and I would catch typographical errors, bad words, etc., that might appear in handouts. Sometimes I failed in that responsibility, and the accusers brought those sheets to court.

In rebuttal, my TAs collected an evidentiary sample of many of my handouts, which I believe mounted to a 30"+ pile. Clarence submitted the stack to Hearing Officer Gallagher for some of her nighttime reading and added a touch something like:

"Although my client admits failing to correct some typographical errors in his handouts, we ask you to review the volume of such work and recognize that a few sloppy sheets that slipped by do not represent the quality of his voluminous work."

Bad odor

NOTICE OF ACCUSATION, March 23, 1972

On December in 17, 1969, Respondent arrived on campus in cut-off trousers and T-shirt and in a dirty and in a rumpled condition.

This actually happened in August, which we corrected for the administration in court, when I came to football practice on my motorbike on a non-school day. Parking 40-50 yards from the administrative offices, I jogged to the field house with no one visibly around. The administration's Clark Kent on that day may have been exposed to a little too much Kryptonite, or not enough Lutein, for I didn't "Look(ed) as though I had crawled out from under a car," as the prosecution contended.

A real Clark Kent would have testified that I wore no grease stains, but I may have graced myself with some saw dust, for I was playing carpenter while building my Rubelian Tree House and staircase.

Prior to this arrival, I had asked fellow coaches if they cared if I came to practice in work clothes before switching to coaching sweats, They gave me another unanimous, but polar opposite to their facial hair vote of "Who cares?"

But to this principal, who had been a football coach, and his administration, they were determined to carry Mrs. Friezner's rule,

"A clean bird is a happy bird"

to another flight level that led to fight time over who smelled worse as a teacher or administrator.

NOTICE OF ACCUSATION, March 23, 1972

On January 26, 1970, Respondent arrived at a faculty meeting and remained there dressed in dirty physical education clothes. His personal cleanliness was deficient as evidenced by a strong body odor.

Said day went like this: After teaching, teachers Conforti, Bell, and myself played some semi-serious hoops with some students. Afterwards, I came to the cavernous faculty/band room, sat in the corner near an open door in my sweats, and found fellow teachers freely choose to sit with me without any uttering an odorous complaint, or donning masks, or moving away under nose hankies. Fellow basket balling teachers Conforti and Bell also received no odorous complaints, but they came about 30 minutes late, after taking a leisurely shower.

The principal, a good 25' away down in the conductor's pit, did not approach our seated group. In court, a true believer could only assume that said conductor was a descendant of the greatest clan of sniffers among hunter-gathers of old. Luckily for the hunted, this greatest of sniffers was now plying his sniffing and preying skills from a principal's perch.

Your objectives are still not acceptable

After Tom King pushed me to flash back in time and thanks to a couple files filled with fading papers refreshing my memory, here's a post glass of cheap Pharm Gallo wine rendition of what was happening back then.

Some of the community powers didn't much like a Pied Piper coming into a comfy town and building what some feared was a teaching process (or read phunny Castle) that built insights differently from how they wanted their homogenized views of suburbs or world taught (or homes built). They wanted forms and standardized tests and objectives (or read suburbanized permits) to drain or kill teachers' (or zany builders') creative time or zeal.

Behind this was an educational battle that marches on today in the early 21st century. The principal's 1972 Memo outlines some of those battle lines:

Principal's Memo

Your objectives are still not acceptable. As I indicated in our last 2 meetings, an acceptable objective must be measurable and it must include the conditions. After re-viewing the materials I have given you, including the Objectives Market Place Game, I find it difficult to understand why you persist in turning in the same type of objective.

Below are listed objectives that would be acceptable using the basic behavior that you want the student to be able to perform.

1. At the conclusion of 9 weeks of study, 90% of my students will be able to list, without the help of notes or other resources, in one class period, 10 differences in interests and philosophies between the Federalists and Jeffersonians.
2. At the conclusion of 10 weeks of study, 80% of my students will be able to contrast, with the aid of notes but no other resources, capitalism, communism and totalitarianism. The student must contrast at least 15 of 20 variables that will be identified in class.
3. When presented with a statement regarding a controversial issue, the student will seek out and examine at least 2 other viewpoints, identify each, compare and contrast and then state within a specified time his final opinion.

sdr
cc: Personal file

p.s. Mr. Martin called to inquire why you had not called the Standard Oil Company nor Edison Company representative for a guest speaker appearance. Please let me know when arrangements are made so that I can call Mr. Martin.

With crowded classes, this teacher wanted to spend less time filling out that formula planning stuff that cuffs a teacher to teach to a test. Time lost in cuffs kills the precious time and energy that could have inspired reading, writing, discussing, debating, daring, and learning. To some, this philosophy of teaching was a problem. Ipso facto, to them I was a problem teacher who had to be sent *ipso packing*.

Glendora Teacher Hits Firing, Sloven Tactics Cited by Board,
San Gabriel Valley Tribune, Dick Lloyd

Since the early days of his employment Hunn has been known for his liberal views on social issues, and it is those reasons, he said, that are at the heart of his ouster. Community pressure, not teaching deficiencies, are causing his removal, he said.

When forty of us were chosen to serve as the Peace Corps first Urban Community Development Group to be sent to Asia, our skills, education, and insights helped determine our selection. In three months of training, Peace Corps tried to build, broaden, and deepen our understanding, language, and skill set. By having a very low administrative staff to volunteer ratio, Sarge Shriver, the Peace Corps first Director, told PCVs to learn, grow, and do on your own. The original Peace Corps sought to engender initiative.

When some of us stumbled onto the Pharm's classrooms, wisened Pharmers taught many of us how to use tools, build with little, and work with others. The Head Janitor didn't like spending time filing plans to build a roof, windmill, tower, or castle. If the shop floor was dirty, use your initiative, grab a broom, and clean it.

When some of us were lucky enough to work with Ed and Joyce Koupal's People Lobby on cleaning up politics and the environment, we learned that they seldom said no to a decent idea, they just asked, "How, will YOU do it?"

When teachers enter the classroom may they be blessed with the time to inspire life long learning rather than fill days with routinized, memorized stuff, which years later few students remember and which today they can *Bingo* with a Goggle generator.

Sarge Shriver, Michael Clarke Rubel, and Edwin and Joyce Koupal were teachers in the best sense of the word. They didn't bury your time and growth under forms, a stifling routine, or quantified objectives that can stifle a classroom or nation filled with unique individuals. This teacher would not gear students to drill for quantified, simplified goals, while the real world was roiling about them. Instead, I tried to expose my students to reading, researching, thinking, discussing, and DOING, while nudging them to get politically and socially involved.

Therein probably laid the gist of the "You're fired" problem. A John Birch influenced community power structure had trouble with an effective, popular teacher, living at and recharging from a different and even more popular Castle, guarded by steely cannons, principled canons, old-fashioned Pharmers, and trusted community old-timers.

Therein lies the gist of some of today's educational battles. Therein is why every town could use a Castle, for in uniquely fortified homes is wherein the spirit of Kipling revives:

If you can keep your head when all about you
Are losing theirs and blaming it on you,
If you can trust yourself when all men doubt you,
But make allowance for their doubting too;
If you can wait and not be tired by waiting,
Or being lied about don't deal in lies
Or being hated, don't deal in hating,
If you can dream—and not make . . .

"What did the Judge say, Mr. Hunn?"

"So what's the verdict, Mr. Hunn?" repeated the student, who had stopped me as I rounded the corner into the school yard at the end of a teaching day.

"Don't know. No word from the judge yet." I replied.

"But they know at the office," he said.

"Who knows?" I asked.

"The Principal and his staff," said the student.

"How do you know that?"

"I open the mail, put it in everyone's mail box . . . I saw stuff from the Judge."

"But John Muraski and I are supposed to get it at the same time they do."

"Well, they got it, and they're having a school board meeting about it tonight."

"They are? No one told me this was being discussed tonight," said a stunned me.

"Can we do anything, Mr. Hunn?" asked one of the other students.

"Well, it might be helpful to spread the word. Might be good to have a few students there, I've got to call Mr. Muraski." I added, as I scurried off.

Glendora School Board Meeting

School board meetings were held in a room that comfortably held about 50 people. When John Muraski and I arrived, we were stunned to find a line wrapped out the door and down the street. The Board decided to move the meeting to the gym at Goddard Junior High. As the Glendora Press reported, the meeting took over 5 hours, with 2 ½ hours in Executive Session.

There was, however, a back story to the Executive Session that the press did not capture. According to my grapevine, it went something like this. As the Board went into Executive Session, Los Angeles' County's Legal Counsel went in with them.

Consequently, John Muraski tried to go into Executive Session too, claiming that "In fairness, Hunn should have representation to offset the County's prosecutorial representation."

County counsel claimed he was only present to explain the findings and Muraski should not be allowed in. The County won that argument.

However, as County Counsel went into Executive Session the Board President Jean Butler issued one caveat, "You'd better remain totally impartial. If you utter anything I deem not impartial, you are gone."

It was not long into that Executive Session before County Counsel explained that the Glendora School Board need not follow the Hearing Officer's findings. He then advised them "To override the Hearing Officer's findings and act as the independent entity you are . . ."

Ain't life ironic?

One of my quiet, fine, competent, ever present students and repeat TAs just happened to be Art Butler, the son of Glendora's School Board President. His mother stuck to her words and kicked County Counsel out of the Executive Session.

After midnight the board returned to the still crowded gymnasium.

Trustees Nix Firing of GHS Teacher,
Glendora Press, July 15, 1972

The audience which had numbered about 300 at the start and waited more than five hours through the regular board meeting and executive session seemed caught by surprise by the decision, responding for a moment in almost complete silence, then exploding in glee as a student muttered, "Man, it's out of sight."

Glendora Schools Keep Controversial Teacher
Pasadena Star News, June 14, 1972

The motions of the board held the crowd in suspense and seemed to lead in the opposite direction until the clincher revealed Hunn was vindicated.

A great many of the audience, which began in numbers at about 300 at the start, were student supporters of Hunn, who admire his teaching manner.

A petition circulated on campus the past week had gathered many signatures of students asking his retention, but that probably had no bearing on the outcome.

Then, even this attentive player became confused as each of the board members, one after the other, read a couple lines from the Hearing Officer's findings. Silence hung over the room for about a dozen seconds as the audience tried to decipher the five members readings. Only after the front row's Rick Dutton, who grew from one of three talented Bee Team quarterbacks to the Varsity starter, uttered some then popular student grunting sounds, did this player think maybe the right team had won.

> **Teacher Wins Fight to Stay At Glendora,**
> San Gabriel Valley Tribune, June 13, 1972
>
> Minutes after trustees said "sufficient cause does not exist" to dismiss Hunn, a partisan crowd of students and teachers erupted into shouts of glee. One student yelled, "Out of sight!"
>
> "He is totally conscientious for his job, and he communicates well with students," said one of Hunn's pupils. "If they had fired him, they would have lost the best teacher in the school."

The AFT and Abe Levy

While living in a conservative town, on a Phunny Pharm, amidst a rising Castle of Junk, where unions were more likely to be verbally battered than praised, the American Federation of Teachers' Union came knocking on my homemade door and offered this Pharmer legal succor.

> *Glendora Teacher Will Retain*
> *Job With Tenure,*
> Los Angeles Times, June 14, 1972
>
> "I like to use discussion techniques in the classroom," he said, instead of a more formal presentation.
>
> Hunn credited the American Federation of Teachers and the students with saving his job.

They offered an attorney to wage a fight on a place imbued with Grandfather Deuel's warning that,

"If you want to have problems, contact an attorney."

Well, Superman Attorney Abe Levy and I had some contact, but I can't remember any problems. Three days of Clarence the Darrow Levy playing in court provided better than *Law & Order* drama, enlightened education, and plain old-fashioned phun.

Of course, most of us know how devastatingly costly even phun-to-watch attorneys can be, and most of us who have dealt with attorneys know the cost of what attorneys do is usually their biggest problem. So, this Pharmer just lived by grandfather's rule #62:

"Don't worry about it (the legal bill) until you can do something about it."

Well, on July 27, 1972 the bill arrived and I was forced to do something about the costly problems attorneys bring as a smiling AFT abandoned me to the financial fates of large costly law firms run by the likes of its founding partner. Below the AFT's aptly phrased letterhead was this bill.

> democracy
> in education
> education for
> democracy

Ah, if only more of us could return to the days of having our own Clarence Darrow for $50 a day.

This "Afterword" is getting long in the tooth. So, I'm going to do a Michael, give a little pout, puff my lips a bit, arch my eyebrows, and prepare to rock in my chair, stare into space, and close my eyes to escape.

American Federation of Teachers

*"democracy in education
education for democracy"*

Dear Dwayne:

Please find enclosed a bill which we received from the Law Firm of Levy & Van Bourg for services rendered in the Dwayne Hunn case in the amount of $300.00. According to our policy if we win, you must pay half and the local pay half after any and all contributions. Please be advised that with an amount that is so low we cannot justify filing a defense application with the State and National Organization. Be advised, therefore, that your half of the cost of the case comes to $150.00 and the local will pay $150.00. Please remit to John Muraski, Treasurer, Foothills Local 1424, 818 E. Virginia, Glendora, Calif. 91740.

Your attention in this matter is greatly appreciated.

Sincerely and fraternally,

Marie Whipp, President FOOTHILLS LOCAL 1424, AFT

Like so many others, I miss Michael and all the joys and joyous people he reincarnated around him. I miss his scribbled *Grandfatherisms* that built foundations from which Michael and much of the country once worked and grew.

So, this book leaves you to ponder how the words that Castle Builder Michael Rubel once left ringing in my ears apply to you and yours . . .

*"Do you know the boo weevil?
It bores down on you.
Sometimes I'm like a boo weevil on you . . .
It's not to pick on you.
It's because you can be so much better . . ."*

Thank you, Michael and Grandfather Deuel and all those wizened old timers for pushing so many of us Pharmers to:

"Plow Deeper."

Because:

"The word "No" never built anything.
It is simply the easiest answer."

And to pursue goals with the right and happy intentions because you:

"Don't defend yourself. History will."

And because Grandfather's words reminded us:

"Man is only as big as the things that bother him."

Well, dear friend,
wherever you are rocking in your chair
and acting as Head Janitor
may you rain down upon the world
the spirit that builds
interesting kids like you that have phun
and build zany Rubelian Castles,
for as Grandfather felt

"Every Town Needs a Castle."

CPSIA information can be obtained at www.ICGtesting.com
Printed in the USA
LVOW121054060112

262547LV00002B/47/P

9 781453 584323